SUPPORTING ADULT CARE-LEAVERS

International good practice

Suellen Murray

First published in Great Britain in 2015 by

Policy Press
University of Bristol
1-9 Old Park Hill
Bristol BS2 8BB
UK
t: +44 (0)117 954 5940
pp-info@bristol.ac.uk
www.policypress.co.uk

North America office:
Policy Press
c/o The University of Chicago Press
1427 East 60th Street
Chicago, IL 60637, USA
t: +1 773 702 7700
f: +1 773 702 9756
sales@press.uchicago.edu
www.press.uchicago.edu

© Policy Press 2015

British Library Cataloguing in Publication Data
A catalogue record for this book is available from the British Library.

Library of Congress Cataloging-in-Publication Data
A catalog record for this book has been requested.

ISBN 978-1-4473-1364-9 paperback
ISBN 978-1-4473-1363-2 hardcover
ISBN 978-1-4473-1366-3 ePub
ISBN 978-1-4473-1367-0 Kindle

Cover design by Double Dagger
Front cover: image kindly supplied by Shutterstock
Printed and bound in Great Britain by CMP, Poole
Policy Press uses environmentally responsible print partners

Author biography

Associate Professor Suellen Murray is Director of Higher Degrees by Research in the College of Design and Social Context at RMIT University in Melbourne, Australia. She has specialised in research in two areas of social policy: the life histories of adult care-leavers and related social policy and social work practice; and violence against women and its related policy and practice responses. Suellen is also the author of *More than Refuge: Changing Responses to Domestic Violence* (UWA Press, 2002) and co-author of *After the Orphanage: Life Beyond the Children's Home* (UNSW Press, 2009), *Half a Citizen: Life on Welfare in Australia* (Allen & Unwin, 2011) and *Domestic Violence: Australian Public Policy* (Australian Scholarly Publishing, 2011).

Acknowledgements

Many people supported my work on this book, and I wish to thank them. Those who I met across the five countries provided invaluable information that helped me make much better sense of the various other sources that I used. In each country, there were some who stood out in terms of their interest in my work and their efforts to help me understand: Phyllis Morgan in Ireland and England; Zachari Duncalf in Scotland; Jim Goddard in England; Janet Longclaws, the Daniels family and John Meston in Canada; and Garth Young in New Zealand. In addition, I wish to thank Eva Wilson Fontaine both for her interest in my work and her warm hospitality. In Australia, I am privileged to have been the beneficiary of the wisdom of a number of people over some years, including Caroline Carroll, Stella Conroy, Jenny Glare and Cathy Humphreys. I acknowledge the contributions made by those whom I have interviewed in the various research projects I have conducted concerned with life after care – their experiences have been central to my understanding of the key policy issues addressed in this book.

I extend my gratitude to the people with whom I work at RMIT University, especially Brían Walsh and Suzana Kovacevic, who provided high-level administrative support that allowed me to find some time to research and write. I also acknowledge the contribution of Alissa Lykhina, who did the initial desktop research seeking information about responses to adult care-leavers internationally. Special thanks to Denise Cuthbert and Gail Green, who encouraged my efforts and generously read a draft of the manuscript. Thanks also to the team at Policy Press for their interest in the topic and their expertise in turning my manuscript into this book. Finally, I thank Libby Best and gratefully acknowledge the many weekends forgone in the writing of this book.

Contents

List of abbreviations

AFA	Alliance of Forgotten Australians
AHF	Aboriginal Healing Foundation
AIATSIS	Australian Institute of Aboriginal and Torres Strait Islander Studies
CEP	Common Experience Payment
CICA	Commission to Inquire into Child Abuse
CLA	Care Leavers' Association
CLAN	Care Leavers Australia Network
CLAS	Confidential Listening and Assistance Service
DHS	Department of Human Services
DoHA	Department of Health and Aging
HIA	Historical Institutional Abuse (Inquiry)
HREOC	Human Rights and Equal Opportunity Commission
IACP	Irish Association of Counsellors and Psychotherapists
IAP	Independent Assessment Process
ICSSS	In Care Survivors Service Scotland
INCAS	In Care Abuse Survivors
IRSRHSP	Indian Residential Schools Resolution Health Support Program
ISASS	Irish Survivors Advice and Support Service
OATSIH	Office of Aboriginal and Torres Strait Islander Health
RCAP	Royal Commission on Aboriginal Peoples
RCIRCSA	Royal Commission into Institutional Responses to Child Sexual Abuse
RIRB	Residential Institutions Redress Board
SCARC	Senate Community Affairs References Committee
SHRC	Scottish Human Rights Commission
TRCC	Truth and Reconciliation Commission of Canada

List of tables, figures and boxes

Tables

Figure

Boxes

ONE

Introduction

"I've struggled all my life ... I've always felt I'm not worthy of anything ... I drifted in and out of drugs and alcohol and drifted in and out of employment basically all my life." (Brian, adult care-leaver, 2011[1])

While some adult care-leavers report positive experiences of growing up in care, others, like Brian, a 60-year-old man who grew up in children's homes in Australia and who is quoted above, reflect on this part of their lives as times of great difficulty and trauma that have had long-term negative impacts. Various inquiries have revealed accounts of abuse and neglect.[2] These experiences of emotional, physical and sexual abuse can result in poor mental and physical health in later life. Often, children experienced a fracturing of family relationships between both siblings and parents and subsequently a lack of knowledge about personal and family history. For Indigenous children, subjected to discriminatory policies of forced removal, this separation could result in disconnection from their community and a loss of knowledge about culture and language. These practices, then, could lead to a loss of sense of identity, social isolation and a lack of emotional and practical support. Limited or disrupted education in some settings has meant that adult care-leavers may also struggle to gain meaningful employment, or have restrictions in their life in a range of other ways.

Generally, childhood experiences can have effects over the life course, so harmful childhood *care* experiences are likely to have impacts in adulthood. In relation to those removed from their families and communities of origin, such as child migrants and

1

Indigenous children, the fact that there would be long-term impacts is not at all surprising. That the aftermath of an abusive childhood in care could be difficult is consistent with what we know about *all* childhoods where children have experienced abuse.[3] So, what can be done to assist those negatively affected by their experiences of care as adults? How can we promote health and well-being over the life course for these individuals and their communities?[4] Or, more simply, how can adult care-leavers be best supported? This book attempts to answer this question.

This book is about social policy responses to adult care-leavers such as Brian in five countries across the English-speaking world: Australia, Canada, Ireland, New Zealand and the UK. While acknowledging that these countries have different policy histories, there are also commonalities. The initiatives under discussion in this book are public inquiries and other forms of investigation, symbolic acknowledgements of time in care such as memorials and apologies, financial redress schemes and other forms of compensation for harm, specialist support services, and access to personal records and family reunification programmes.[5] In addition, I consider the important work of advocacy groups that have typically prompted the advent of such responses. For each form of response, I provide an international overview based on a desktop review and contact with a range of key agencies in each country and then highlight examples of good practice in the form of case studies. Thus, the responses discussed here are not the only responses that could occur, but, rather, the ones that have been most commonly put in place to date. This is an emerging area of social policy and practice, and in the conclusion to this book, I consider what other possibilities there could be.

By focusing on these initiatives in this book, I am not suggesting that all those who grew up in care need 'responses' such as specialist support programmes. Nor am I suggesting that adult care-leavers are passive victims awaiting support from others – far from it. As I have indicated, and will explore further in Chapter Eight, it is the work of advocacy groups comprising adult care-leavers themselves that, by and large, have brought about the existence of such services. However, we do need to acknowledge that care has had long-term detrimental effects, especially for those abused in care and for those who have experienced a loss or lack of knowledge about their family and culture of origin. What we know from the various biographical accounts, government inquiries, programme evaluations, advocates' research and the academic literature is that specialist support and other programmes are of assistance to some adult care-leavers.

Approach

My approach to the topic of this book is informed by the Law Commission of Canada's report *Restoring Dignity: Responding to Child Abuse in Canadian Institutions*.[6] While not dissimilar in some respects to the approach of other public inquiries, the Law Commission of Canada most clearly articulated the principles from which it operated. First, the Commission approached the topic with the view that responses were needed, not *whether* they were needed. The Commission was charged with the responsibility of identifying 'what types of processes would best address wrongdoing, while affording appropriate remedies, and promoting reconciliation, fairness and healing'.[7] I also came to the topic with the position that, given what we know about the harms that have been perpetrated against children in care in the past, social policy responses are needed. Second, the Law Commission took an adult care-leaver-centred approach by framing its research 'by asking how those adults who had been abused as children understood their needs'.[8] I also took the position that social policy needs to respond to the long-term effects of care as understood by adult care-leavers themselves, and that they need to be involved in the development and oversight of such initiatives.

Consistent with this focus, my approach was also informed by what social work academic Cathy Humphreys and her colleagues call the 'knowledge diamond', that is, that social policy knowledge draws from four sources, each an essential part and found at one of the four points of a diamond: 'survivor [adult care-leaver] experience, practice wisdom, policy data and research evidence'.[9]

Figure 1.1 The knowledge diamond

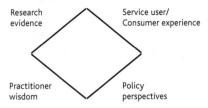

Source: Humphreys, C. and Kertesz, M. (2012) 'Personal identity records to support young people in care', *Adoption and Fostering*, vol 36, no 1, pp 27–39. Reproduced with permission

As Humphreys explains:

> at the heart of any profession are claims to knowledge and hence to power.... It is therefore unsurprising that what counts as evidence, or what counts as knowledge, is contested ... it raises the question of whose knowledge counts and who is allowed to speak and be heard.[10]

What is striking about the experiences of adult care-leavers to date is their restricted capacity as children – and as adults – to speak, and be heard. To some extent, public inquiries have provided opportunities to speak; the extent to which they have been heard and their concerns acted upon is the focus of this book. So, in the same way that 'the voices of survivors brought the knowledge of domestic violence into the public realm', adult care-leavers' accounts of their experiences are 'an important source of knowledge' about care and its aftermath; however, their value is, as yet, not fully realised.[11] The knowledge diamond attempts to draw in these various sources of knowledge, including that of adult care-leavers themselves.

This book is written for practitioners and policymakers in social work, social care and related professions working with people who grew up in care. As noted, this work is an emerging area of practice. In 2014 in the UK, for example, in recognition of the significance of personal records, statutory guidance has been introduced to encourage the provision of support to adult care-leavers when receiving their records from local authorities. While some local authorities have well-developed practice in this area, for others, it will be new territory. Staff will require education and training, both in terms of the release of records and also in the background that leads to the need for such practice. Another area of developing need is related to the ageing of adult care-leavers. There will be demand for a skilled care workforce who understand the impacts of childhood institutionalisation and what the implications might be for those who live in nursing homes or other supported accommodation.

Key concepts

Before going further, some clarification of the terminology and key concepts found in this book will be useful. First, by 'care', I mean the various forms of 'out-of-home' or 'out-of-family of origin' support that have been used since the mid-20th century, including both foster care and institutional forms of care, such as orphanages, industrial schools, children's homes, residential schools, cottage homes and family group homes.[12] To a lesser extent, it also includes other institutional settings such as remand homes, reformatories or other forms of juvenile justice facilities, mental health institutions or hospitals in which children resided long-term, and homes for children with disabilities. These forms of care were used in different ways over time and, to some extent, with the various population groups of children in care in the countries under discussion. These varying social policy histories are discussed further in Chapter Two. It is important to note that there was significant diversity in the site – or sites – of children's care: 'some children spent a few months with a foster family. Others spent entire childhoods in a succession of orphanages, cottage (group) homes and hospitals'.[13]

I acknowledge the contested use of the term 'care' and that many did not experience it as 'caring'. I use the term 'care' as a shorthand way of identifying out-of-home and out-of-family of origin care. When discussing 'care', it is often assumed that the focus is (historic) abuse (in care). While this book is concerned with the long-term *individual* effects of *child abuse*, it is not exclusively about this. The impacts of care on childhood attachment, identity and separation from family and community are not always identified as key effects of care, and while they can be understood as a form of emotional abuse, I name them separately to ensure that attention is paid to them and that they are not lost with a focus on other forms of abuse. Indeed, it is important to acknowledge that adult care-leavers experienced varied harms in care. In addition, care has had the wider *societal* effects of loss of language and culture for Indigenous communities due to generations of children leaving to grow up in care. I return to a fuller discussion of care in Chapter Two.

Second, in this book, an 'adult care-leaver' refers to a person, older than 25 years of age, who grew up for all or part of his or her childhood in 'care'. This, then, refers to a group of people who, in 2015, were born before 1990. Hence, the book is not concerned with children in care or young people who are transitioning out of care or are immediately post-care. While, in some instances, grandchildren (or other descendants) may have an interest in some of the programmes discussed in this book (for example through researching family history), my primary interest is with programmes for the adult care-leavers themselves, and their societal transgenerational effects. The term 'adult care-leaver' is one of several terms to name this group of people – others include 'home child', 'former resident', 'orphan', 'survivor' and 'ward of the state'. There are also other names for specific population groups, mentioned later.

As noted by Joanna Sköld, 'adequate statistics on how many children have been subjected to care ... are surprisingly often lacking'.[14] In Australia, for example, it is estimated that around 500,000 children were in care during the 20th century.[15] In Ireland, over the middle decades of the 20th century, the Commission of Inquiry into Child Abuse reported that there were 170,000 children in care, but this figure is now considered an overestimation.[16] Even when such inaccuracies are taken into account, these numbers suggest that adult care-leavers form a sizeable portion of the total population.

The age demarcation of over 25 years is important, and contested.[17] To date, some attention has been paid to young people leaving care and the period of five years post-care through, for example, the work of Mike Stein in the UK and researchers in other countries.[18] To differentiate between those who are older from the younger group, I include the term 'adult'. This age demarcation means that this book does not discuss programmes for children in care or leaving care and immediate post-care or transitional support programmes for (younger) care-leavers. This is not to say that a (younger) care-leaver would not use one or other of the specialist programmes discussed in this book, such as a service providing support to access personal records. Some of the programmes discussed, however, are specifically targeted at the older (post-25 years) age group. Some argue that the age demarcation for adult care-leavers should be older than 25 years – over 30 years or 40 years – to better reflect the specific needs of these older age groups. For the purpose of this book, I have used over 25 years as this age most clearly differentiates young people leaving care from (older) adult care-leavers.

Within the group of adult care-leavers there are three distinct populations and not all are present in each of the five countries under discussion. First, there are Indigenous people in Australia (Aboriginal and Torres Strait Islanders, also known as members of the Stolen Generations), Canada (First Nations, Inuit and Métis peoples) and New Zealand (Māori). The second group are former child migrants who were taken from the UK and Malta to Australia, Canada and New Zealand (as well as Rhodesia [now Zimbabwe] and South Africa). Specialist responses have been developed for some of these specific population groups. For these two groups – Indigenous children and child migrants – placement in care occurred as a result of public policies that targeted such children and that were abandoned by around the 1970s (but as late as the 1980s in Canada), which are discussed later in this chapter. This is not to say that Indigenous children were no longer in care; rather, that the assessment for their need for care was not explicitly based on their indigeneity as it had been at times in the past. However, socio-economic circumstances could mean that Indigenous families (and poor non-Indigenous families) were placed in care at greater rates than others despite the provision of caring homes because these families were assessed as not meeting what was deemed to be the necessary material standards of care.[19]

The third group of adult care-leavers comprises people who are neither Indigenous nor former child migrants and who form the largest group in each country or, in the case of Ireland and the UK, the only group. Within this group, there is non-Indigenous ethnic diversity reflecting that of the wider population. These children typically entered care for one or more reasons, which may include: family poverty; neglect; the death or ill-health of one or both of their parents; 'illegitimacy', or having been born to an unmarried mother; domestic violence, child abuse or other violence in the family; or their family breakdown, including 'desertion' of one parent. There was also a smaller group of 'status offenders' who were in 'reformatories' or other forms of juvenile justice institutions, even though their offences may have been more about their protection from 'moral danger' or their assumed engagement in sexual activity, for example, in the case of young women and girls.[20] In addition, there were smaller groups of children who, due to ill-health or, in some cases, intellectual disability, were placed in medical and other facilities for substantial periods of their childhood. These circumstances may have also contributed to the removal into care of Indigenous children and child migrants, but for these two groups, as noted, public policy specifically targeted them in earlier decades.

For the older adult care-leavers, entry to care did not necessarily occur as a result of state intervention. In the mid-20th century, families could 'voluntarily' enlist the support of orphanages to care for their children during hard times. In addition, for children in all three groups, being an *actual* orphan – a child with one or both parents who had died – was the exception rather than the rule, despite the use of '*orphan*ages' to care for them.

Some may argue that because of the different policy circumstances in which these three groups came into care, they should not be named together as 'adult care-leavers' and discussed as a single group. While I appreciate that there are significant differences, paying attention to the similarities in relation to both time in care and its aftermath across the three groups can be useful. A striking example of this occurred when I was researching adult care-leavers' access to records and the need for improved services. In Australia, there is a comprehensive and well-developed service system in place for members of the Stolen Generations known as Link-Up (discussed in Chapter Seven). More recently, initiatives have been put in place for non-

Indigenous adult care-leavers; much could be learned from the work of Link-Up. So, my discussion of 'international' responses is not just *across* nations, but also *within* nations. Having said that, at times, it is important to identify the specific group to which the initiatives are directed as the nature of the support provided reflects the impacts of the specific policy history.

Third, what do I mean by 'international' in choosing these particular countries? One reason for the choice of Australia, Canada, Ireland, New Zealand and the UK was pragmatic: they are all English-speaking (although Canada is officially bilingual) and I am monolingual. Another important reason is that all these countries have been a 'welfare state' in some form or other since the middle decades of the 20th century. By 'welfare state', I mean a society in which the state provides a minimum income, some level of economic security for its citizens during old age, disablement, ill-health or unemployment, and a range of social services. In addition, the existence of such welfare provisions has resulted in what these countries have considered to be protective interventions in the lives of children who are deemed to be at risk of neglect or abuse and, consequently, for some children, their entry into care. Moreover, the conduct of these care arrangements in all five countries has been similar. For example, typically religious organisations were initially the main providers of care in all five countries. As well as similar environments that allowed entry into care, these five countries have also shared some level of concern about its long-term effects. Relatively recently, all have provided some resourcing of support services and other programmes for adult care-leavers. In other words, these countries cared for children in broadly similar ways and have all since begun to respond to the needs of adult care-leavers.[21] In all five countries, as with their involvement in the provision of care, religious and other non-government organisations are also involved in programmes and other support services for adult care-leavers. The focus of this book is mostly on government responses.

While there are these important broad similarities in social policy among these five countries, there are also major differences. As discussed further in Chapter Two, a major reason for social policy differences is their varying constituent populations. In addition, the five countries differ according to population and geographic sizes. In 2012, New Zealand and Ireland had similar populations of 4.4 and 4.6 million, respectively, Australia had 22.7 million, Canada had 34.8 million and the UK had 63.7 million (comprising 53.5 million in England, 5.3 million in Scotland, 3.1 million in Wales and 1.8 million in Northern Ireland).[22] Their geographies are also varied, with Australia and Canada having much larger land masses, both with significant remoteness. While they are all democracies and share some elements of similar parliamentary traditions (and four are members of the Commonwealth), due to their varying histories and sizes of population and geography, how they are administered on the ground differs markedly – and this has an impact on the provision of programmes and support services in each of the countries. Thus, programmes and other initiatives are located at varying levels within governments across the five countries.

Outline of the book

In this chapter, I have explained my approach and key concepts and, in doing so, established the scope of the book. In Chapter Two, I turn to a brief overview of the policy contexts in which care has occurred and review the literature relevant to the support of adult care-leavers. Overarching all areas of support for adult care-leavers is the need for them to be heard and to have attention paid to their harmful experiences of care and their long-term negative effects. As discussed in Chapter Three, public inquiries into the experiences of care and their aftermath have played a watershed role in bringing attention to these concerns. Public inquiries have an important function in providing a forum in which adult care-leavers can recount their experiences in care and the community can be made aware of the needs of those affected. However, being heard is not just about speaking out; it is also about having these experiences formally acknowledged. Chapter Four, then, is concerned with the various forms of acknowledgement, including apologies. There have also been other ways that adult care-leavers have been heard and their experiences made visible, and that is through memorials and the development of oral history collections and museum exhibitions, also discussed in Chapter Four. While financial reparation has rarely compensated for lost income, it can be a further acknowledgement of harm, as argued in Chapter Five. In Chapter Five, the importance of redress programmes and financial compensation is presented.

As discussed in Chapter Two, there are a number of ways in which the health and well-being of adult care-leavers have been affected. Support for mental health and assistance to gain further education and develop life skills are ways that the lives of adult care-leavers can be enhanced. For Indigenous people and their communities, there can be a need for support for cultural reconnection and revitalisation. These forms of specialist assistance are discussed in Chapter Six. Loss of identity and disconnection with family point to the need to gain access to records in an effort to better understand personal and family histories, with the goal, for some, of family reunification. The ways in which support can be provided to facilitate access to records and family reunification are presented in Chapter Seven. Change in relation to support for adult care-leavers has come largely through the actions of advocates and their champions and Chapter Eight discusses this work. Chapter Nine concludes the book by reviewing what has been done to date, suggesting good practice and considering what else could be done to address the long-term harms experienced by adult care-leavers.

TWO

Care and its aftermath

Witnesses reported that the abuse experienced in childhood had an enduring impact on their lives.
(Commission to Inquire into Child Abuse, 2009[1])

The Irish Commission to Inquire into Child Abuse, reporting in 2009 and quoted above, documented shocking levels of physical, sexual and emotional abuse and neglect, and 'the failure to provide for [children's] safety, education, development and aftercare had implications for their health, employment, social and economic status in later life'.[2] The Commission was a landmark inquiry that provided opportunities for thousands of Irish people who had grown up in care to present an account of their childhood experiences and the impact that it had on their lives. Similar testimonies have been heard in each of the countries where inquiries have been held. These public inquiries have been important in providing evidence about the aftermath of care and the need for support from the perspectives of adult care-leavers themselves.

Before we examine the various social policy initiatives in place to support adult care-leavers, we need to consider the nature of care and its aftermath. In this chapter, first, a brief history provides context to the provision of care in the five countries over the second half of the 20th century. Second, a review of the literature identifies the effects of a childhood in care and the subsequent support needs of adult care-leavers.

Background to childhoods in care

There are similarities in the social policy related to care in the countries under discussion, and also significant differences. To make sense of these similarities and differences, sociologist Jeff Hearn and his colleagues argue that an assessment of 'the broad historical background and the context of the welfare state' in the countries under study is required.[3] To illustrate this point, in Australia, according to historian Nell Musgrove:

> [t]here is great diversity in the approaches that have been taken to addressing this issue [of care] in various parts of the nation at different times.... In addition to differences in policies across locations, it is also vital to consider the complex relationships between government and non-government arms of child welfare, the distinctions drawn between Indigenous and non-Indigenous children, and the broader social conditions which limited the possibilities and influenced the thinking of welfare officials and workers.[4]

However, the scope of this book does not allow for such a detailed analysis.[5] Instead, in this brief overview, I focus on the overall trends and suggest some of the key differences, particularly in relation to diverse population groups. I highlight relevant areas of social policy concerned with child welfare, child protection and family support, and the treatment of Indigenous children and child migrants specifically. Shifts in the form of out-of-home care provided – whether institutional or family-based – are also addressed.

As noted by Hearn, 'child welfare and child protection take place in the context of more general state, welfare, social and economic policies', and these can also impact on whether children went into care and under what conditions.[6] Historically, income support has been a particularly important factor, and this overview commences with this discussion. As this book is largely concerned with responses to people who spent time in care, are still alive and are now at least 25 years old, this overview is focused on the social policy of the mid- to latter decades of the 20th century.

Income and social support

Wider social policy – particularly in relation to income support – significantly influenced the use and provision of care. Historically, one of the main reasons children entered care was due to family poverty. In Ireland, for example, in the 1940s, at least a third of all children in industrial schools at that time were there because of their parents' inability to support them financially. It was recommended that government funds be used to support families to care for their own children rather than place them in institutions.[7] As we shall see, this change was not to occur for another four decades. Other reasons for children being placed in care typically meant that one parent was then responsible for the care of their children; reasons such as serious ill-health, 'illegitimacy' or single motherhood, or family breakdown. There was little financial support for single parents before the 1970s and caring for children and earning an income were often incompatible. Access to financial and social support, then, could be a major factor in whether children were placed in care or not.

Over time, there were changes that enabled children to remain at home in family circumstances of impoverishment. In Britain, for example, the Children and Young Persons Act 1963 'made it the duty of local authorities to provide advice, guidance and assistance such as might reduce the need to receive children into or keep them in care'.[8] Material and financial assistance became available to support families in efforts to prevent children coming into care. The single mother's pension, implemented during the 1970s, significantly reduced the number of children coming into care. Ensuring that women had access to financial support meant that they were more likely to care for their children, rather than them being placed in the care of the state or adopted.[9] Instead of funding institutions to care for children, these financial resources, in effect, were directed to families to support them to keep their children at home.

Child welfare and child protection

As noted by historian Bronwyn Dalley, 'many of the developments in child welfare philosophy and practice stemmed from changes in attitudes to children and young people'; how children are understood has significant implications for the use of care such that they could be seen as 'victims of society or as threats to it, and sometimes as both at once'.[10] Hence, child welfare could be concerned with control rather than care; indeed, in the mid-19th century, 'legislation was to protect the state from the danger believed to be posed by destitute children'.[11] In Ireland, following their establishment in England and Scotland in the mid-19th century, 'reformatory and industrial schools were designed for the children of the poor, who were perceived as a threat to the social order'.[12]

The child rescue movement of the late 19th century began to challenge these understandings. Philanthropic and religious organisations provided assistance to abandoned, orphaned and neglected children. They were now perceived as victims with a need for 'protection from parents or guardians who were failing in what were now defined as their core responsibilities'.[13] Protective child welfare policies emerged from these initiatives of the child rescue movement. However, this is not to say that children could not also require control in some circumstances: those engaged in unruliness were redefined as juvenile delinquents requiring reform.

By the first half of the 20th century, in Australia, the state began 'taking greater responsibility for looking after children's welfare, and [there was] the increased use of legislation to enforce appropriate standards of care'.[14] Similarly, in the UK, there was an 'extension of state responsibilities in child protection and substitute care'.[15] In Ireland, while there was state involvement through the funding of care, with the care increasingly provided by Catholic religious congregations and orders, this did not guarantee engagement in the maintenance of the standards of care.[16] As historians Maria Luddy and James M. Smith note: 'with that development came less and less public accountability for the work being done in these institutions'.[17] This was partly because of the mode of funding. Funding for care was derived from a capitation grant (or payment per child), only to be replaced by an annual budget or block grant in the mid-1980s. This mechanism allowed for greater control of the management and admission policies of children's homes, a change that had been made in the UK more than six decades earlier.[18] From the 1960s, state engagement in care was to escalate after concern about child abuse and its composition expanded to include physical, sexual and emotional forms, and neglect.[19] Criminologist Adam Tomison reminds us that:

> It is only quite recently, in the last 50 years in particular, that the mistreatment of children has created ongoing, widespread public concern and led to the development of government and non-government services designed to protect children from harm and prevent the occurrence of maltreatment.[20]

Moreover:

> public concern for the welfare of children and the need for expertise in the assessment and treatment of cases of child abuse and neglect has led most communities to develop some form of distinct, professionally staffed, child protection service, located within social service agencies or government departments.[21]

Thus, from the mid-20th century, there was increasing professionalisation of state childcare services. In the UK, this had occurred as a result of 'public outcries over scandals involving children in care which were attributed to poor supervision and coordination'.[22]

While the family has been seen as central to the care of children, the extent to which the family has been deemed capable of providing a suitable environment for children has varied across time and location. Tomison explains these social policy shifts about when to remove a child from their family and place them in care:

The dilemma of determining when to remove a child at risk of harm [into care] highlights the conflicting values of child protection work – to protect children while maintaining or preserving families. Over time, the 'threshold' for protective investigation and intervention (taking statutory action to remove a child) has continually shifted in response to public concerns and resource issues.[23]

These decisions involve 'striking a balance between children's well-being and the integrity of the family'.[24] For example, social policy has promoted family preservation and paid greater attention to keeping children with their birth or natural family as a result of increased understandings of the importance of identity, particularly in relation to Indigenous children. When there has been greater attention to removal of children, there have been resourcing consequences, as Tomison explains: 'In the late 1990s, statutory child protection services in the Australian states and territories, like those in other western countries, were struggling to cope with ever-increasing numbers of reports of suspected child maltreatment and fewer resources'.[25]

To attempt to deal with this overload of child protection services, there was a reorientation to providing greater support to families through the broader child and family welfare system. There was a 'renewed focus on addressing family ills holistically, to supporting children and families, in order to prevent the development or recurrence of child abuse and neglect'.[26] Thus, in the UK in the 1990s and elsewhere, due to the overwhelming number of families brought into the child protection system, the attention shifted from 'procedurally narrow investigations' to a greater focus on family support.[27] Also influential has been the 1989 United Nations Convention on the Rights of the Child, to which all five countries discussed in this book are signatories. The Convention reframed and extended the need for children to be protected and provided with the means for their development.[28] Consistent with these broad shifts in the conduct of child welfare in New Zealand, Australia and the UK, in Canada, similar trends are evident, including, over time: increased professionalisation of the service system; greater government responsibility for public funding and oversight; and 'a shift from institutional and protection-oriented services to non-institutional and prevention-oriented services'.[29]

Shifts in the understanding of child welfare are also reflected in the form of care provided to children whose families were deemed to be unable or unwilling to care for them. The large 19th-century orphanages and industrial schools housing hundreds of children had developed out of the workhouses and reformatories of earlier times. Over time, and with greater understanding of child development and the importance of attachment to carers, residential institutions reduced in size and number from around the 1950s, but later in Ireland.[30] In some settings, at some times, foster care – or boarding out as it was also known – was the dominant form of care.[31] Across all five countries, there has been increasing use of home-based foster and kin care rather than institutional or residential forms of care in recent decades. However, the policy shift away from institutional to foster care was not without resistance. As noted in New Zealand:

> Churches were the main providers of institutional childcare at a time when government policy had favoured foster care for some time. Churches wanted to shore up membership at a time of declining attendance. They believed institutions were the easiest and best way of instilling moral and spiritual values in children. They were also often left money through bequests which had to be spent on institutions.[32]

In Ireland, the Department of Education showed 'a very significant deference' towards the Catholic congregations that ran the industrial schools where children in care resided and 'this deference impeded change'; it was only after a public inquiry in 1970 that the dismantling of 'a long out-dated system' began.[33] While there were sound child developmental reasons for the widespread adoption of foster care as the primary means of care, it has also not been without its difficulties.[34]

The way in which child welfare is administered varies across the five countries. For example, in Australia, child welfare is dealt with by the individual states and territories, resulting in variations in the definitions of abuse and neglect, and in service structures and processes. Regardless, as Tomison reports, 'each service plays a similar role and each service has been affected by a number of inter-related issues that have impacted on the provision of child protection and child welfare/family support services across the western world'.[35] In Canada, the child welfare system is decentralised, with over 300 provincial and child welfare agencies operating under the jurisdiction of the 13 Canadian provinces and territories. In addition, there are over 120 federally funded Indigenous child welfare agencies. Similar to Australia, in Canada, as noted by Sinha and Kozlowski, 'all provincial and territorial child welfare systems share certain basic goals and characteristics; nonetheless, they vary considerably in terms of their organization of service delivery systems, child welfare statutes, assessment tools, competency-based training programs, and other factors', with variation in Indigenous children's services 'even more pronounced'.[36] However, it is typically *not* the child welfare system that provides services to adult care-leavers, other than through the provision of records as they usually remain the responsibility of child welfare departments.[37] The other forms of responses discussed in this book – public inquiries, apologies, redress schemes and specialist support services – are the responsibility of a range of other parts of governments, which, again, vary across countries, reflecting their different governance structures.

What is most different across the five countries is their constituent population groups. As noted in Chapter One, Australia, Canada and New Zealand have Indigenous populations and the same three countries received child migrants from the UK. The UK and Ireland have neither populations of Indigenous people nor child migrants. It is to a discussion of social policy related to these two groups that we now turn.

Child migration

From the mid-1800s, over 130,000 unaccompanied child migrants from the UK were sent to Canada, Australia and New Zealand. The earliest child migration programmes were those to

Canada from the 1860s to 1939. The first in Australia were in 1911 and in New Zealand in 1920, ceasing in 1970 and 1954, respectively. Since the Second World War, Australia received the majority of child migrants – in the order of 3,300 children – with about 600 to New Zealand.[38] About a hundred of the children who came to Australia were Maltese. At the time of migration, most children were aged between three and 14 years, with the majority aged seven to 10 years.[39]

The majority of child migrants who travelled to Canada are no longer alive or are very elderly. There is considerable interest in them by their families and researchers but, as we shall see, less by government.[40] For some families, there is a desire for an official apology to make right the harms endured and to gain recognition for their forebears, as well as to learn about their lives and to undertake genealogical research.[41] The history of child migration to Canada is a way into understanding the context and motivations for this now much criticised practice. It commenced in the context of the child rescue movement, as noted by Parker:

> Various circumstances thus conspired to create the opportunity for a reconsideration of emigration as a solution to the intensified social and economic problems of Britain in the late 1860s. Children came to be regarded as an especially appropriate group of candidates. Child-saving motives could be blended with the wish to see the poor rates relieved and society protected from the dangers of unbridled street-children. Compulsory education was still in the future, while in both the industrial towns and in the countryside new technologies reduced the call for child labour.[42]

In Canada, there was demand for both farm labourers and, to a lesser extent, domestic servants, and both occupations could be undertaken by children. In particular, there was a shortage of seasonal farm labour and child migrants took up this work, with most living in these rural areas on farms.[43] While Canadian children in institutional care were also placed on farms, this occurred to a much lesser extent, partly because of the fewer number of children and the need for institutions 'to be kept full to encourage subscriptions and thus to enable such visible charitable activities to continue', as was noted previously in relation to children in other countries.[44]

According to the advocacy organisation Child Migrants Trust, child migrants 'were sent overseas by specialist agencies … established specifically for the purpose of migrating young children to populate the empire with "good, white British stock"'.[45] Indeed, after the Second World War:

> a popular immigration slogan was 'the child, the best immigrant'. They constituted a particularly attractive category of migrant because they were seen to assimilate more easily, were more adaptable, had a long working life ahead and could be cheaply housed in dormitory style accommodation.[46]

In other words, even though it was claimed at the time that sending the children overseas would provide them with greater opportunities in life, there were other social policy reasons, 'none of which gave first priority to the needs of the children involved'.[47]

A range of religious and charitable organisations were involved in the work of child migration. The Fairbridge Society was set up specifically for the purpose of child migration and others, such as Barnardos, the Church of England, the Methodist Church, the Salvation Army and the Catholic Church, were major providers of care in the destination countries. In Australia, unlike in Canada, child migrants were to live in institutional care rather than with farming families. There were over 30 homes approved by the Australian government for the housing of child migrants, most run by religious or non-government organisations.[48] In Western Australia, the Australian state to where most child migrants were sent, homes included the Christian Brothers orphanages known as Bindoon and Castledare. The Fairbridge farms in Western Australia and New South Wales were also places where many child migrants lived.[49] In New Zealand, children

were typically fostered.[50] Barnardos' current view of their work
of this period reflects changes in the understanding of care:

> Since the early 1980s we have been one of the
> strongest critics of the policy of child migration
> and have publicly acknowledged the hurt that was
> caused to many child migrants. However, between
> 1921 and 1965, consistent with the mistakes made in
> child welfare at the time, we were one of the leading
> advocates of child migration. Now we understand
> how incredibly important it is for children to have
> contact with their birth families so that they know
> where they have come from.[51]

Indigenous children

There are similarities in the policies of Australia and Canada
where children were removed from their families and placed
in care on the basis of their indigeneity. In both cases, from
the 19th century, it was intended that their experiences of
care would bring about their accelerated assimilation into the
dominant non-Aboriginal society. These practices have had
devastating consequences for individuals, their families and
wider communities in terms of language, culture and kinship.[52]

Australian Aboriginal and Torres Strait Islander children

During the period 1910–70, an estimated 100,000 Aboriginal
and Torres Strait Islander children were removed from their
families, between a tenth and a third of all Australian Indigenous
children.[53] During much of this period, Australian states
administered Aboriginal affairs, not the federal government as
in Canada.[54] All states except Tasmania developed a separate
child welfare system for Indigenous children in addition to
the system in place for non-Indigenous children. As historian
Margaret Jacobs explains, this 'gave the state and its ministers
unprecedented powers over Aboriginal families. State authorities
became legal guardians over *all* Aboriginal children'.[55] By the
late 19th century, there were 'systematic removal practices being

implemented through a range of assimilation and "protection policies"'. These policies varied from state to state. For example:

> [i]n Queensland and Western Australia, the Chief Protector was able to enforce protection policies to the effect that Indigenous people could be removed into large, highly regulated government settlements and missions. Children were removed from their mothers at about the age of four years and placed in dormitories away from their families. At about the age of 14 years, the children were sent off the missions and settlements to work.[56]

In New South Wales, policies were oriented towards assimilation for some Indigenous people and 'protection' for others depending on the perceived degree of Aboriginality. Aboriginal children, however, were typically removed from their families and placed in institutions, where they were trained in unskilled labour such as domestic service or farm work.[57] This policy of assimilation was in place nationally by the early decades of the 20th century. At the 1937 national Aboriginal Welfare Conference of commonwealth and state Aboriginal authorities, it was agreed that:

> The destiny of the natives of aboriginal [sic] origin, but not of the full blood [sic], lies in their ultimate absorption by the people of the Commonwealth.... all efforts should be directed to that end ... efforts by all state authorities should be directed towards the education of children of mixed aboriginal blood [sic] at white standards, and their subsequent employment under the same conditions as whites with a view to their taking their place in the white community on an equal footing with the whites.[58]

Assimilation was reaffirmed as official Australian policy over the middle decades of the 20th century.[59] However, in response to Indigenous resistance, the formal policy of assimilation was abandoned, and forced removals ceased from as recently as

1970. By the 1980s, it was acknowledged that, despite these changes, practices concerned with the removal and placement of Indigenous children could still be discriminatory and large numbers of these children are in care.[60]

Canadian Aboriginal children

Between the 1870s and 1980s, approximately 100,000 First Nations, Métis and Inuit children were placed in residential schools across Canada. These schools were funded by the Canadian government and operated by the Catholic, Anglican, Presbyterian and United Churches. Over this time, there were 130 schools and, at its peak, 80 in operation at any one time. The reason for such schools was:

> the assumption that aboriginal [sic] culture was unable to adapt to a rapidly modernizing society. It was believed that native children could be successful if they assimilated into mainstream Canadian society by adopting Christianity and speaking English or French. Students were discouraged from speaking their first language or practising native traditions. If they were caught, they would experience severe punishment.[61]

Residential schools have been described as the 'centrepiece' of Canada's assimilation strategy.[62] The intention was that Aboriginal children would abandon their traditions and adopt mainstream Canadian culture and practices and, in turn, pass on these values to their own children. An economic motive was also in operation: 'the disappearance of the Indians as distinct peoples would free the lands for settlement at no financial cost to the nation'.[63]

During the second half of the 20th century, residential schools were closed down and responsibility for Aboriginal child welfare shifted to the provincial or territorial child welfare systems. At this time, there was then a sharp increase in the number of Aboriginal children placed in care, many permanently through adoption. This occurred as a result of concerns about child welfare that were often related to socio-economic disadvantage and other social problems for which support was not provided. This period is known as the 'Sixties Scoop' and describes a time when from up to a third of the child population in some Aboriginal communities were adopted and a third of all children in care were Aboriginal. In the 1960s, special programmes were in place for such adoptions to take place, including to families in the US.[64] Since the 1960s, due to concerns about the scale of the removal of Indigenous children, First Nations groups have developed child welfare agencies with funding from the federal government.[65]

In the 1990s, former residential school students successfully challenged the federal government and churches in the largest Canadian class action settlement. As a result, the Indian Residential Schools Settlement Agreement has provided compensation to former students and established the Truth and Reconciliation Commission of Canada.[66] (For further discussion, see Chapters Three, Four and Five.)

New Zealand Māori children

In contrast, in New Zealand, Māori children were not placed into institutional care in large numbers until the 1960s at a time when there was increasing migration of Māori people from rural areas into the cities. Before this time, they were typically placed in foster care with Māori families. While Māori children came to be over-represented in care, and they were exposed to similar processes of assimilation through the lack of attention to their cultural heritage, there were not specific policies or programmes targeting Māori children (nor, more recently, as adult care-leavers).[67] In this book, they are not discussed as a separate group from the wider New Zealand population of adult care-leavers.[68]

Literature review

Before proceeding to review the literature about care and its aftermath, it is important to reiterate that some people recall positive experiences in care that stood them in good stead for their later adult lives.[69] This is not in any way to diminish the difficulties that some have experienced, but rather to acknowledge the diversity of outcomes. Others, despite adverse beginnings, have had mixed experiences across their lifetime. Even though some had tough times both in care and before entering care, many have gone on to live satisfying and fulfilled lives, seeking support at times as others in the community also do. Others have struggled. For this group, the impact has been the greatest, as reflected in the findings of the Commission to Inquire into Child Abuse in Ireland:

> witnesses reported that their adult lives were blighted by childhood memories of fear and abuse. They gave accounts of troubled relationships and loss of contact with their siblings and extended families. Witnesses described parenting difficulties ranging from being over-protective to being harsh and commented on the intergenerational sequelae of their childhood abuse.... Witnesses also described lives marked by poverty, social isolation, alcoholism, mental illness, sleep disturbance, aggressive behaviour and self harm. Approximately 30% described a constellation of ongoing, debilitating mental health concerns.[70]

Other inquiries reporting on the long-term impact on Indigenous people who were removed from their family and community described the devastating loss of their language, culture and spirituality.[71] Thus, this literature review considers the following questions: what are the long-term individual and collective harmful effects produced by childhoods in care? What do we know about the support needs of adult care-leavers? What might this tell us about how to best provide support?[72]

Acknowledging the complexities

In reviewing the literature, there are two important considerations to bear in mind. One is the difficulty in identifying relationships between care experiences and lifelong outcomes. As social policy researcher Roy Parker explains in relation to child migrants, which is equally applicable to other children in care:

How children react to the trauma of uprooting will, of course, depend on many things: for example, their age, their personality, the completeness of the severance from their past and, not least, on the kinds of misfortunes that have already befallen them.[73]

Adult outcomes are also likely to be affected by the length of time in care, the forms of care experienced and the experience of care itself. Here, we can consider such factors as: their access to, and support for undertaking, education; how 'caring' the care environment was; the level of emotional and physical safety provided; and whether children were supported to retain their cultural identity and family relationships. The quality and quantity of basic necessities such as food and health care are also important elements of childhood experience and potentially affect long-term outcomes in adulthood, as is the level of support provided when leaving care and their age of independence post-care.[74]

Having established the range of factors likely to affect adult outcomes, identifying their long-term effects is not straightforward. There can be difficulties in drawing links between care experiences and adult outcomes as the time period since life in care increases.[75] In some instances, identifying a direct relationship between specific care and adult life experiences, and distinguishing these outcomes from those attributable to other non-care-related events, can be complex. As Parker notes: '[m]uch remains to be understood about the influence of such factors, about their interactions, and about their short- and long-term psychological and physical consequences'.[76] In relation to Canadian Indigenous peoples:

> Narratives and life histories suggest that the residential school experience has had enduring psychological, social and economic effects on survivors.... Of course, the links between events and outcomes made by individuals in their narratives do not prove causality, but they give a clear picture of how suffering is understood and identify plausible connections for more systematic study.[77]

This suggests the need for further research in this area to better understand the long-term impact of harmful experiences in care. While acknowledging these uncertainties, I work from the premise that care experiences are a contributing factor – sometimes a major factor – to what comprises an adult life post-care.

A second important consideration is the sources from which knowledge about the long-term outcomes of care and adult care-leavers' need for support have been derived.[78] Much relevant information about experiences of care and its lifelong effects can be found not only in the academic literature, but also in other genres, such as biographies, public inquiries, programme evaluations and materials produced by advocacy groups. These various genres reflect the range of sources identified in the 'knowledge diamond' – adult care-leavers, practitioners, policymakers and researchers.

First, many adult care-leaver biographical accounts describe damaging childhoods or overcoming adversity to lead successful and fulfilling lives.[79] Some accounts emphasise mixed experiences of care, drawing attention to those aspects that were harmful but also highlighting individuals or aspects of their environment that were helpful in the longer term.[80] For Indigenous populations in both Australia and Canada, the loss of family, culture and identity are powerful themes.[81] These biographical accounts cannot be regarded as representative experiences of care, but their variety and depth give us insights into the impact of the past on the present. In addition, while usually not written specifically to seek support for the individual concerned, these testimonies typically provide compelling evidence of the ways in which care had impacted on their lives, and how, in some instances, support may have been beneficial.[82]

Public inquiries have been a second and powerful means by which detailed evidence of the lives of adult care-leavers has been revealed. Johanna Sköld notes that 'knowledge of how life turned out for adult care leavers was sparse before the inquiry commissions started asking these questions of the care leavers themselves'.[83] Like biographical works, inquiries tend to present negative outcomes since, as explained in Chapter Three, they often stem from abuse investigations, and so the findings may not be generalisable to all those who grew up in care. There have been few evaluations specifically targeting programmes or services for adult care-leavers, but to the extent that this has occurred, there are some in which they have reflected on their experiences and engaged with policy processes.[84] Such evaluations are noted in the discussion of specialist support in Chapter Six.

Materials produced by advocacy organisations are a fourth source of information about adult lives after care. These organisations, discussed further in Chapter Eight, campaign around a number of issues, including historical abuse and access to records. A specific form of research being undertaken by some advocacy organisations is membership surveys, such as those conducted in Australia, Ireland and the UK.[85] Such surveys typically provide evidence for the need for support in a range of areas. What is important about these four sources is that adult care-leavers themselves have been central to the accounts of care and its impact.

From these various sources and the academic literature, a number of overlapping harmful impacts of care can be identified: mental ill-health; poor educational outcomes, including in relation to life skills and subsequent restricted employment opportunities and socio-economic disadvantage; troubles with interpersonal relationships and parenting; and loss of identity, fractured family relationships and cultural disconnection. There is also a lack of understanding in the wider community that has contributed to limited support for the plight of adult care-leavers. As a result, for some adult care-leavers, there has been the need to recount and gain acknowledgement for these harmful experiences and their long-term impacts. A summary of the literature pertaining to each of these areas follows.

Mental health

Research with adult care-leavers has suggested higher levels of mental ill-health than that in the wider community.[86] Physical, sexual and emotional abuse during childhood are risk factors for mental ill-health in adulthood. Anxiety disorders (including post-traumatic stress disorder), depression, self-harm and alcohol and substance abuse have been found to be linked to experiences of child abuse.[87] These impacts of child abuse have been found to occur 'well into late life'.[88] The institutionalised environments in which many children lived in past decades, and the fracturing of families and disconnection from parents, siblings and communities, increased social isolation and vulnerability to mental ill-health. As noted by Laurence Kirmayer and his colleagues, among Canada's Indigenous people, 'the policies of forced assimilation have had profound effects on Aboriginal peoples at every level of experience from individual identity and mental health, to the structure and integrity of families, communities, bands and nations'.[89]

Common themes are evident internationally regarding social policy responses to the mental ill-health of adult care-leavers. Long-term counselling was considered very important to a group of adult care-leavers who had given evidence to inquiries into child abuse in residential institutions in England and Wales, but that support had not been available to all. Some preferred self-help groups.[90] In Scotland, Moyra Hawthorn highlighted the importance of consulting with adult care-leavers to identify their support needs. Moreover, she recommended that counsellors have additional training to gain specialist expertise in working with adult care-leavers.[91] Similarly, a study of the mental health of Irish adult care-leavers recommended that evidence-based psychological treatment should be available, that the personnel providing these services should be properly trained to work with this group and that evaluations of such services should be undertaken.[92] In Canada, psychologist David Wolfe and his colleagues concluded that 'the field of mental health needs to become familiar with [victims of historical abuse] particular assessment and treatment needs'.[93] Most recently, a guide developed for welfare professionals working with Irish adult care-leavers in the UK is likely to prove to be very useful and adaptable to other social policy contexts.[94]

While, as these studies suggest, some attention has been paid to the mental health of adult care-leavers, particular attention has been paid to Indigenous adult care-leavers and their communities due to the impact of policies of colonisation and assimilation, including the forced removal of children. As noted by Indigenous psychiatrists Mason Durie, Helen Milroy and Ernest Hunter: 'mental health services have often struggled to accommodate indigenous worldviews and traditional healing alongside more conventional psychiatric methods'.[95] Despite these challenges, they argue that, since the 1980s, four different approaches have been used: the utilisation of traditional healing services; the incorporation of ethnic values and customary practice in treatment programmes; the development of ethnicity-centred psychological therapies; and an increase in the Indigenous mental health workforce.[96] In relation to the use of traditional healing for adult care-leavers, in Canada, psychologist Joseph Gone noted that there are few rigorous assessments of such programmes.[97] In response, he analysed the therapeutic approach and explored the meaning of healing in a community-based counselling programme that was established to address the historical trauma of the Canadian residential schools.[98] Also in Canada, psychologist Rod McCormick described modes of counselling that combine elements of 'mainstream psychological approaches and traditional healing approaches in a complementary fashion'.[99]

Educational attainment, employment and related socio-economic disadvantage

The educational attainment of children in care has typically been lower than that of others in the community.[100] The provision of poor educational facilities, the requirement to undertake domestic, farm and other work, and the impact of abuse all contributed to educational performance at levels lower than other children.[101] For those in foster care, the disruption to schooling through changes in placement was also disadvantageous to educational attainment. These factors could result in low literacy and numeracy. Worth noting, however, is that despite difficult educational experiences as children, some research indicates that adult care-leavers return to study in later life at rates seemingly higher than their counterparts.[102]

As adults, low educational attainment could result in employment in unskilled, poorly paid occupations, or mental or physical ill-health may have prevented long-term participation in the workforce.[103] The combination of these factors could result in lifelong socio-economic disadvantage.[104] Various authors have argued for redress schemes to address this disadvantage, particularly in Australia, where they have been limited in their implementation.[105]

Interpersonal relationships and parenting

The Australian Senate Community Affairs References Committee's report *Forgotten Australians* highlighted the plight of this group:

> A fundamental, ongoing issue is the lack of trust and security and lack of interpersonal and life skills that are acquired through a normal family upbringing, especially social and parenting skills. A lifelong inability to initiate and maintain stable, loving relationships was described by many care leavers who have undergone multiple relationships and failed marriages.[106]

There is evidence from public inquiries suggesting that some adult care-leavers need greater support to parent because of their own difficult experiences of being parented.[107] In relation to Canadian Indigenous people, transgenerational effects of the residential schools include 'the transmission of explicit models and ideologies of parenting based on experiences in punitive institutional settings'.[108] Compounding these circumstances are the fracturing of family relationships that can lead to reduced social networks and support for parenting. However, the limited research that has been done in this area is somewhat contradictory; it may be that a major reason for parenting difficulties is that adult care-leavers have children at a younger age.[109]

Identity, family relationships and cultural connectedness

A sense of personal identity and belonging is central to good mental health and well-being.[110] As we have seen, families were broken up and children were removed from their communities to be placed in care, sometimes from a young age and for many years. Adult care-leavers may not know who their families are or their own personal history. If they did know their family, in care, children were routinely separated by age and gender, so children may not have grown up with their siblings and may have been discouraged from having contact with them. Unlike what is considered to be good practice today, children in care in previous decades were not routinely encouraged or supported to have information about themselves and their family.[111]

There are two bodies of literature relevant here. First, there is an emerging literature specifically concerned with enhancing identity and family reunification through access to personal records, including those held by care institutions and child welfare departments. Research conducted primarily in the UK and Australia has focused on areas such as highlighting the importance of records to care-leavers, promoting the supported release of records and identifying the need for adult care-leaver-specific legislation such as that which exists for adoptees.[112] A guide developed for staff in the UK who release care records is very useful and adaptable to other social policy contexts.[113]

Second, there is a body of literature concerned with the impact of removal from, and reconnection with, Indigenous families and communities. In Australia and Canada, the removal of Indigenous children from their families and communities and discouragement to engage with their language and cultural practices resulted in their loss of traditional knowledge and disconnection from their heritage.[114] As noted by the Law Commission of Canada:

> deprived of their native languages, cultural traditions and religion, many Aboriginal children in residential schools were cut off from their heritage and made to feel ashamed of it. As a result, the residential school system inflicted terrible damage not just on individuals but on families, entire communities and peoples.[115]

Thus, as well as the ways in which care has impacted on an individual's sense of identity, health and well-being, there are more systemic effects. Removal of children over generations and the subsequent attempts to assimilate them into non-Aboriginal society devastated not just families, but also communities (and nations) as their loss impacted on the transfer of language and culture across time. This is not to say that those communities have not survived in many instances; rather, that such removal policies have had significant negative effects.[116] Laurence Kirmayer highlights the centrality of healing practices to the revitalisation of Indigenous cultures and communities. He argues that '[f]or many indigenous peoples, systems of healing are important expressions of traditional forms of spirituality, social organisation and worldview'.[117] Such healing practices have been incorporated into social policy responses to Indigenous Canadian adult care-leavers.[118]

Wider community understandings: telling their story and being acknowledged

Another systemic effect is the lack of understanding in the wider community about the aftermath of care and its impact on individuals. Limited understanding has contributed to a lack of accountability for harms perpetrated.[119] This at least partly reflects the marginalisation of children who were in care typically due to their family circumstances, socio-economic status or indigeneity, and the stigmatisation that they experienced because of this, both as children and adults. Some were too frightened to complain and others were actively silenced in attempting to reveal their experiences of care.[120] As David Wolfe and his colleagues explain, in relation to research conducted with male survivors of institutional abuse:

> On several occasions a child's efforts to disclose the abuse were thwarted by the strong community support for the institution, as well as the resources and power of the institution itself. Because the institution was located in a small, closely knit community that was bound by cultural, ethnic, and religious identities, formidable resistance still remains to acknowledging the men's abusive experiences and ongoing needs.[121]

That some adult care-leavers in Australia have become known as 'Forgotten Australians' reflects this view that, as a group, they had been marginalised. As noted by the Alliance of Forgotten Australians: 'telling their story is important.... Although it is painful for them, they want history recognised. Unpleasant truths are better understood than kept in darkness'.[122] The report of the Irish Commission to Inquire into Child Abuse noted that the most common reasons for giving evidence was 'to have the abuse they experienced as children officially recorded and to tell their story'.[123] Moreover, 'Most witnesses expressed the hope that a formal record of their experiences would contribute to a greater understanding of the circumstances in which such abuse occurs and would assist in the future protection of children'.[124] Thus, speaking out is not just about conveying the experiences of care-leavers themselves; it also expresses a concern for those children in care today and in the future.

Conclusion

In this chapter, we have briefly considered the policy context in which the care of children has occurred since the mid-20th century, and an overview of the impact of care and support needs have been outlined. While there is a growing literature concerned with the impact of harmful experiences of care, less research has been about social policy responses to these specific harms and the support that can be provided. It is with this that this book deals.

Those areas suggested by the literature, and for which there are initiatives in place, include: giving adult care-leavers the opportunity to tell their story of care and its impact; having these experiences acknowledged; offering redress for the damage caused; and providing specialist support in relation to mental health, education, social engagement, cultural reconnection, access to records and family reunification. Public inquiries have been a forum in which adult care-leavers have told their life stories, and they are an important source of information about the aftermath of care for those harmed as children. The scene is set, then, for a closer examination of the various public inquiries in Chapter Three.

THREE

Public inquiries

With knowledge comes responsibility. (Helen Holland, adult care-leaver and advocate, 2013[1])

Helen Holland, quoted here, is a founding member of the Scottish advocacy and support organisation In Care Abuse Survivors (INCAS). INCAS has lobbied for a full public inquiry into care and has had input into Scotland's National Confidential Forum, discussed later. Such inquiries produce knowledge, and Holland draws our attention to their implicit purpose: that this knowledge must then be used to inform responses. Advocacy groups such as INCAS play an important role in campaigning for public inquiries, which, in turn, have typically been the impetus to bring about system reform of varying degrees. Inquiries of one sort or another have been held in all five countries under discussion in this book, and include those with national reach, which are largely the focus of this chapter.[2] Other more local or organisational enquiries have also been held. While public inquiries are the focus of this chapter, it is important to note that there are other forums in which knowledge about care and its outcomes have been identified. The Law Commission of Canada's report of 2000, *Restoring Dignity: Responding to Child Abuse in Canadian Institutions*, in discussing redress, very helpfully details the range of ways in which such information may be gathered. Criminal justice prosecutions, civil law actions, criminal injuries compensation programmes, ombudsman's inquiries and other community initiatives are all ways in which this may occur.

In this chapter, we first consider, generally, the purpose and nature of public inquiries. We then turn to a specific discussion of care-related public inquiries. While these inquiries have typically, but not always, had a focus on abuse in care, they have taken various forms, and the range is presented from across the five countries. Variations in the scope of these inquiries include how abuse is defined and whether specific forms of abuse are targeted, the range of population groups included, the time period covered, and the forms of care analysed.[3] While highly significant, attention to identity issues and disconnection from family and community are not always identified as an initial key concern of public inquiries. The distinguishing features of public inquiries are highlighted, including the circumstances of their establishment and their structure, sources, findings and outcomes. In particular, I pay attention to the three countries where national public inquiries have been held: Australia, Canada and Ireland. Then, in the conclusion to the book, I will return to this discussion having considered in detail the outcomes of the inquiries across subsequent chapters by considering whether knowledge has brought responsibility.

Public inquiries – their purpose and nature

According to the Law Commission of Canada, a public inquiry is 'an official, independent public investigation ordered by a federal or provincial cabinet'.[4] Such inquiries are differentiated from those conducted by government officers, with their credibility and standing enhanced through the appointment of judges as commissioners. While they have their terms of reference determined for them, their independence is evident in other ways. Typically, public inquiries:

> determine their own procedures. They may retain researchers to conduct studies on any matter within the mandate of the inquiry. Public hearings are common, and a broad range of people may be invited to participate, often in innovative ways. Some public inquiries adopt court-style hearings in which individuals and organisations are represented

by lawyers who present evidence and cross-examine witnesses.[5]

Through access to this wide range of sources of evidence, matters that have both affected individuals and were systemic in nature can be investigated, and recommendations can be made on actions to be taken to remedy harms. Such recommendations could include that 'a prosecution be launched, a compensation be paid, or that an institution be redesigned or closed'; however, public inquiries have 'no power to impose formal sanctions on individuals or organisations or to implement any of their recommendations'.[6] For this reason, a public inquiry may be called a 'toothless tiger'. Public inquiries thus rely on their credibility and standing to engage government, other relevant organisations and the wider community to ensure that the recommended actions are undertaken.

Public inquiries have an important function in providing a forum in which concerns can be raised and the community can be made aware of the suffering of those affected. Participants in a public inquiry are given the opportunity to recount their experiences, they are listened to and there are commitments made that action will be taken to address the issues that they have raised. Sometimes, individuals may wish to participate in an inquiry but not present their contributions in a public forum due to the sensitivity of the topic, or for other reasons. Public inquiries can hold hearings that are conducted privately and written submissions can be held in confidence or published anonymously.

Public inquiries typically produce a report that serves the function of documenting the topic in detailed ways that have not been done before. This public record has both practical and symbolic importance. Identifying that the topic is worthy of such attention is particularly significant when inquiries deal with matters that have previously been considered unimportant by those in authority or deal with marginalised groups of people. Inquiries, then, can 'give voice' to individuals and groups who may not have had the opportunity to speak publicly about their experiences before. Reports may make liberal use of the oral and written evidence of those affected, as well as historical photographs, and some have produced videos for public education purposes. Some reports have been intentionally written in plain language or with summary plain-language versions to facilitate access to the findings by the wider community.

Inquiries serve the function of promoting accountability for the actions under investigation. As indicated earlier, evidence derived from public inquiries can be forwarded to other agencies, such as the police, for further investigation, or the inquiry may have similar powers to investigate. However, as noted by the Law Commission of Canada in relation to child abuse:

> accountability should not necessarily be seen as synonymous with punishment or the imposition of liability. Some survivors may be satisfied just to see the record set straight and the perpetrators identified; at a minimum, this would expose the disbelief and denial of those in authority at the time the abuse took place. There is, in other words, value in making findings of accountability, even if legal liability is not attached to those findings. In fact, there are times when the law is powerless to impose civil liability despite the acknowledgement of personal responsibility; this happens, for example, when a claim for damages is barred by a statute of limitations.[7]

Importantly, inquiries can promote accountability not just in terms of past actions, but also for the future by informing policy and practice. A common concern of those affected by institutional child abuse is to ensure that children in care today do not suffer the same experiences.

Establishment, purpose and structure of care-related inquiries

While public inquiries related to adult care-leavers were conducted before 1990, this book focuses on the most recent ones. From the 1990s, inquiries have been concerned with 'hearing survivor testimony', and are therefore of particular interest.[8] There has also been an increased incidence of inquiries over the last 25 years and this has occurred as least partly because of a greater appreciation of children's rights to be protected and to live in environments that facilitate their development. A legal framework identifying these rights was enshrined in the 1989 United Nations Convention on the Rights of the Child. Harm in care, then, could be understood as an abuse of their rights, and rights-based approaches have been used in challenging governments about their histories of care.[9]

Table 3.1 provides an overview of the major inquiries undertaken in the five countries in the period between 1990 and 2015. There are considerable differences internationally, and in the next sections, the establishment, purpose and structure of key inquiries from each country are explained.

Australia

Australia has been a leader in conducting inquiries into care and care-related abuse, with major public inquiries into the circumstances of the three population groups – Indigenous people, former child migrants and those who are neither Indigenous nor former child migrants – in that order since the mid-1990s.[10] Responsibility for child welfare is largely handled at the level of state and territory governments in Australia, but the federal government also has an interest in wider related social policy and in Indigenous matters. For these reasons, inquiries have occurred at both state and federal levels. As well as the three Australian national inquiries into matters related to adult care-leavers, and one ongoing into institutional responses to sexual abuse, others have been held at state level.

Then Senator Andrew Murray, a former British child migrant to Rhodesia who moved to Western Australia as an adult, was instrumental in bringing about two enquiries that investigated, first, child migration and, later, the experiences of Forgotten Australians, reporting in 2001 and 2004, respectively.[11] These inquiries followed on from an earlier national enquiry instigated by the Human Rights and Equal Opportunity Commission (HREOC), reporting in 1997, which investigated the circumstances of Indigenous children who had been removed from their families.[12] In Australia, in contrast to other countries,

Table 3.1: Key public inquiries concerned with adult care-leavers, 1990–2015

Country	Inquiry and body responsible	Key report	Date of conduct of inquiry
Australia	**Western Australia** – Removal of Children Inquiry, Aboriginal Legal Service of Western Australia	*Telling our Story: A Report by the Aboriginal Legal Service of Western Australia (Inc) on the Removal of Aboriginal Children from their Families in Western Australia*	1994–95
	Australia – National Inquiry into the Separation of Aboriginal and Torres Strait Islanders Children from their Families, Human Rights and Equal Opportunity Commission	*Bringing Them Home: Report of the National Inquiry into the Separation of Aboriginal and Torres Strait Islanders Children from their Families*	1995–97
	Western Australia – Inquiry into Child Migration, Select Committee, Legislative Assembly, Western Australian Parliament	*Select Committee into Child Migration: Interim Report*	1996
	Queensland – Commission of Inquiry into Abuse of Children in Queensland Institutions, Queensland Parliament, Minister for Families, Youth and Community Care	*Commission of Inquiry into Abuse of Children in Queensland Institutions: Final Report*	1998–99
	Australia – Inquiry into Child Migration, Australian Senate, Community Affairs References Committee	*Lost Innocents: Righting the Record. The Report of the Community Affairs References Committee on Child Migration*	2000–01
	Australia – Inquiry into Children in Institutional Care, Australian Senate, Community Affairs References Committee	*Forgotten Australians: A Report on Australians who Experienced Institutional or Out-of-home Care as Children*	2003–04
	Tasmania – Review of Claims of Abuse from Adults in State Care as Children, Tasmania Ombudsman and Department of Health and Human Services	*Listen to the Children: Review of Claims of Abuse from Adults in State Care as Children*	2003–04
	South Australia – Commission of Inquiry (Children in State Care), South Australian Parliament	*Children in State Care: Commission of Inquiry. Allegations of Sexual Abuse and Death from Criminal Conduct*	2004–08
	Victoria – Investigation into the Storage and Management of Ward Records by the Department of Human Services, Victorian Ombudsman	*Investigation into the Storage and Management of Ward Records by the Department of Human Services*	2011–12
	Victoria – Parliamentary Inquiry into the Handling of Child Abuse by Religious and Other Non-Government Organisations, Victorian Parliament, Family and Community Development Committee	*Inquiry into the Handling of Child Abuse by Religious and Other Organisations*	2012–13
	Australia – Royal Commission into Institutional Responses to Child Sexual Abuse, Australian Parliament	*Interim Report, Volumes 1 and 2 (and ongoing)*	2013–

Public inquiries

Country	Inquiry and body responsible	Key report	Date of conduct of inquiry
Canada	Canada – Royal Commission on Aboriginal Peoples, Canadian Parliament	Report of the Royal Commission on Aboriginal Peoples	1991–96
	British Columbia – Treatment of Children in Jericho Hill School, Ombudsman of British Columbia	Public Report No 32: Abuse of Deaf Students at Jericho Hill School	1992–93
	New Brunswick – Treatment of Children in Kingsclear Training School and Two Other Institutions in That Province, Commission of Inquiry	Report of the Commission of Inquiry – Miller Inquiry	1992–95
	Quebec – Treatment of 'Duplessis Orphans', Quebec Ombudsman	The 'Children of Duplessis': A Time for Solidarity	1992–99
	Nova Scotia – Inquiry into institutional abuse, Investigation led by Former Chief Justice of New Brunswick, Stuart Stratton	Report of an Independent Investigation in Respect of Incidents and Allegations of Sexual and Other Physical Abuse at Five Nova Scotia Residential Institutions (Stratton Report)	1994–95
	Canada – Inquiry into the Abuse of Children in Institutions, Law Commission of Canada	Restoring Dignity: Responding to Child Abuse in Canadian Institutions	1997–2000
	British Columbia – Treatment of the Sons of Freedom Doukhobor Children, Ombudsman of British Columbia	Public Report No 38: Righting the Wrong – The Confinement of the Sons of Freedom Doukhobor Children	1999
	Nova Scotia – Inquiry into institutional abuse, Independent Review by Fred Kaufman, QC	Searching for Justice, An Independent Review of Nova Scotia's Response to Reports of Institutional Abuse (Kaufman Report)	1999–2002
	Canada – Truth and Reconciliation Commission of Canada	Honouring the Truth: Reconciling for the Future. Summary of the Final Report of the Truth and Reconciliation Commission of Canada	2008–2015
New Zealand	New Zealand – Ministry of Social Development	Social Welfare Residential Care, 1950–1994	2006
	New Zealand – Ministry of Social Development	Understanding Kohitere	2006
	New Zealand – Confidential Listening and Assistance Service, Department of Internal Affairs		2008–2014

43

Country	Inquiry and body responsible	Key report	Date of conduct of inquiry
United Kingdom	England – Pindown Inquiry, Staffordshire County Council	The Pindown Experience and the Protection of Children	1991
	England – Inquiry into Sexual Abuse of Residents by Head of Home and Staff Members, Leicestershire County Council	The Leicestershire Inquiry	1993
	Wales – Inquiry into Child Abuse in Clwyd Council's Children's Home, internal social service inquiry conducted by an independent panel	Unpublished report known as the Jillings Report	1994–96
	Wales – North Wales Tribunal of Enquiry	Lost in Care: Report of the Tribunal of Inquiry into Abuse of Children in Care in the Former County Council Areas of Gwynedd and Clwyd since 1974 (Waterhouse Report)	1996–2000
	England and Wales – Children's Safeguards Review, Department of Health	People Like Us: The Report of the Review of the Safeguards for Children Living Away from Home	1997
	Scotland – Safeguarding Children Living Away from Home, Scottish Government	Children's Safeguards Review	1997
	United Kingdom – Inquiry into the Welfare of Former British Child Migrants, House of Commons Health Committee	Health – Third Report – An Inquiry into the Welfare of Former British Child Migrants	1997–98
	Scotland – Edinburgh Inquiry, City of Edinburgh Council	Edinburgh's Children: The Report of the Edinburgh Inquiry into Abuse and Protection of Children in Care	1998–99
	Scotland – Fife Council Independent Enquiry, Fife Council	Fife Council Independent Enquiry Established by the Chief Executive Following the Conviction of David Logan Murphy for the Sexual Abuse of Children	2001–02
	Scotland – Investigation into the Systemic Factors Which Had Allowed Abuse to Take Place in Children's Homes and Residential Schools, 1950–1995, Scottish Government	Historical Abuse Systemic Review	2007
	Scotland – Independent Inquiry into Abuse at Kerelaw Residential School and Secure Unit, Scottish Government and Glasgow City Council	Independent Inquiry into Abuse at Kerelaw Residential School and Secure Unit	2009
	Scotland – Time to be Heard Forum, Scottish Government	Time to be Heard: A Pilot Forum	2010–11
	Scotland – National Confidential Forum, Scottish Government	Learning the Lessons: Operation Pallial	2014–
	Scotland – National Inquiry into Historical Child Abuse, Scottish Government	Ongoing	2015–
	Wales – Independent Investigation Examining Claims of Historical Abuse at Children's Homes in North Wales, Operation Pallial, National Crime Agency	Ongoing	2012–
	Northern Ireland – Inquiry into Historical Institutional Abuse, Northern Ireland Assembly	Ongoing	2012–
	England and Wales – Independent Panel Inquiry into Child Sexual Abuse	Ongoing	2014–

Country	Inquiry and body responsible	Key report	Date of conduct of inquiry
Ireland	**Ireland** – Commission to Inquire into Child Abuse	*Final Report of the Commission to Inquire into Child Abuse (Ryan Report)*	2000–09
	Ireland – Inter-departmental Committee to Establish the Facts of State Involvement with the Magdalen Laundries	*Inter-departmental Committee to Establish the Facts of State Involvement with the Magdalen Laundries (McAleese Report)*	2011–12
	Ireland – Ascertain responses to *McAleese Report*	*Magdalen Commission Report (Quirke Report)*	2013

these three inquiries were specifically concerned with adult care-leavers and had a broader focus than abuse. As historian Shurlee Swain and her colleagues have argued:

> Before the enquiries and subsequent apologies, Forgotten Australians [and former child migrants and members of the Stolen Generations] were confronted by a cultural silence which denied them the language, concepts and accepted narratives within which to construct and narrate their own experiences.[13]

Commencing in 2013, a Royal Commission is being held into institutional responses to child sexual abuse, which includes many adult care-leavers in its ambit.[14] In its first year, more than 1,000 victims gave evidence to the Royal Commission, with over 40% having experienced abuse in either children's homes or foster care.[15] By January 2015, nearly 3,000 people had spoken to the Commission, with another 1,500 waiting to do so. In addition, by this time, over 3,000 written submissions had been received.[16] The impetus for the Royal Commission came very much out of the lobbying of the advocacy organisation Care Leavers Australia Network (CLAN), whose work in this area is discussed in Chapter Eight. Despite appreciation of the advent of this inquiry, some advocates have expressed concern that its focus is confined to sexual abuse and does not include investigation of other forms of abuse typically experienced by many who grew up in care. Others have been less than enthusiastic, expressing concern that there have been similar inquiries that have produced substantial knowledge that was not subsequently 'translated into practice'. They argue that the 'considerable expenditure of money and human resources' could be better spent on furthering 'a broad Australian child protection and abuse responses agenda and services'.[17] While this may be true, what the Royal Commission does do, as well as producing knowledge, is provide a forum for those affected to present their accounts and receive acknowledgement.

Like the current Australian Royal Commission, the HREOC inquiry came about as a result of lobbying from two key Indigenous organisations: the Secretariat of the National

Aboriginal and Islander Child Care and Link-Up (New South Wales). They expressed concern that 'the general public's ignorance of the history of forcible removal was hindering the recognition of the needs of its victims and their families and the provision of services'.[18] Highlighting these concerns, the Royal Commission into Aboriginal Deaths in Custody, completed in 1991, found that 'half of the deaths investigated were members of the Stolen Generations'.[19] In 1994, the Aboriginal Legal Service of Western Australia undertook research into the removal of Indigenous children in that state.[20] The following year, the national inquiry was established, with the terms of reference including:

a) trace the past laws, practices and policies which resulted in the separation of Aboriginal and Torres Strait islander children from their families by compulsion, duress or undue influence, and the effects of those laws, practices and policies;

b) examine the adequacy of and need for any changes in current laws, practices and policies relating to services and procedures currently available to those Aboriginal and Torres Strait Islander peoples who were affected by the separation under compulsion, duress or undue influence of Aboriginal and Torres Strait Islander children from their families, including but not limited to current laws, practices and policies relating to access to individual and family records and to other forms of assistance towards locating and reunifying families;

c) examine the principles relevant to determining the justification for compensation for persons or communities affected by such separation.[21]

In undertaking this inquiry, public evidence in the form of both oral and written submissions was taken from Indigenous organisations and individuals, and government, Church and other non-government representatives; confidential evidence was also taken from Indigenous people affected by forcible removal and their families. Over 500 Indigenous people throughout

Australia contributed evidence regarding their experiences of forcible removal. An Indigenous Advisory Council provided advice on both the collection of this evidence and its analysis.[22]

As well as these national inquiries, four of the six Australian states have conducted inquiries into care or care-related topics. The earliest of these inquiries reported in 1999; the most recent in 2013.[23] All were concerned with abuse – some were limited to children in institutional state care; others included non-institutional forms of care and other providers of care.

The Royal Commission into Institutional Responses to Child Sexual Abuse is a good practice example of the ways in which participation in a public inquiry may be encouraged and supported. The Royal Commission provides for both private sessions and public hearings, as well as telephone and written submissions. Advice in plain language is available on the Commission's website on how to present a submission and how the private sessions run, as well as protocols for appearing at the public hearings.[24] Openness about these proceedings is further facilitated through the public hearings being webcast and their transcripts being lodged on the Royal Commission's website. Much further information about the conduct of the Royal Commission, the commissioners and related matters are found on the website. Importantly, support services are identified because the process of participating in a public inquiry, either privately or in a public hearing, can be emotionally difficult. As the Royal Commission website explains: 'making contact can be challenging for survivors. It may be the first time you have told anyone about the abuse, or it may bring back memories which are very hard to deal with'.[25] The contact details of support services are listed, which have received additional funding to work with those affected by the Royal Commission.

Canada

In Canada, as indicated in Table 3.1, there have been several investigations into abuse in various provinces and territories.[26] In addition, two key national public inquiries were held during the 1990s and a truth and reconciliation commission was completed in 2015. While public inquiries have targeted Indigenous people and the wider population, there has not been a public inquiry into the experiences of child migrants (known as home children in Canada) as there has been in Australia.

The 1996 Royal Commission on Aboriginal Peoples was established by the federal government and paid considerable attention to residential schools.[27] A second Canadian inquiry, completed in 2000, was initiated through a reference from the justice minister to the Law Commission of Canada. It was specifically concerned with addressing the harms inflicted on children who lived in institutions that were run or funded by the government, including residential schools for Indigenous children and other institutions such as orphanages, schools for the deaf and long-term health-care facilities. As argued by law academic Margaret Hall, a factor that contributed to the instigation of this inquiry was that the Canadian government was facing 'mass civil litigation' in the order of 'thousands of civil cases [having] been initiated by former pupils' of the residential schools; additionally, at this time, the churches were concerned that 'they may be bankrupted'.[28]

As noted in Chapter One, the Law Commission of Canada's task was to identify 'what types of processes would best address wrongdoing, while affording appropriate remedies, and promoting reconciliation, fairness and healing'.[29] In other words, this inquiry commenced with the knowledge that serious harm had been caused by the abuse that had occurred, and investigated what could be done about it in terms of redress for those affected, with the aim that something would be done. This is markedly different to other inquiries, where the starting point has been to discover the extent and nature of abuse, and to explore the possibility of responses. While the Law Commission inquiry had a major focus on Indigenous people (drawing on the earlier inquiry specifically about this group), it also paid attention to the non-Indigenous population. However, former child migrants were not identified as a population group.

Reflecting the aim of addressing harms, the Law Commission of Canada's inquiry was framed to investigate how those adults who had been abused as children understood their needs. Abuse was understood broadly, and included sexual, physical, spiritual, cultural, emotional and psychological forms.[30] A series of research reports was commissioned and overseen by specialist expert study panels, including those that analysed the needs of survivors of the residential schools for Indigenous children and other institutions.[31] These needs were summarised as: establishing a historical record and remembrance; acknowledgement; apology; accountability; access to therapy or counselling; access to education or training; financial compensation; and prevention and public awareness. The possible responses to these needs (including criminal justice prosecutions, civil law actions, criminal injuries compensation programmes, ombudsman and public inquiries, community initiatives, and redress schemes) were considered through an analysis of eight criteria, reflecting the identified needs: respect, engagement and choice; fact-finding; accountability; fairness; acknowledgement, apology and reconciliation, compensation, counselling, and education; needs of families, communities and peoples; and prevention and public education.[32] Further consultation occurred though the development of discussion papers that were made available in a range of ways for feedback about the proposed policy recommendations.

The most recent inquiry, the Truth and Reconciliation Commission of Canada, finalised in 2015, is a particular form of public inquiry. It partly arose as an outcome of the Law Commission of Canada's inquiry and was also a result of the largest class-action settlement in Canadian history, the Indian Residential Schools Settlement Agreement. While partly functioning as an inquiry, the Commission has operated much more as a means of improving understanding, promoting healing and renewing respectful relationships among the Canadian population. The Truth and Reconciliation Commission had a mandate 'to learn the truth about what happened in the residential schools and to inform all Canadians about what happened in the schools', and sources have included:

> records held by those who operated and funded the schools, testimony from officials of the institutions that operated the schools, and experiences reported by survivors, their families, communities and

anyone personally affected by the residential school experience and its subsequent impacts.[33]

In 2015, a National Research Centre will be opened at the University of Manitoba in Winnipeg to hold all these records and to make them available to the public. As part of its work, the Truth and Reconciliation Commission engaged in extensive public education activities to promote reconciliation, including through national, provincial and local events, and is supported by an impressive web presence.[34]

Ireland

In Ireland, the Commission to Inquire into Child Abuse conducted an extensive investigation examining experiences of abuse in care across much of the 20th century. Its report, published in 2009 and known as the *Ryan Report*, ran to over 2,500 pages and led to changes in Irish social policy and the position of the Roman Catholic Church in Ireland.[35] The release of this report has been described as 'a painful event in the history of modern Ireland'.[36] While there had been an earlier and influential inquiry in 1970 (resulting in the so-called *Kennedy Report*) that had recommended the closure of industrial schools, it had not revealed the extent of abuse in care. It had, however, engendered a political and social environment much more concerned about the rights of children in care, including the introduction of modernised child welfare legislation in 1991.[37]

In addition, in the 1990s, several key public events spurred concern about the increasingly recognised incidence of abuse in care. The programme *Dear Daughter*, broadcast in 1996 on Irish national television (RTÉ), outlined the experiences of physical and emotional abuse endured by Christine Buckley and other women who had grown up in the Irish Catholic orphanage Goldenbridge.[38] In 1999, the three-part series *States of Fear*, also broadcast on RTÉ, provided further shocking evidence of widespread and systemic abuse in Irish industrial schools, reformatories and other care institutions.[39] At the same time, a number of advocacy groups, such as One in Four, Irish Survivors of Child Abuse, the Aislinn Centre (founded by Christine

Buckley) and the London Irish Women's Group, campaigned for action to be taken by the Irish government.[40]

As noted by social policy academic Fred Powell and his colleagues, 'the survivors' voice became the basis of the Ryan Report'.[41] Indeed, the centrality of the evidence of abuse of survivors was laid down in its underpinning legislation. A principal function of the Commission was to 'provide for persons who have suffered abuse in childhood in institutions during the relevant period, an opportunity to recount the abuse, and make submissions, to a Committee'.[42] The Commission established two committees to which survivors provided evidence of their experiences of abuse in care. The Confidential Committee heard from 1,090 witnesses who spoke in confidence and were not interrogated. The Confidential Committee was 'conducted in an atmosphere that was as informal and as sympathetic to, and understanding of, the witnesses as was possible in the circumstances'.[43] The information gathered through the Confidential Committee was used to make 'proposals of a general nature' to inform the recommendations of the Commission.[44]

In contrast, the Investigation Committee had greater powers and was concerned more widely with the context and circumstances in which children were in care, and the institutions in which they resided, including their systems of management, operation and regulation.[45] The Investigation Committee also drew on a wider range of sources. As well as statements from the complainants, the Committee considered responses from those named by the complainants and the congregations affected by the allegations and relevant government departments, plus extensive documentation. Reflecting the powers of the Investigative Committee, it could 'compel witnesses, order the discovery of documents and impose penalties for refusal to testify and document destruction'.[46] There were major difficulties in the operation of the Investigative Committee leading to significant changes, including in relation to the selection of witnesses and not naming perpetrators of abuse. There were also ongoing concerns regarding the presence of large numbers of lawyers at the hearings. These were controversial decisions, and despite the widespread support for the inquiry, these matters drew considerable criticism.[47] A number of experts were also engaged to further investigate some aspects related to institutional child abuse. Their reports drew on a range of archival and other sources.[48] The release of the *Ryan Report* in June 2009 was greeted with mixed feelings. While, on the one hand, that the extent of abuse had been revealed was welcomed, on the other, there was dissatisfaction from advocacy groups about the level of redress and support provided at that time. Thousands of people participated in a silent march of solidarity through Dublin from the Garden of Remembrance to the Dáil (Parliament House). Petitions were delivered to Parliament and religious orders, stating that: 'We the people of Ireland join in solidarity and call for justice, accountability, restitution and reparation for the unimaginable crimes committed against the children of our country by religious orders in 216 institutions'.[49] RTÉ News reported that 'demonstrators left children's shoes at the Dáil entrance to symbolise the innocence of child abuse victims'.[50] The march was led by advocate leaders, including Christine Buckley, who carried a banner with words drawn from the 1916 Proclamation of the Irish Republic 'Cherishing all of the Children of the Nation Equally'.[51]

New Zealand

In New Zealand, there have not been the open, national and comprehensive public inquiries of the kind held in Australia, Canada and Ireland. Indeed, there are also no plans for a public inquiry despite there having been a campaign for there to be so.[52] A justification for the lack of a public inquiry is provided in the following explanation of the work of the Ministry of Social Development's Historic Claims team (which provides forms of redress and is discussed in Chapter Six, being formerly known as the Care Claims and Resolution Team). The Historic Claims team investigates individual claims and 'works with claimants to seek resolution and help get on with their lives'. Their work also:

> looks into the meaning of the claims collectively. To date, it has found no evidence of systemic failure,

and the total known claims make up less than 1 per cent of former State Wards. For this reason, claims are predominantly investigated as individual matters.[53]

Moreover, in response to the United Nations Committee against Torture that had requested information about allegations of historic abuse, the New Zealand government reiterated that:

> as the claims [of historic abuse] generally do not involve claims of broad systemic or institutional failure but are, predominantly, concerned with particular incidents and experiences of individuals, such an approach is not feasible here. The Government has also determined that, for the same reasons, a public inquiry is not an appropriate mechanism.[54]

As well as the internal investigations carried out by the Historic Claims team:

> many claims have been filed in the courts, which provide an independent, well-tested means of hearing and responding to serious allegations. The Government acknowledges that the Court process can be difficult for claimants in particular, and can be time consuming.[55]

In effect, the New Zealand government has introduced a redress scheme without undertaking an inquiry, and continues to resist the need for such an inquiry. More extensive research has been conducted in two instances that involved in-depth interviews with former residents in one case and analysis of personal records in the other.[56] These, however, did not lead to a wider inquiry.

While not a *public* inquiry, since 2008, there has been an additional forum in which those who have been abused in state care in New Zealand can speak about their experiences. The Confidential Listening and Assistance Service (CLAS) is not dissimilar to the Confidential Committee of the Irish inquiry (except a major difference being that there was no equivalent Investigation Committee in New Zealand).[57] CLAS was established as a means of providing and accessing redress and is discussed further in Chapter Four. Investigation of allegations of abuse is possible, but not by CLAS. Individual cases can be referred to the police with the consent of the complainant. CLAS's functions, however, were amended when it became clear that it was important to report collectively on the findings due to evidence that suggested systemic failings. Whether these findings will result in the New Zealand government taking further steps to address abuse in care is still to be seen.

As noted in Chapter Two, Māori adult care-leavers have not been identified as the subject of public inquiries, as Indigenous people in Australia and Canada have been, and nor have child migrants who came to New Zealand.[58]

United Kingdom

In the UK, there have been numerous local inquiries, such as those in Leicestershire, Staffordshire and North Wales, but like New Zealand, there has been resistance to the establishment of far-reaching country-wide public inquiries.[59] Forms of such inquiries are under way in Northern Ireland and Scotland, and these constitute the basis of the discussion here. Advocate groups, including the Care Leavers' Association, have lobbied for wide-reaching public inquiries in England and Wales. Commencing in 2012, in North Wales, there has been a re-investigation of the earlier inquiry into abuse in several children's homes, as well as an investigation of new allegations in these homes.[60] In late 2014, the Independent Panel Inquiry into Child Sexual Abuse was set up 'to consider whether, and the extent to which, public bodies and other non-state institutions have taken seriously their duty of care to protect children from sexual abuse in England and Wales'.[61] While not focused exclusively on children's homes or all forms of abuse, those who experienced abuse in care are likely to form a significant cohort of those providing evidence.

The most comprehensive public inquiry in the UK is occurring in Northern Ireland. Like inquiries elsewhere, it was established as a result of lobbying from advocacy groups and with increasing community concern about the extent and severity of abuse that had been experienced by children in care, and the long-term impact. The Irish Commission to Inquire into Child Abuse contributed to this awareness of the depth of the issues.[62] The Historical Institutional Abuse (HIA) Inquiry, established in 2013 and due to complete in 2016, is examining whether there were 'systemic failings by institutions or the state in their duties towards those children in their care' during the period 1922–95.[63] Over 400 people registered to participate in the inquiry, two thirds of whom live in Northern Ireland, with others in Australia, Ireland and Great Britain.[64]

The structure of the Northern Ireland inquiry is similar to the Irish inquiry in that there are both confidential and investigative elements. The Acknowledgement Forum provides for participants to recount their experiences of abuse in care confidentially; the Statutory Inquiry is investigative and involves complainants providing a formal statement via a legal interview and their possible participation in a public hearing. Additional evidence is sought from government and institutional records. The HIA Inquiry is organised so that the Acknowledgement Forum has been conducted first and its findings inform the Statutory Inquiry. The report of the HIA Inquiry will be presented to the Northern Ireland Executive and will include:

> Recommendations and findings of institutional or state failings in their duties towards the children in their care and if these failings were systemic; an apology – by whom and the nature of the apology; recommendations as to an appropriate memorial or tribute to those who suffered abuse, and the requirement or desirability for redress to be provided by the institution and/or the Executive to meet the particular needs of victims.[65]

In Scotland, there is a long and tortuous history of attempts to establish an inquiry. In 2002, institutional abuse survivor and adult care-leaver Chris Daly petitioned the Scottish government to undertake a public inquiry and for both government and religious orders who undertook the care to apologise for wrongdoings.[66] A government apology was forthcoming in December 2004, at which time a debate was held in the Scottish

Parliament on an inquiry into past institutional child abuse. In 2005, a National Strategy for Survivors of Childhood Abuse was initiated, with its aims being to 'raise awareness of childhood abuse, increase awareness of its long-term consequences, improve support services and enhance the health and wellbeing of survivors'.[67] Subsequently, an investigation was conducted into the management, operation and monitoring of children's homes in Scotland. This research, released in 2007 as the *Historical Abuse Systemic Review*, was records-based and did not investigate individual cases. Only later in the investigation were former residents and staff interviewed as part of the research.[68]

In 2008, the Scottish government announced that it would put in place 'a form of truth commission', which has since become known as the 'Acknowledgement and Accountability Forum'.[69] In 2009, the Scottish Human Rights Commission (SHRC) was commissioned to develop a human rights framework to inform this public inquiry and other remedies. The SHRC drew on the experiences of inquiries that had taken place in other countries (including Australia, Canada and Ireland), an analysis of international human rights law and consultations with survivors of institutional abuse.[70] However, before the framework was released, the Scottish government announced that a pilot of the forum would be undertaken in 2010. The form of this inquiry, which was called 'Time to be Heard', was based on the Irish confidential committee model and had a non-statutory base. It aimed to 'test the appropriateness and effectiveness of a confidential forum in giving former residents of residential schools and children's homes the opportunity to recount their experiences in care, especially abusive experiences, to an independent and non-judgmental panel'.[71]

In addition, the pilot was a means of creating a historical record of abuse in care in Scotland and providing information about support services to participants. While taking into account some elements of the recommended approach by the SHRC, many advocates were concerned that it fell a long way short of what they had expected and important decisions had been made without their involvement. Other concerns were that participants in the pilot were restricted to former residents of one children's home, Quarriers, and that there was no capacity for accountability measures to be implemented.[72]

In 2013, the Scottish government announced the establishment of a National Confidential Forum, building on the Time to be Heard pilot. Remarkably, it was almost 10 years since the government apology when the inquiry had first been debated in Parliament.[73] In relation to the work of the SHRC, over 2013 and 2014, a parallel stream of facilitated negotiation, known as InterAction, occurred between adult care-leavers, academics and representatives of government and former and current providers of care in order to develop an action plan to deliver 'justice for victims of historic abuse of children in care'.[74] In May 2015, the Scottish government announced its National Inquiry into Historical Child Abuse.[75]

Key findings and their outcomes

Having established the nature and purpose of key public inquiries across the five countries, we now turn to their findings and outcomes. Here, we focus on the three countries where national inquiries have been conducted, and concluded: Australia, Canada and Ireland. While it is important to acknowledge that the inquiries have identified ways in which children in care were well looked after, it is the nature of inquiries (and, in many cases, their purpose) that what was investigated in detail was the care that was harmful and not done well. Hence, the focus here is on findings that were concerned with harm and poor care practices, their detrimental long-term effects, and the responses to them.

Without exception, each report of the inquiries documented 'the shocking and horrific treatment of children criminally abused in the very organisations and institutions that were supposed to care for them'.[76] In Canada, the Royal Commission on Aboriginal Peoples found that 'physical and emotional abuse and neglect were features of the institutions and that sexual abuse occurred in many of them'.[77] More than this though, they were 'at pains to demonstrate that these abuses were not isolated or sporadic but systematic and sustained, and that they were known to the responsible church and government officials of the day'.[78] The later Law Commission of Canada inquiry made the point that:

> the Commission feels obliged to emphasise that wrongdoings were pervasive enough, both within certain institutions and across a significant enough number of institutions, that the recent and ongoing revelations of child abuse cannot be dismissed as isolated episodes. These revelations paint a picture of wide-ranging and serious inadequacies in the design of these institutions, their recruitment and training processes, their supervisory and management procedures, and their child placement decisions.[79]

In Ireland, the Commission to Inquire into Child Abuse provided:

> harrowing accounts of the lives of children in the institutions and detail[ed] incidences of abuse of all types.... The Commission found that physical abuse and emotional abuse and neglect were features of the institutions and that sexual abuse occurred in many of them. Physical abuse was pervasive and severe.... The Commission found a disturbing level of emotional abuse suffered by disadvantaged, neglected and abandoned children.[80]

A further matter commonly raised in these inquiries, and one that can be understood as a form of emotional or cultural abuse and a contravention of rights under the United Nations Convention of the Rights of the Child, is the loss of identity associated with enforced separation from family and community.

Due to a lack of acknowledgement of these damaging experiences in care, the inquiries found that there were few social policy responses to address the resultant harms. Typically, the inquiries have then recommended the sorts of initiatives discussed in the following chapters, such as apologies, memorials, redress schemes and specialist support services, including support to access personal records and family reunification.

In some instances, the evidence was so overwhelming and the public support so great for the plight of those affected that such initiatives were put in place over the course of the inquiries and in advance of the final reports.

There are two common responses to the recommendations of the inquiries into care. Despite evidence of the nature and extent of the abuse, one response suggests that those who cared for the children did the best that they could under the circumstances, and with the best intentions of the day. There is an acknowledgement that abuse did occur, but that these were isolated events. Responses are therefore geared towards individuals, with the aim of improving their health and well-being through the provision of therapeutic services. Alternatively, where the systemic nature of the abuse is acknowledged, compensation, justice and redress underpin the responses, which may also include individually targeted support.[81]

Canada and Ireland have most clearly taken the approach whereby there has been an acknowledgement of the systemic nature of the harms. In Canada, it is most evident in relation to their Indigenous populations where 'the importance of a holistic approach to redress and healing for Aboriginal survivors and their communities is a direct consequence of the policies and practices that lay behind the residential school system'.[82] Similarly, in the foreword to the Irish government's implementation plan in response to their public inquiry, the Minister makes clear that action will be taken:

> The litany of terrible wrongs inflicted on our children, who were placed by the State in residential institutions run by religious orders, was collated by the Commission and presented for Ireland and the world to read. The healing process involves listening to, understanding and consulting with survivors on how the wrongs of the past can be addressed and how their needs can be catered for in the future.[83]

The Irish government accepted all 20 of the inquiry's recommendations and an implementation plan outlined how each would be addressed. While many of the recommendations were concerned with changes to policy and practice related to children in care today, some related to the needs of adult care-leavers, including the erection of a memorial, the ongoing provision of mental health support through counselling services and family tracing services.[84] The Irish government had previously apologised and already had in place a comprehensive redress programme, which has since been further developed. Discussion of these initiatives is in the following chapters.[85]

In Australia, the national inquiries, reporting to a conservative government, were less successful in the implementation of their recommendations. Indeed, the outcomes have been more in line with individualistic responses rather than those that recognise the systemic nature of mistreatment. For example, the Australian government's response to many of the recommendations of the 2004 *Forgotten Australians* report, while giving support to the various proposals, declined to take responsibility and stated that they were 'matter(s) for state and territory governments, churches and agencies to consider'.[86] In relation to an apology, it was considered that 'it would not be appropriate for the Australian Government to issue an apology for a matter for which it does not have responsibility'.[87] The 1997 HREOC *Bringing Them Home* report had also recommended a formal apology to members of the Stolen Generations. The then Prime Minister John Howard refused to apologise. Other social policy responses, such as financial compensation schemes, memorials and specialist support services, were also recommended by both inquiries; again, not all were implemented.

In particular, the *Bringing Them Home* report included recommendations that the Commonwealth government 'provide reparations for the injury suffered by Indigenous people affected by removal policies' and 'legislate to implement the 1949 Convention on the Prevention and Punishment of the Crime of Genocide with full domestic effect as part of official recognition that removal policies of the past are over and will not be repeated'.[88] *Bringing Them Home* understood the treatment of Australia's Indigenous children as genocidal and a gross violation of human rights, a claim denied by the government; 'instead the Government has emphasised the idea that the removal of Indigenous children was often perpetrated by people of "good will" and that it was consistent with the "standards of the day"'.[89] In 2000, HREOC took this to the United Nations Committee on the Elimination of Racial Discrimination, who stated that:

> Concern is expressed that the Commonwealth Government does not support a formal national apology and that it considers inappropriate the provision of monetary compensation for those forcibly and unjustifiably separated from their families, on the grounds that such practices were sanctioned by law at the time and were intended to 'assist the people whom they affected'. The Committee recommends that the State party consider the need to address appropriately the extraordinary harm inflicted by these racially discriminatory practices.[90]

Subsequently, a Motion of Reconciliation was passed in the federal Parliament in 2000 but it did not contain the 'necessary elements of an apology' as identified in *Bringing Them Home*; moreover, it did not 'specifically mention forcible removal policies'.[91]

Even though the Australian Royal Commission into Institutional Responses to Child Sexual Abuse is still in progress at the time of writing, it is already clear that there are likely to be major shifts in social policy as a result of their investigations. For example, the Catholic Church has committed to raising the maximum level of compensation payments, and there is discussion of a national redress scheme, funded through government and other organisations that provided care.[92]

Implementing the recommendations of these inquiries is subject to political will, wide public support and the capacity to deal with the financial consequences. In Ireland, all these factors were in place, and we see the most comprehensive outcomes there. Some years later, and with an Irish economy much less buoyant, commentators have made the point that such responses would not have happened a decade later. In Canada, there has been a comprehensive response to their Indigenous peoples but not other groups. In Australia, with a change of government, one of the first acts of new Prime Minister Kevin Rudd in 2008 was to apologise to members of the Stolen Generations – an act that received universal support. The following year an apology was given to former child migrants and Forgotten Australians. For all three groups, there has been funding for memorials and other forms of acknowledgements, as well as specialist support services. The lack of national financial compensation schemes for any of the three Australian groups has been most controversial, and is discussed in Chapter Five.

Conclusion

Public inquiries have arisen for a range of reasons, including due to concerns about discriminatory policies and practices in relation to Indigenous peoples and child migrants, as well as the occurrence of widespread (or specific forms of) ill-treatment and its negative long-term consequences, and not necessarily specifically about the experiences of adult care-leavers. In some instances, inquiries have targeted particular groups and this inquiry has led to another within the same country, such as in Australia. Advocates have been central in each case to their initiation and establishment. New Zealand is noteworthy for its unwillingness to conduct a national inquiry.

Public inquiries have taken various forms and had differing levels of authority to access information. Notably, where national inquiries have been held, the highest levels of authority have been exercised through Commissions of Inquiry (or a Royal Commission, as in Australia and formerly in Canada). These have included both written and oral submissions, with public hearings, extensive archival research and detailed investigation of complaints. Others have included confidential forums in which opportunity is provided to recount experiences privately. An important part of these inquiries has been the ways in which people have been assisted to participate in them through access to information about the process and counselling or other therapeutic support services. Having considered the public inquiries, we now turn to the initiatives that have arisen from them and, first, those forms of acknowledgement that commemorate experiences in care.

FOUR

Apologies, memorials and other acknowledgements

The apology from Mr Rudd [Australian Prime Minister] and Turnbull [Leader of the Opposition] – some of them were jumping around: 'Oh I'm relieved'. 'What do you mean? You're still the same. You can't eat an apology.' It's nice to receive it but you'll still be the same tomorrow and the day after. (Ray, adult care-leaver, 2011[1])

There are mixed feelings about apologies and other symbolic acknowledgements of harms caused by a childhood in care. Ray, a man now aged in his 80s who grew up in care from a baby for all of his childhood, came to Parliament House to hear the apology from the Prime Minister to the Forgotten Australians in 2009. Even though he knew others found great consolation in their words, he left feeling somewhat ambivalent. Some adult care-leavers have found these symbolic acknowledgements important ways to assist in reconciling the trauma of their childhood. Others, like Ray, have found them less helpful and have sought more practical forms of recognition, as discussed in the following chapters. In Australia, while there has been a range of programmes put in place to support adult care-leavers, the federal government apologies have not included financial redress, unlike in Ireland and Canada.

Typically, in response to the various inquiries, formal apologies have been issued by some governments, non-government agencies and religious organisations.[2] Other forms of official remembrance have also been initiated, such as memorials and museum exhibitions. To acknowledge the importance of the children's homes to former residents, plaques have been laid at these sites to commemorate and honour the lives of the children who lived there. All these initiatives attempt to change the way in which the past is understood and remembered. They contribute to shifts in understandings of care and present-day relationships between adult care-leavers and the wider community.

In this chapter, we first consider the forms of acknowledgement, their purpose and importance, and key characteristics. We then review what has occurred in each of the countries under investigation. Specific examples of the various forms of acknowledgements are analysed to see to what extent they include features that have been identified as critical to their performance as acknowledgements. Particular attention is paid to Australia, Canada and Ireland, where national apologies and remembrance initiatives have been put in place.

Acknowledging lives in care and their aftermath

An acknowledgement adds to the public record and identifies wrongdoing and its cause. As described in relation to public inquiries, acknowledgements are also a means of providing accountability for what has occurred. The Law Commission of Canada explains that an acknowledgement is 'naming the acts done and admitting they were wrong', in the following three ways:

> [an acknowledgement] must be specific, not general, and forthright, not reticent; nothing less than a detailed and candid description of persons, places and acts is required. Second, it must demonstrate an understanding of the impact of the harms done; acknowledgement requires recognition of the consequences of the acts perpetrated. Third, it must also make clear that those who experienced the abuse were in no way responsible for it; acknowledgement means there can be no shifting of blame on to survivors.[3]

Reports of public inquiries, then, can form a substantial acknowledgement, but there are many other forms. These three criteria will form the basis of our analysis of the various forms of acknowledgement to be discussed later in this chapter. While acknowledgement can be directed at a specific person, our interest here is with that to *groups* of people harmed by their experiences of care by those who were responsible for providing the care, and monitoring its quality. However, more than that it be directed to a group, there is also the need to identify the way that, as a group, there might have been systemic effects. So, it is not just that a group of individuals has been affected, but that the wrong, for example, in relation to Canadian Indigenous people, has been 'culturally abusive in its very conception'.[4] Even so, when directed at a group, it can impact individually as acknowledgements can function in a very personally affecting way. For those who have been unable to talk about their experience of care because of fear of what response they might get or because of the silencing that has occurred due to abuse, having it publicly acknowledged means that there is likely to be a greater level of understanding in the community.[5]

An apology is a particular form of acknowledgement and is both 'a means of recognising that an injustice has been done and a means of accepting responsibility for the harm and suffering brought about by that injustice'.[6] Thus, an apology includes an acknowledgement, as well as 'accepting responsibility for the wrong that was done; the expression of sincere regret or remorse; assurance that the wrong will not recur, and reparation through concrete measures'.[7] Alice MacLachlan identifies three elements to an apology, which she describes as narrative, disavowal and commitment. First, the narrative of an apology identifies 'the wrongdoing as such, the apologizer as responsible for it, and the victim or addressee as wrongfully harmed by it'; disavowal involves distancing from the acts being apologised for and, at the same time, taking responsibility for them; then there is commitment to the disavowal and to make efforts to repair the wrongs.[8]

Recognition of past suffering and its legacies is an important part of an apology.[9] Apologies in themselves can be a form of reparation, whereby the redress of past injustices is done through symbolic measures. While, as suggested, redress through material means is part of an apology – discussed further in the following chapters – 'often the point of primary significance to the claimant has been recognition of the narrative of their suffering which has been marginalised in or excluded from the hegemonic accounts of the past'.[10] The apology, then, is 'a confirmation of their symbolic inclusion in the national (or other) community – their painful memories are institutionally incorporated in "our shared memory" and "our history"'.[11] In effect, an apology and other forms of acknowledgement, such as museum exhibitions and memorials, produce a 'change in the authoritative historical record'.[12]

In response to concerns about the politicisation of apologies, Melissa Nobles argues that 'reparation politics', of which apologies are a part, are 'a tactic used to enhance citizenship and a response to the government's failure to address enduring and deeply rooted inequalities'.[13] In attempting to deal with the politicisation of apologies, Michael Murphy identifies four criteria as grounds for an apology: a wrong or an injustice needs to have been committed; there need to be identifiable victims; the apologiser must be responsible for the actions, and 'transgenerational responsibility' can apply here, whereby a government carries responsibility over time; and reparation, even if only symbolic, needs to be offered.[14] Then, if an apology is to be offered, and to be made as meaningful as possible, consideration needs to be given to practicalities, such as: 'Who is to offer the apology; what substantial issues should the apology address; where is the apology to be offered; when is the apology to be offered; and how is the ceremony surrounding the apology to be configured?'[15] Engagement of those to whom the apology is offered in its preparation is vital to ensure that how and what is presented holds the greatest meaning and significance.

While not all adult care-leavers want an apology, many identify receiving an apology as one of their highest priorities. There are arguments put forward not to apologise, but there are also situations where there are compelling reasons for an apology to be made.[16] To not make an apology, given what is known, 'signals an indifference to past injustice and the indignities suffered by those who were victimized'.[17]

Apologies are not the only form of acknowledgement. Other forms of acknowledgement also take challenging the way we remember the past as their starting point, and contribute to the production of an alternative historical narrative. As Dacia Viejo-Rose reminds us: 'this constructed historical narrative is reflected in many formats from school curricula to comic books and films and is reinforced through commemorative practices'.[18] National remembrance initiatives can challenge how the past is remembered, and they are important because 'the way the past is represented conveys information about present relations'.[19] Moreover, remembrance is about 'knowing the past' and also 'reflecting the needs of the present'.[20] Central to this process of memorialising is that is it selective: 'choices are made about what to explicitly "remember" or deliberately silence'.[21] Thus, these initiatives can be 'open-ended with implications for the present, or limited, so that the present-day is safeguarded from the implications of the past'.[22] For example, retaining the focus on children rather than the adults that they have become is a way that legacies of their childhood experiences are not dealt with in acknowledgements.

Memorials are an 'aspiration to remembrance' and have the intention of preserving memory, especially in relation to loss.[23] They can include physical structures, but also ceremonies, commemorative days and creative arts and theatre productions, as well as other forms. Memorials can be created not only as sites of remembrance, but also as a means of bringing a community together, creating a focus for commemoration and making a political statement.[24] As noted by Joanne Laws, through the use of memorials, 'moments of great national tragedy have been poignantly acknowledged, with the aim of marking and preserving them in the present-day collective memory'.[25]

Museum exhibitions, oral history collections and documentaries are all other forms of remembrance-based acknowledgements and are ways that the state contributes to producing a more inclusive history. A final way that acknowledgement occurs is through programmes of public education, separate to those conducted through memorials and museums, often initiated by, and conducted with the involvement of, adult care-leavers themselves. These programmes can serve the dual purpose of both informing the wider community and also having healing effects upon those engaged in them.[26]

We now turn to a selection of these various forms of acknowledgement. Drawing on the characteristics identified by the Law Commission of Canada, several case studies are discussed in more detail and are considered in terms of their specificity, indication of harms done and recognition of responsibility, and in the case of apology, the extent to which they offer reparation for these harms. Some aspects of the practical considerations of who, how, where and when apologies and other acknowledgements are offered are also noted.

Apologies

Apologies have not been offered by the national governments in all of the countries under review, and within countries, there have been apologies to some groups and not to others. New Zealand, England and Wales have not offered apologies. The UK offered an apology to British child migrants, following on from the one given to child migrants in Australia (which was also given to those who were not child migrants or Indigenous). In contrast, Canada has not offered an apology to child migrants. Apologies have been given to the Indigenous peoples of Canada and Australia. Ireland and Scotland have given apologies to their adult care-leavers. An apology to adult care-leavers in Northern Ireland has, as yet, to be offered, but the framing of their inquiry (ongoing in 2015) suggests that this will occur.

Importantly, in Australia and Canada, state, territory and provincial governments have also given apologies in some instances. It is worth remembering that, in many cases, it was these governments that implemented and administered the child welfare policies and so have the greatest responsibility for the actions that were taken. Regardless, that a national government apologises, even if there was limited direct involvement in the provision of care or the development of its policies, can hold great symbolic significance.

In Ireland, widespread ill-treatment of children in care was apparent before its public inquiry was held and an apology was made in advance of the inquiry's commencement. In May 1999, the Taoiseach (Prime Minister) Bertie Ahern announced the establishment of a commission of inquiry and other measures. He said in part:

> On behalf of the State and of all citizens of the State, the Government wishes to make a sincere and long overdue apology to the victims of childhood abuse for our collective failure to intervene, to detect their pain, to come to their rescue.[27]

At the release of the report of the inquiry, this apology was reiterated and all recommendations of the report were accepted by the government.[28] The report was a significant acknowledgement of harm and both apologies included measures to address the wrongs through a range of practical and symbolic measures, including the establishment of a memorial (discussed later in this chapter) and funding for a redress programme, counselling and family tracing services. The Irish apologies were specific, clearly identified the harms done, recognised failed responsibility and offered significant reparation.

In 1998, after the Royal Commission on Aboriginal Peoples, the Canadian government acknowledged their suffering in a Statement of Reconciliation, which stated in part:

> One aspect of our relationship with Aboriginal people over this period that requires particular attention is the Residential School system. This system separated many children from their families and communities and prevented them from speaking their own languages and from learning about their heritage and cultures. In the worst cases, it left legacies of personal pain and distress that continue to reverberate in Aboriginal communities to this day. Tragically, some children were the victims of physical and sexual abuse. The Government of Canada acknowledges the role it played in the development and administration of these schools. Particularly to those individuals who experienced the tragedy of sexual and physical abuse at residential schools, and

who have carried this burden believing that in some way they must be responsible, we wish to emphasize that what you experienced was not your fault and should never have happened. To those of you who suffered this tragedy at residential schools, we are deeply sorry.[29]

As an acknowledgement, the statement was specific, identified harms, placed responsibility with the state and was accompanied by a range of reparation measures. However, its focus was more on individual impacts rather than those that were systemic.[30] While generally well received, it was widely understood not to be an apology, at least partly because it was not named as such and did not use the words 'apology' or 'apologise' in its text; nor was its delivery given the gravitas expected of an apology. The statement was delivered by the Minister of Indian Affairs and Northern Development rather than the Prime Minister, who was not present in Parliament at the time, although in Ottawa, suggesting that it was less meaningful than it might have been due to the lesser standing of the person delivering it.[31] In contrast, when an apology was given in 2008, there was more attention paid to who was involved, adding to its symbolic significance. In delivering the apology, the Prime Minister said:

> The government recognizes that the absence of an apology has been an impediment to healing and reconciliation. Therefore, on behalf of the Government of Canada and all Canadians, I stand before you in this Chamber so central to our life as a country, to apologize to Aboriginal peoples for Canada's role in the Indian Residential Schools system.... The Government of Canada sincerely apologises and asks the forgiveness of the Aboriginal peoples of this country for failing them so profoundly.[32]

The Prime Minister's address was followed by statements from all other political party leaders and a response from National Chief Phil Fontaine of the Assembly of First Nations, in full ceremonial headdress. Present in Parliament House were also leaders of the Métis and Inuit populations. Most importantly, 'this was the first time that indigenous leaders had been invited onto the floor of the house in their capacity as representatives of *nations* and had been granted permission to speak in that capacity'.[33]

The 2008 Canadian government's apology to its Indigenous people meets the criteria for an acknowledgement: specificity, indication of harms done and recognition of responsibility. In this case, the apology followed the establishment of reparations, the Indian Residential Schools Settlement Agreement having been established in 2007 and comprising financial compensation, funding for healing programmes, commemorative activities and the establishment of the Truth and Reconciliation Commission.[34] Indeed, in his speech, the Prime Minister acknowledged the importance of both reparations *and* apology.[35]

In contrast to these responses to its Indigenous people, in Canada, there have been no national apologies to the two other groups of adult care-leavers, even though child migrant advocates have a petition seeking one.[36] In response to the advent of the apologies by Australia and the UK to child migrants, the Canadian Minister for Immigration Jason Kenney was reported as saying that there was 'no need for Canada to apologize for abuse and exploitation suffered by thousands of poor children shipped here from Britain' and that there was 'limited public interest in official government apologies for everything that's ever been unfortunate or a tragic event in our history'.[37] Instead, other initiatives were put in place, including a home child stamp, museum exhibitions and the designation of a Year of the British Home Child, as discussed shortly.[38]

In the UK, a somewhat belated apology was given by Prime Minister Gordon Brown to former child migrants in 2010, three months after the apology that was given to child migrants by the Australian government:

> To all those former child migrants and their families
> … we are truly sorry. They were let down. We are
> sorry they were allowed to be sent away at the time
> when they were most vulnerable. We are sorry that
> instead of caring for them, this country turned its

back. And we are sorry that the voices of these children were not always heard, their cries for help not always heeded. And we are sorry that it has taken so long for this important day to come and for the full and unconditional apology that is justly deserved.[39]

The apology went on to identify the range of harms caused by child migration, including the loss of family relationships, inadequate education and abuse. Reparations were limited, with funding made available to assist in family reunifications, but not otherwise. The apology received support from child migrant advocates, including Harold Haig from the International Association of Former Child Migrants and their Families, who described it as 'a momentous day'.[40]

In Australia, former child migrants and Forgotten Australians received a joint apology a year after that given to the members of the Stolen Generations. Unlike those from the Irish and Canadian governments, the Australian apologies were accompanied by limited reparations and did not include financial compensation payments to individuals (although four of the state-based apologies have done so). The apology to members of the Stolen Generations was a 'historic' and 'emotional' event, but was delayed as former Prime Minister John Howard had refused to apologise.[41] As a result of the *Bringing them Home* report, some initiatives had been put in place, such as a large oral history project managed by the National Library of Australia, and funding for family reunification services and counselling and other support.

In contrast to that of the Howard government, the Australian community response to the *Bringing them Home* report was 'almost overwhelming'.[42] At events held around Australia on the newly instituted national Sorry Day, hundreds of thousands of people signed 'Sorry books'. On this first anniversary of the report's publication, over a million people marched in support, and by the end of 1997, most governments of Australian states and territories had apologised to their Indigenous people. In stark contrast, an apology from the Australian government was not to occur for another 11 years.[43]

A major consultation process occurred in the development of the apology, with members of the Stolen Generations meeting with the Minister, and many others responding to a survey canvassing questions such as who the apology would address, how the apology would be delivered and what the nature of the event at which the apology would occur should be. On the day before the apology, for the first time and in another act of great significance to Indigenous people, the Australian Parliament was welcomed to (Indigenous) country by the traditional owners of the Canberra region.[44]

That the apology was going to be made was well known as it had been a promise made at the preceding federal election. Thousands of Indigenous Australians came to see the apology delivered in Parliament House and many other Australians watched it on television and big screens in city squares and other public places. In part, Prime Minister Rudd stated:

> We apologise for the laws and policies of successive Parliaments and governments that have inflicted profound grief, suffering and loss on these our fellow Australians. We apologise especially for the removal of Aboriginal and Torres Strait Islander children from their families, their communities and their country. For the pain, suffering and hurt of these Stolen Generations, their descendants and for their families left behind, we say sorry. To the mothers and the fathers, the brothers and the sisters, for the breaking up of families and communities, we say sorry. And for the indignity and degradation thus inflicted on a proud people and a proud culture, we say sorry. We the Parliament of Australia respectfully request that this apology be received in the spirit in which it is offered as part of the healing of the nation.[45]

The apology was complemented by a range of other initiatives, including increased funding for support services for members of the Stolen Generations, but no financial redress programme. There were mixed responses to the apology from among Indigenous people. For many, the 'acknowledgement of their suffering was personally significant and ... they now felt part of the national story'.[46] Others welcomed the apology but did not believe that it went far enough; others believed that it was 'a hollow gesture without accompanying compensation'.[47] Of greatest concern was that at the same time as the apology was made, the government endorsed and retained the highly contested 'Northern Territory intervention' that had been introduced by the former Howard government, which placed restrictions on the use of welfare payments in Indigenous communities.[48]

Despite being among the 'most apology-friendly [nations] in the world', Australia's approach is not without its critics.[49] In an analysis of Australian apologies, Denise Cuthbert and Marian Quartly found a shift from what was initially a focus on indigeneity and social injustice in the protracted lead-up to the apology to members of the Stolen Generations, and towards a focus on childhood experiences. They argue that 'the prevailing discourse became one of sentimentalization centred on the suffering of children rather than political and other restitution for Indigenous Australians'.[50] In doing so, the focus of the apology shifted from the injustice done to Indigenous people towards a focus on a 'more generalized "historical abuse"'.[51] What is more, the apologies were addressed to the children, rather than the adults who they had become, a strategy that Cuthbert and Quartly argue reduces accountability.[52] Their childhood is in the past, so the apology addresses the past, not their current circumstances. This, then, means that the apology focuses 'on the past suffering of children and glance[s] only obliquely at the ongoing suffering and injustices of Australia's first peoples'.[53] Moreover:

> it is not enough to say sorry without fully articulating the grounds on which the wrongs were done. It is only though a sustained and historically informed acknowledgment of the power structures that lead to such injustices that we can ensure that they are not repeated.[54]

This focus on childhood experiences of suffering has enabled, and is also reflected in, the subsequent apologies to former child migrants and Forgotten Australians. These groups have been included in '"national membership" through the apology delivered to them more as innocent children who were wronged by the state decades ago and less as the adults they have become'.[55] To some extent, this lack of attention to the circumstances that created the need for an apology, and their aftermath, is demonstrated through the lack of due attention to other social policy responses. There has been acknowledgement, but less accountability, as is discussed in Chapter Five.

Memorials

Memorials and other forms of commemoration have been part of the reparation measures of apologies and a significant means of acknowledgement. In Canada and Ireland, in particular, there have been major processes around the design and development of national memorials to the legacy of abuse in care. In addition, there are a myriad of local memorials; some examples are noted here.

In Canada, the Indian Residential Schools Settlement Agreement included a $CDN 20 million programme that supported national, regional and local initiatives that 'honour, educate, remember, memorialize and/or pay tribute to former Indian Residential School students, their families or communities'.[56] These funds have now been allocated and 145 varied projects across Canada were initiated, including: the establishment of commemorative plaques at the sites of all former residential schools, with an accompanying website and application to search and access these sites; a work performed by the Royal Winnipeg Ballet developed in collaboration with the Truth and Reconciliation Commission of Canada; and a series of radio documentaries on the residential schools and their students.[57] In 2012, one of the national projects was unveiled at Parliament House in Ottawa. A commemorative stained-glass window was installed above the west entrance to the centre block of the federal Parliament buildings. Entitled 'Giniigaaniimenaaning' ('Looking Ahead') it was designed by Métis artist Christi Belcourt. The stained-glass window acknowledges the apology given by the Prime Minister in 2008, reflects on the history of the residential schools and also looks to the future, with healing, reconciliation and renewal.[58] The window is an acknowledgement of great beauty. While sending a powerful message to the parliamentarians who enter through the door below where it is placed, because this is an area with tight security measures in place, most Canadians will unfortunately never see the window and appreciate its significance.

In Ireland, a more contained form of commemoration programme was put in place: a €500,000 fund to erect a memorial that would include an inscription of the words of the apology made by the Taoiseach in 1999. The memorial was a recommendation of the *Ryan Report* in 2009, but more than five years later, it has yet to eventuate. After an extensive consultation process, the committee overseeing the project sought expressions of interest for a memorial that:

> appropriately and respectfully acknowledges, on behalf of the State and of all citizens of the State, the pain and suffering experienced by former residents of institutions, who as children were subjected to physical abuse, emotional abuse, sexual abuse and neglect.[59]

The winning entry, 'Journey of Light', was to be installed adjacent to the Garden of Remembrance in Parnell Square, Dublin, and had been approved by the Dublin City Council. However, an appeal of this decision was upheld in late 2013. As noted by the *Irish Examiner*:

> While victims were split on the issue, many will see this as another form of maltreatment at the hands of officialdom. Rightly or wrongly, they will regard it as a sign that modern Ireland has failed to come to grips with the appalling treatment of thousands of children by those supposed to be caring for them. The latest twist in this long running saga will further convince them in that view.[60]

Consequently, no Irish memorial to those abused in care has yet to be established.

In Australia, all three national enquiries recommended the establishment of memorials. The aforementioned Sorry Day was one of these recommendations, and there are memorials in all states and territories honouring members of the Stolen Generations, Forgotten Australians and child migrants. The inaugural Sorry Day of 26 May 1998 was the anniversary date of the tabling of the *Bringing Them Home* report in the federal Parliament and aimed to 'commemorate the history of forcible removals and its effects'.[61] As we have seen, Sorry Day has been a powerful way in which Australians have expressed support for members of the Stolen Generations. Other memorials are found in Reconciliation Place, which is located in a prominent part of the national capital in Canberra and placed 'physically and symbolically at the heart of Australia's democratic life and institutions'.[62] There, among a collection of 16 Indigenous public artworks, two are on the theme of the separation of children from their families. One of these incorporates an image of a boy in care, an empty coolamon, or traditional Aboriginal vessel for carrying a baby, and a recording of an Indigenous lullaby. With this sadness, there is also hope and reconnection, with Indigenous words for baby and child inscribed in glass panels.[63] Other memorials are now located in sites across Australia.[64]

In response to both the *Lost Innocents* and *Forgotten Australians* reports, the federal government pledged up to $AUS 100,000 for state memorials.[65] A memorial to the British and Maltese child migrants who came to Western Australia was unveiled in 2004 in the grounds of the Maritime Museum in Fremantle, where the children arrived by ship. The memorial depicts two life-size bronze children arriving with a suitcase each – a not uncommon image of child migrants and one that firmly places the experience in childhood.[66] In contrast, a somewhat more abstract memorial in Adelaide takes up the aftermath of care as its focus. Unveiled in 2010, it consists of four stainless steel daisies (one of which is over two metres tall), with the flowers in various stages of opening. The artwork is a memorial to Forgotten Australians and symbolises 'hope and healing for children (now adults) who suffered harm in out of home care'.[67]

There are also memorials to children who died in care. In Scotland, In Care Abuse Survivors (INCAS) led a campaign to have the 100 babies and children honoured who had died while in care in Smyllum orphanage in Lanark near Glasgow. The children's graves had been unmarked and records were not kept of many of those who had died. An untended gravestone engraved with the words 'Sweet Jesus have mercy on the souls of the children of Smyllum' in the local cemetery was the only acknowledgement of the children's existence. In contrast, the nuns who ran the orphanage were also buried in this cemetery, but in graves with headstones and crosses.[68] INCAS campaigners successfully sought funds from the Sisters of Charity to install a monument but were unable to find the details of all those who had died. The memorial, inscribed with the following words, was unveiled in a moving ceremony in 2004:

> Life so short, no world to roam, they were taken so young, they never went home. So, spare a thought for them as you pass this way – a prayer if you remember day by day. Our lives so short in need of love but found in the arms of God above. Jesus said: Suffer little children come unto me.[69]

Other forms of acknowledgement and remembrance

There is a range of other ways in which lives in care and their aftermath have been acknowledged and remembered by the state, including through museum exhibitions, oral history collections, documentaries and other forms of public education.[70] Just like museums that 'preserve, interpret and memorialize' by their 'constructed representation of the past', all these forms of acknowledgement serve an important function in presenting a 'change in the authoritative historical record'.[71]

In Australia, the involvement of two of the most significant historical institutions – the National Museum and the National Library – highlights the country's intention to include those who grew up in care in the national narrative. The National Museum of Australia's travelling exhibition 'Inside: Life in Children's Homes and Institutions' came about as a commitment that was part of the national apology. The exhibition, first opened in 2011 and running until 2014, includes the stories, photographs and personal objects of those who were in care, including Forgotten Australians, former child migrants and members of the Stolen Generations. The exhibition is based on personal histories and 'is a voice for those who were inside and a chance for others to understand'.[72] There is also an extensive website that accompanies and further explains the exhibition, including additional material from those who resided in the institutions and an education kit for teachers. As well as this government-supported exhibition, the advocacy organisation Care Leavers Australia Network has set up a permanent exhibition in their Sydney office, known as the National Orphanage Museum, with many items available for viewing on their website.[73]

The National Library of Australia has a large oral history collection comprising, in total, around 45,000 hours of recordings. Two collections document the experiences of adult care-leavers, derived from two separate projects. The Bringing Them Home oral history project was established after the release of that report and consists of over 300 interviews with members of the Stolen Generations and others involved in or affected by the child removal practices collected between 1998 and 2002.[74] Accompanying the collection is a book based on these oral histories.[75] The Forgotten Australian and Child Migrants oral history project came about as a result of a commitment of the national apology to these groups. Over 200 interviews were conducted from 2010 to 2012 and the collection is accompanied by a booklet.[76] Many of the interviews in both collections are available online and have transcripts available. These interviews are moving first-hand accounts of being in care and its aftermath.

Another way that acknowledgement has occurred is through film and television, some of which has had state support, including the previously mentioned television programmes aired in Ireland in the 1990s – *Dear Daughter* and *States of Fear*. Regarding child migrants, television programmes such as the Australian Broadcasting Commission's *The Leaving of Liverpool* (1992) and Canada's *Childhoods Lost: The Story of Canada's Home Children* (2010) have contributed to changing the public record about the nature of childhoods in care.[77]

In Canada, to memorialise child migration, a stamp series was produced in 2010.[78] This is a somewhat surprising initiative because, in Canada, there have been few other official acknowledgements of this group, including the lack of an apology, despite both Australia and the UK apologising in 2009 and 2010, respectively. It may be that such initiatives as the stamp and the designation of the Year of the British Home Child were undertaken in lieu of an apology. Indeed, home children (and their descendants) have protested at the lack of an apology. While the stamp may first have been seen as a welcome acknowledgement, at least one advocate soon thought otherwise. John Willoughby ran the Canadian Centre for Home Children and was disappointed in the stamp initiative:

> I have had time to consider the postal stamp announcement, and it is loaded with irony. Here is a 4 million strong community [of home children and their descendants] deliberately kept separate for generations. They have tried hard to find each other, mostly with little success. So the Minister of Immigration announces a new stamp featuring Home Children. NOW if we only knew who they are – and where they live, we could use the stamp to contact them.[79]

Accessing records and family reunification has been a major focus of the child migrant advocacy groups in Canada.

The other official way that Canadian home children have been recognised is through the designation of 2010 as the Year of the British Home Child. Instead of acknowledging their suffering through an apology, this initiative paid more attention to the group's strengths. In announcing the initiative, the Minister for Citizenship, Immigration and Multiculturalism Jason Kenney stated:

> the Government of Canada recognizes the hardships suffered by British Home Children and their perseverance and courage in overcoming those hardships. Over the next year, the Government

of Canada will honour the great strength and determination of this group of child immigrants, and reflect on the tremendous contributions made by former Home Children and the descendants to the building of Canada.[80]

Little information about how this initiative developed over time was found and the website and resources associated with it are no longer available.

In recognition of the large number of child migrants who went to the Canadian province of Ontario, in 2011, the provincial government declared 28 September as British Home Child Day. In doing so, again, strengths were emphasised, as stated in the British Home Child Act: 'With remarkable courage, determination, perseverance and strength, these children overcame the obstacles before them ... British Home Child Day is intended to recognize and honour the contributions of the British home children who established roots in Ontario'.[81] The declaration of this day came about through a private member's bill introduced by former Member of Parliament Jim Brownell, whose grandmother had been a home child.[82] The Ministry of Children and Youth Services maintains a website that includes links to resources and personal stories of home children.[83] Local groups organise events to recognise the day, such as in 2013, when an event memorialising home children was held at the historical site of Upper Canada Village in Ontario.[84]

Public education programmes

Public education programmes have also been ways that have contributed to changing the national historical narrative. As we have seen, memorials and other forms of acknowledgement and remembrance need not be physical structures; instead, they can 'serve an active, educational role'.[85] There are particularly significant examples from Canada, where there have been substantial levels of support from the state. The Indian Residential Schools Settlement Agreement sought to begin repairing the harm caused by residential schools.[86] Two elements of the agreement engage directly with public education. First, the Truth and Reconciliation Commission of Canada has a mandate:

> to learn the truth about what happened in the residential schools and to inform all Canadians about what happened in the schools. The Commission will document the truth of what happened by relying on records held by those who operated and funded the schools, testimony from officials of the institutions that operated the schools, and experiences reported by survivors, their families, communities and anyone personally affected by the residential school experience and its subsequent impacts.[87]

The Truth and Reconciliation Commission was established for five years from 2008, with a budget of $CDN 60 million; this was extended to 2015. At the time of writing, it is winding up and work is being undertaken to establish the National Research Centre. The Truth and Reconciliation Commission has collected information about the experiences of residential schools through statement-gathering from former students and their families. In addition, public education activities have included both national and community events. For example, the first national event in 2010, titled 'It's about respect – a journey of survival, strength and resilience', took place in Winnipeg, and commenced with:

> a sunrise ceremony … at the Forks National Historical Site. Located where the Red and Assiniboine rivers meet, the Forks has a long history as a gathering site … an average of 10,000 Aboriginal and non-Aboriginal people per day came together in the spirit of understanding and respect, to learn about residential schools and honour the experiences of survivors. For many, the event was their first exposure to the residential school story. For many survivors, it was their first opportunity to speak publicly about their experiences.[88]

Other such events have taken place across Canada. The Aboriginal Healing Foundation commenced in 1998 for 11 years with a $CDN350 million grant from the Canadian government, which was extended with additional funding from the Indian Residential Schools Settlement Agreement to 2014. It came about as a result of the action plan subsequent to the Royal Commission on Aboriginal Peoples:

> We see our role as facilitators in the healing process by helping Aboriginal people and their communities help themselves, by providing resources for healing initiatives, by promoting awareness of healing issues and needs, and by nurturing a broad, supportive public environment. We help Survivors in telling the truth of their experiences and being heard. We also work to engage Canadians in this healing process by encouraging them to walk with us on the path of reconciliation.[89]

In doing so, the Aboriginal Healing Foundation was involved in the provision of public education activities, with some specifically targeted to school children. The Foundation developed a range of resources, such as a directory of residential schools in Canada, a bibliography of sources on residential schools and a poster series about residential schools and healing.[90]

In Australia, the Alliance for Forgotten Australians, with funding from the federal Department of Social Services, has produced a range of resources, including a DVD comprising a series of moving accounts of life in care and its aftermath and a booklet to inform health-care professionals about some of the possible effects of a childhood in care (discussed in Chapter Six).[91] Their president, Caroline Carroll, routinely engages in public speaking to inform the wider community about the lifelong impacts of care.

Conclusion

A robust acknowledgement must satisfy three key criteria: it must be specific; it must demonstrate understanding of the harms done; and it must take responsibility for these harms. There are a variety of forms of acknowledgements, including memorials, museum exhibitions and oral history collections, commemorative days, plaques, and public art works. While an acknowledgement can stand alone, invariably, acknowledgements are part of a suite of initiatives introduced to support adult care-leavers. An important feature of an acknowledgement is that it is durable over time. Acknowledgements contribute to the public record and change the historical narrative by including those who have been marginalised. Engagement with those affected in the development of acknowledgements and their delivery is paramount to ensuring their significance and meaning.

One of the most well-known forms of acknowledgement is an apology. In making a mature apology, there is recognition of the harms perpetrated and a commitment to make amends. However, not all apologies have come with comprehensive redress measures, as Ray, who we met at the beginning of this chapter, alludes to. In his experience, 'you can't eat an apology'. In Chapter Five, then, we turn to a consideration of what redress could entail.

FIVE

Reparation and redress

To provide 'redress' is to remedy or rectify a wrong.
(Royal Commission into Institutional Responses to
Child Sexual Abuse, 2013[1])

In Chapter Three, we found that public inquiries have
consistently identified harms or 'wrongs' experienced in care.
In Chapter Four, we considered acknowledgements of these
harms and that a crucial aspect of an apology is reparation.
Indeed, acknowledgement and apology are parts of reparation,
or redress, and are means of remedying or rectifying harms, as
explained by the Australian Royal Commission into Institutional
Responses to Child Sexual Abuse in the opening quotation. In
particular, 'state redress responds to authorized wrongful acts of
state'.[2] Broadly speaking, redress is:

> a remedy or compensation, and it can include
> financial compensation, provision of services,
> recognition and apologies and the like. It includes
> damages, or financial compensation, obtained
> through civil litigation, as well as schemes or processes
> established by governments or institutions to offer
> compensation, reparation and/or services.[3]

This chapter considers the forms that reparation has taken,
in particular, where financial compensation has been put in
place. To differentiate 'schemes or processes established by
governments or institutions to offer compensation, reparation
and/or services' from the wider forms of reparation, I use the

term 'redress' (programmes or schemes), and these are the focus of this chapter.[4] As noted, reparation can be provided in other ways, such as through criminal injuries compensation or as a result of civil litigation. Here, I discuss redress where the state has made specific arrangements for the group or individuals affected. While reparation can occur in other ways, such as through the provision of universal specialist support services, they are discussed in the next chapter.

Some form of redress has been available in all countries under discussion in this book. However, the nature of redress varies, with some elements present in some countries and not others, and their availability not necessarily to all groups in each country. Redress schemes can include ex gratia payments, specific assistance to gain educational qualifications or vocational expertise, and counselling or other individual support. In this chapter, we first consider what redress entails and why it has been a contentious area. We then establish four key models and turn to an analysis of the various redress initiatives across the five countries. Finally, drawing on these examples, we consider what is good practice in the implementation of redress programmes.

Redress

The central goal of any approach, as noted by the Law Commission of Canada, is to 'redress the harm suffered by survivors of institutional abuse'.[5] To achieve this goal, there are two key elements to redress. First, such programmes involve negotiation with the recipients about what would redress the harms experienced. Second, while typically including financial compensation, they do not necessarily only include cash payments. As explained by legal academics Reg Graycar and Jane Wangmann:

> the traditional legal remedy for harm is damages, and it follows that the traditional understanding of redress or reparations usually involves some form of financial compensation. However, if redress is seen as an attempt to address the multiple needs of victim/ survivors of abuse, this involves looking at multiple

dimensions of the process, including but not limited to financial remedies. It involves instituting a process that is more respectful of the harms that are claimed to have been experienced, and one that acknowledges the multiple ways in which these harms impact on a person.[6]

The process of developing redress programmes

According to Graycar and Wangmann, some redress approaches are characterised by an emphasis on 'financial compensation' and an 'adherence to more legalistic notions of responsibility, causation, validation and witness credibility'.[7] In contrast, they emphasise the importance of having the engagement of claimants in all aspects of developing redress programmes, and shared decision-making.[8] They also argue that such redress processes may be considered a form of therapeutic jurisprudence or, at the very least, a way of dealing with some of the anti-therapeutic elements of traditional forms of litigation. The therapeutic elements are likely to be that harm is acknowledged, accountability is placed on the perpetrator and claimants are treated with respect.[9] Moreover, 'the emphasis on process is important' as it 'can tell us much about whether a process is empowering to victim/survivors … [and] whether it responds to their needs'.[10] In this process of negotiation, an important element is support to the claimant, a point to which we will return later in this chapter when discussing good practice. In the conclusion of the Canadian inquiry, Nathalie Des Rosiers, former president of the Law Commission of Canada, explains:

> We invited governments to take a proactive stand and move toward responding to the harm in innovative ways – ways which included more than financial compensation and sought not to re-victimize survivors in the process of 'responding' to their past suffering. This encouragement to move to non adversarial methods of resolution was at the core of our approach. We suggested that any process ought to be articulated around the principles of respect and

engagement of the victim, and provided him or her with information and support.[11]

An important element of redress schemes is their ability to compensate for intergenerational effects, as has occurred to some extent in Ireland, Australia and Canada. As redress schemes are negotiated settlements, they can meet the needs of individuals, as well as their families and communities and the wider society. In addition, redress schemes can accommodate a much broader view of harms and abuse, incorporating emotional, psychological and cultural abuse, as well as the more typically considered sexual and physical abuse. In the Canadian context, but applying elsewhere as well:

> the impact of abuse suffered by individual Aboriginal children can only be totally understood when it is placed within its larger social context: families and communities have been profoundly harmed. Nor is it enough to look at possible redresses as if it were only necessary to redress physical and sexual abuse, although that is a priority. Developing an understanding of the link between degradation and disconnection caused by physical and sexual abuse and the context within which it took place requires approaches that also address emotional, psychological and spiritual harm. In other words, the adequacy of any redress mechanism must be evaluated according to how well it addresses the full range of harms experienced by individuals, families and communities.[12]

A reason put forward for the implementation of redress schemes is the fear of major litigation against government and churches. In 2002, Jennifer Llewellyn described a 'recent flood of civil litigation suits' that were brought against the Canadian government and four churches by former students of the residential schools, and that this threatened to 'overwhelm the court system and bankrupt several of the Church organizations'.[13] One of the key concerns of civil litigation is its cost, and redress schemes can be a cheaper option for a government facing such financial circumstances. However, civil actions can also be costly for claimants. Netta Christian, founder of the Care Leavers Trust New Zealand, recounted her dismay at winning compensation for harms done to her as a child while in care, but then losing all of this $NZ 10,000 in payment for legal fees.[14] Rosslyn Noonan from the New Zealand Human Rights Commission backed her and noted that an independent commission that would investigate and have the power to respond would mean that care-leavers would not need to spend their compensation funds on legal fees. The New Zealand government's Ministry of Social Development, although a separate unit in the form of the Historic Claims team, investigates claims and offers redress (see later) but is not independent of government.[15]

A criticism of some redress models and, in particular, the one recommended by the Law Commission of Canada is that they do not deal satisfactorily with allegations of abuse. As Hall remarks:

> The Report recommends that redress processes be sensitive to survivors, fair to alleged abusers and enhance public education and the development of prevention protocols.... If fairness to survivors requires a less adversarial and intimidating process, fairness to alleged abusers may demand such a process.... It may be more fair to abusers, however, to acknowledge this limitation and more honest to say that redress programmes nevertheless remain the most successful and accessible approach for survivors. Unless this limitation is acknowledged, the implication is that victim compensation proved the allegation of abuse.[16]

Typically, redress programmes require claimants to indemnify the state, meaning that they foreclose the possibility of taking civil actions against the state.

Financial compensation

Legal academic Ben Matthews has noted that 'a central feature' of redress schemes is financial compensation and that its provision for those who 'have suffered damage at the hands of the state is a moral imperative'.[17] As noted by the Compensation Advisory Committee of the Commission of Inquiry into Child Abuse in Ireland:

> no amount of money can truly compensate those who have been abused. And we agree with the Government that it is vital that a comprehensive package of services and other forms of assistance is put in place for the benefit of survivors. But we acknowledge that the award of appropriate financial redress can provide some tangible recognition of the seriousness of the hurt and injury caused to the survivors of child abuse, and that it may enable some survivors to pass the remainder of their years with a degree of comfort which would not otherwise be readily attainable.[18]

However, redress schemes that involve financial payments are often considered controversial. Sometimes, it is argued that those harmed in care should not receive special treatment through the offer of cash payments for childhood experiences that occurred long ago and, generally, it is believed, were well intended (although we can now clearly recognise discriminatory practices that underpinned some of these schemes). Others argue that what occurred does not warrant compensation at all. In contrast, public inquiries and other forms of investigation have been well able to establish that harm has been caused – harm that in any other circumstance would warrant financial compensation.[19] In relation to 'special treatment', the Law Commission of Canada notes that:

> whenever large numbers of people are harmed in significant ways as a result of the policies, acts or omissions of public authorities or large organisations,

the response should not necessarily be restricted to traditional processes. In certain cases, the response must be informed by a sense of what is right and what is necessary, both to mitigate the effects of the harms done (especially where those harms directly affect subsequent generations) and to take steps to prevent their recurrence. This type of approach should apply whenever that combination of circumstances arises.[20]

If compensation is considered possible, then there are concerns about providing money, and the difficulty of knowing how much to award in such cases. Moreover, there may be undetected false claims resulting in the waste of public money. In response to whether money should be provided to those who have been harmed in care, the Law Commission of Canada explains:

> Money is the way the Canadian [and other] legal system compensates people for injuries wrongfully caused by others. Of course, survivors must be able to demonstrate, according to the standards set by whatever judicial or extra-judicial process is being invoked, that they were injured by the wrongs committed against them. But once they have fulfilled that obligation, they are entitled to compensation, just like all other victims of a crime or a civil wrong. Financial compensation is, in some ways, the most basic material need of survivors, because it has the potential to provide for a range of other needs, such as therapy and education.[21]

As the earlier discussion highlighted, it is also important to acknowledge that many reparation schemes are not just about providing financial compensation. Indeed, none of the programmes discussed in this chapter are exclusively concerned with financial payments. Based on research with survivors of the residential schools and other forms of institutional and foster care in Canada, it was clear that much more than financial compensation was important.[22] Also, while not wanting to deny claimants' agency or to patronise them, there are sometimes good reasons to provide non-monetary compensation due to the risks associated with the receipt of large lump-sum payments, or to ensure that intensive support is available to those who are at risk, particularly as a consequence of recounting their history of abuse.[23]

In relation to how much financial compensation there should be, the Law Commission of Canada continues:

> It is not easy to establish the right amount of compensation for injuries that cannot be compensated by money, in any true sense. Yet courts perform these calculations every day in ordinary civil actions for damages. What is fair and reasonable as financial compensation for the abuse experienced by children in institutions will vary depending on the redress process adopted and the jurisdiction in which it takes place.[24]

In some redress schemes, a multiple-tier or matrix system is used to assess the severity of harm; however, as Graycar and Wangmann note, it is important to consider both the experience and its impact in determining the severity of harm.[25] In Ireland, such factors were taken into account when a scheme was devised that identified different categories of abuse and injury. In doing so, it was considered essential that redress was provided which was 'fair and reasonable having regard to the unique circumstances of each applicant'; moreover, the scheme required 'a suitable degree of predictability, sensitivity and flexibility', with the goal of providing payments that were 'comparable with amounts awarded in respect to other types of serious personal injury'.[26]

As to whether the cost of financial compensation might be too much, the Law Commission of Canada argues that:

> Whatever the monetary cost of negotiating a redress program and providing compensation to those who meet the criteria of eligibility, this cost is small when compared to the cost of not acting. The secondary and ongoing damage – to survivors, to their families and to the community – caused by failing to address

harms arising from institutional child abuse is incalculable. In view of this fact, it seems misguided and short-sighted to suggest that redress programs are too costly to undertake.[27]

Finally, the concern that large-scale fraudulence may occur is one that the Law Commission of Canada resists:

> It is true that the standard of proof for civil, and especially criminal, trials reduces the likelihood of fraudulent claims or charges to succeed. But there are many other, existing compensation programs that do not require claimants to undergo extensive cross-examination in an adversarial setting. The criminal injuries compensation process is an example. Those who hear and determine criminal injuries compensation claims have acquired a level of expertise and experience that helps them to detect unfounded claims. There is no reason to believe that similar processes for filing and supporting claims, and similar techniques for achieving validation cannot be incorporated into any redress program.[28]

Having justified why a financial payment would be a central element of a redress scheme, we now turn to the various models.

Models of redress schemes

Criteria have been identified that categorise the redress schemes in place in the five countries under study. These first criteria are the defining characteristics[29]:

- Universal or targeted – all those in care or only some groups or circumstances within a given jurisdiction.
- Not assessed or validated – having been in care is sufficient to gain redress (but usually subject to confirmation of evidence of having been in care) (ex gratia) or validation through assessment of claims is required to gain redress (resolution).

Within these two categories, there are variations according to whether compensation is:

- calculated according to a flat sum or is matrix-derived – all receive the same amount or the amount is related to the assessed degree of harm and impact of that harm;
- a cash payment and/or provision of an individually targeted identified service such as counselling or education (in-kind);
- accompanied by other initiatives (such as an apology, funding for a memorial and support services) or not.

A redress scheme could include a combination of both criteria of one category in different elements of their scheme (eg both a non-assessed, flat-sum payment, plus a further payment derived from a matrix dependent on the degree of harm experienced, subject to validation).

First, a redress scheme, or a part of a scheme, can be universal and non-assessed, so all who experienced care in that country are entitled to some redress, which may be a flat sum or awarded according to a matrix depending on the degree of harm, resulting in cash or in-kind payments. In this instance, the nature of care is deemed to be intrinsically harmful, and by virtue of being there, all are entitled to some form of compensation upon verification of having been in care.[30] Second, there are programmes that target particular groups or circumstances of care and are not assessed. They may be offered cash payments or in-kind contributions for an identified need, or both. Like the universal non-assessed model, having been in care for this particular group or in this circumstance is considered sufficient to be entitled to redress.

Third, there are redress programmes that are available universally to all who experienced care but validation is required to gain redress, and payments can be a flat sum or matrix-derived, and include cash and/or in-kind payments. Fourth, there are redress programmes that are targeted to particular populations, and claims require validation to determine compensation. In summary, the four models (with some variations within each according to the other criteria) are: universal and non-assessed; targeted and non-assessed; universal and validated; and targeted and validated. Before proceeding to discuss examples of these four models in more detail, an overview of redress schemes in the five countries will set the scene.

Overview

Across the five countries, there has been varying implementation of redress schemes. Table 5.1 provides examples of redress schemes from across the five countries, with a summary of their components to the extent to which this information is available. Two points are highlighted. First, the majority of these redress schemes include a financial payment, in varying amounts. Second, they all include other elements such as an apology and funding for counselling support.

In Australia, the federal government has refused to implement a redress scheme involving cash payments for any of the adult care-leaver population groups, and there are ongoing calls for such schemes to be put in place.[31] Instead, there has been funding for a range of initiatives, such as support services (discussed in Chapter Six) and acknowledgements (discussed in Chapter Four). However, it is possible that a national redress scheme will be an outcome of the Royal Commission into Institutional Responses to Child Sexual Abuse.[32] The state governments of Queensland, South Australia, Tasmania and Western Australia have each had universal redress schemes that involved the validation of claims resulting in cash payments to those harmed while in care in that state. The Tasmanian scheme identified members of the Stolen Generations in particular, but the others did not differentiate between the three population groups. Child migrants have had access to government funds to support family reunification through travel to the UK.[33]

Like these Australian state-based redress schemes, Ireland and New Zealand have implemented universal schemes that are available to any person who had experienced harm in care, subject to their claims being assessed (or validated). Ireland has a cash payment redress scheme subject to the validation of claims (the Residential Institutions Redress Board [RIRB]), as well as a number of universal, non-assessed programmes, including therapeutic support. There is a second redress scheme, previously

Table 5.1: Redress schemes for adult care-leavers

	Title/location	Date	Key features	Outcomes of financial payments
Ireland	Residential Institutions Redress Board (also Education Finance Board)	2002–14 (2006–11)	Financial payments – five tiers from €50,000 to €300,000 plus apologies, psychotherapy services, phone counselling, memorials, public and confidential inquiries, funding for educational support	15,100 awards; total cost close to €1 billion, average award of €62,500
	Caranua (Residential Institutions Statutory Fund)	2014–	Funding for health, housing and education support	Ongoing; at March 2014, 2,100 eligible applicants; 38 payments; total expected fund of €110 million provided by congregations
	Magdalen laundries	2013–	Non-assessed financial payments of €11,500 to €100,000, depending on length of time; plus apology and other supports, including enhanced pension	600 women expected to claim; likely total cost of €58 million

	Title/location	Date	Key features	Outcomes of financial payments
Canada	Indian Residential Schools Settlement Agreement, and earlier initiatives	1998–	Common Experience Payment (CEP) – $CDN10,000 for first year and $CDN for subsequent years Independent Assessment Process (IAP) – assessed according to matrix of abuse and wrongful acts, harm and loss of opportunity up to $CDN275,000, plus Statement of Reconciliation, Action Plan, $CDN350 million +$CDN125 million Aboriginal Healing Fund, Apology, Truth and Reconciliation Commission, $CDN20 million Commemoration; Resolution Health Support Program – mental health and cultural supports	CEP: $CDN1.9 billion fund; 79,200 payments at average of $CDN19,400 IAP: $CDN2.2 billion ongoing; 23,600 payments at average of $CDN115,300
	British Columbia, Jericho Hill Individual Compensation Program	1995–99	Financial payments – three-tier awards from $CDN3,000 to $CDN60,000; plus $CDN1 million fund for advancement of the deaf community in British Columbia	233 awards; total cost of $CDN8.38 million in total compensation, average award of $CDN35,600
	Quebec, Orphans of Du Plessis	2001–06	Apology, non-assessed and assessed claims: lump sum of $CDN15,000 and $CDN1,000 for each year, plus an additional $CDN15,000	1,500 claimants, $CDN41 million in two instalments
	Ontario, Grandview Training School for Girls	1994–2000	Financial compensation – four tiers from $CDN3,000 to $CDN60,000, personal and public apologies, therapy services, tattoo and scar removal, and support for education upgrading	350 awards, total of $CDN16.4 million, average award of $CDN37,700
New Zealand	New Zealand, Ministry of Social Development	2008–	Ex gratia payment plus Confidential Listening and Assistance Service, counselling	At 2012, 272 awards, highest award of $NZ80,000; total of $NZ3.55 million paid out

	Title/location	Date	Key features	Outcomes of financial payments
Australia	Australia – Some separate programmes for members of the Stolen Generation and other adult care-leavers	1999–	No financial compensation paid; apologies, commemoration, funding for Indigenous-specific and generic support services; funding for national care records website (Find and Connect); funding for former child migrants to reunite with family in UK	No (national) financial redress
	Queensland – Former residents of institutional care and who were abused in care	2007–08	Two-tier financial payments – $AUS7,000 and up to $AUS40,000, plus support service, public inquiry, memorial, apology	7,400 awards, total of $AUS100 million scheme
	South Australia	2008–	Ex gratia payments via the Victims of Crime Act 2001	At June 2014, 82 offers accepted to a total of $AUS1.167 million
	Tasmania – Members of the Stolen Generations	2007	Two-tier financial payments – $AUS60,000 for those wrongfully removed, $AUS5,000 for their children up to $AUS20,000 for a family group, plus apology, counselling	106 claimants; $AUS5 million total fund
	Tasmania – Abused wards of the state	2003–08	Up to $AUS60,000 ex gratia payment, plus apology, oral history collection, memorial	Total funding of $AUS27.5 million
	Western Australia – Former residents of institutional care and who were abused in care	2008–09	Four-tier financial payments – between $AUS5,000 and $AUS45,000 plus apology, memorial	Total funding of $AUS114 million
United Kingdom	British child migrants to Australia, Canada, New Zealand and Zimbabwe	2010	Family Restoration Fund: covers cost of two-week trip including return economy flights and accommodation, plus apology	Total funding of £6 million

Sources: Aboriginal Affairs and Northern Development Canada, 'Statistics on the Implementation of the Indian Residential Schools Settlement Agreement' (from 19 September 2007 to 30 September 2013), available at: https://www.aadnc-aandc.gc.ca/eng/1315320539682/1315320692192 (accessed 1 June 2014); Caranua, 'FAQ', available at: http://www.caranua.ie/who_we_are/frequently_asked_questions (accessed 13 November 2015); BBC News Europe, 'Magdalene laundries support scheme unveiled', 26 June 2013, available at: http://www.bbc.com/news/world-europe-23064112 (accessed 1 June 2014); Child Migrants Trust, 'Family Restoration Fund', available at: http://www.childmigrantstrust.com/resources/uploads/files/FRF%20Information%20Pack%20-%20Jan%202014.pdf (accessed 1 June 2014); Graycar and Wangmann, 'Redress packages for institutional child abuse'; Matthews, 'Queensland government actions to compensate survivors of institutional abuse', pp 28–31; Residential Institutions Redress Board (RIRB), *A Guide to the Redress Scheme Under the Residential Institutions Redress Act, 2002 as Amended by the Commission to Inquire into Child Abuse (Amendment) Act, 2005* (3rd edn), RIRB, Dublin, 2005; RIRB, 'Updates: newsletter, 23 December 2013', available at: http://www.rirb.ie/updates_article.asp?NID=128 (accessed 1 June 2014); RCIRCSA, *Consultation Paper*, Appendices A & B; Angela Sdrinis and Penny Savidis, 'How can care leavers achieve justice?', paper presented at CLAN 10th Anniversary Conference, July 2010, Sydney; Shea, 'Redress programs relating to institutional child abuse in Canada'; Claire Trevett, 'Bennett tells abused state victims to claim', *New Zealand Herald*, 27 June 2012, available at: http://www.nzherald.co.nz/nz/news/article.cfm?c_id=1&objectid=10815735 (accessed 1 June 2014); Stephen Winter, *Transitional Justice in Established Democracies: A Political Theory*, Palgrave Macmillan, Basingstoke, 2014, pp 201–2; Stephen Winter, 'Australia's ex gratia redress', *Australian Indigenous Law Review*, vol 13, no 1, 2009, pp 48–61, 52.

known as the Residential Institutions Statutory Fund, now known as Caranua, which commenced in 2014 and targets improvements in health, housing and education. Caranua is available to those who have been in receipt of RIRB awards, as well as those who received awards through the courts or settlements. New Zealand's redress is more limited in its scope, providing a financial payment and limited counselling and other targeted support. New Zealand also worked with child migrants, providing support to find families and travel to the UK to meet with them.[34]

In Canada, there has been a national redress scheme for Indigenous people and schemes in several provinces that were targeted and responded to particular institutional situations of abuse. The Indian Residential Schools Settlement Agreement, in place from 2006, was an outcome of negotiations between the state, churches and Indigenous advocates and came about as a result of the largest settlement in Canadian history in an agreement with the nine Canadian courts in which legal action was being undertaken. Claimants did not have to accept the terms of this agreement; they could opt out and continue to pursue litigation. From 2003, there had also been in place an alternative dispute resolution process that had proved to be 'challenging'.[35] The Settlement includes both cash payments and a range of accompanying initiatives. There are no identified programmes for child migrants. One universal programme is British Columbia's Residential Historic Abuse Program, commenced in 1992, which provides intensive long-term therapy to adult care-leavers who experienced sexual abuse in that province.[36]

In the UK, there have not been the universal schemes as in the states of Australia, New Zealand or Ireland. Nor has there been the range of other initiatives. A redress scheme that aimed to support family reunification of child migrants provided targeted funds for travel to the UK.[37] It is likely that the Scotland and Northern Ireland inquiries will recommend some form of redress once they have been finalised.

Universal and non-assessed redress

In this group of universal and non-assessed redress schemes (or, rather, specific programmes within them), there are none that include financial payments. However, there are a number of examples of service responses that have been made universally available. These are discussed in more detail in Chapter Six (as forms of specialist support or access to records and family reunification programmes) and include the government-funded National Counselling Service and Connect telephone counselling service in Ireland. In addition, in Ireland, Barnardos Ireland Origins service assisted care-leavers to access their personal records and find their families. In Australia, universal and non-assessed redress initiatives include state-based support services such as Lotus Place in Queensland.[38]

Targeted and non-assessed

There are several examples of targeted and non-assessed elements of redress schemes. Two examples are provided of those that include financial payments. In Canada, former residential schools students party to the Indian Residential Schools Settlement Agreement were eligible for the Common Experience Payments (CEP) of $CDN 10,000 for the first year or part of a year that they attended school, plus $CDN 3,000 for each subsequent year. Acceptance of the CEP released the government and churches from all further liability relating to the residential school experience, except in cases of sexual abuse and serious incidents of physical abuse.[39] This is one aspect of a much larger package, including an apology, the funding of memorials and other acknowledgements, the Truth and Reconciliation Commission of Canada, and additional payments for experiences of sexual abuse that are assessed (discussed later).

In the Australian state of Tasmania, members of the Stolen Generations received non-assessed cash payments for wrongful removal in addition to being eligible for assessable awards available to all adult care-leavers in that state. Also, additional funding was granted to the family reunification support service Link-Up (discussed in Chapter Seven).

An example of a redress package that includes a number of targeted and non-assessed components comes from Ontario in Canada. This package did not include a non-assessed cash payment. The Grandview Training School for Girls, in operation from 1933 to 1976, incarcerated Aboriginal and non-Aboriginal girls aged between 12 and 18 years for up to four years. Deemed as being in 'moral danger' was a key reason for entry, typically related to sexist and racist perceptions of the interactions of sexuality and gender.[40] Survivors revealed experiences of severe physical, sexual and psychological abuse during their time as state wards in Grandview. Through a 'detailed negotiating process' with the government, representatives of the survivors support group and their lawyer agreed to a package of measures, including therapeutic support, which was put in place during the negotiations.[41] Other elements of the redress included 'group benefits' that applied to all women under the agreement without assessment of their claims, such as tattoo removal, a telephone crisis line and a public apology. 'General benefits' included the development of a documentary that aimed to create a 'historical record'. Finally, accessing 'individual benefits' required an assessment and validation of claims 'on the balance of probabilities', and resulted in financial compensation, education and training assistance, therapy, and a personal apology.[42]

The UK Department of Health's redress programme for former child migrants also does not provide a financial payment. The Family Restoration Fund 'help[s] to reunite former child migrants with their families so that they can build relationships, be involved in significant family events or urgently visit relatives in times of crisis such as serious illness or death'.[43]

Universal and assessed

Ireland has two universally available and assessable redress schemes. The first, the Residential Institutions Redress Board (RIRB), since finalised, provided individual awards of up to €300,000. Claims were assessed by reference to two key factors according to a 'weighting scale': the severity of the abuse and the severity of the injury resulting from the abuse. The latter was broken down according to medical evidence, psychosocial effects and loss of opportunity. The level of redress was then identified according to the 'band' level previously determined through the principles of general damages in Ireland.[44] From 2014, those who received payments from the RIRB or through other settlements can apply for additional support from Caranua, which funds services such as dental treatment, home care, home adaptations and counselling, psychological and psychiatric services.[45]

Universal and assessed redress schemes have operated in some states of Australia. In Western Australia, for example, a redress scheme (known as Redress WA) was put in place, with awards of up to $AUS 80,000. With a change of government and advice that the programme was underfunded, the maximum payment was reduced to $AUS 45,000, with assessments made on the basis of having experienced abuse, and the impact of that abuse.[46] In New Zealand, former wards of the state can apply for a financial settlement to the Ministry of Social Development. At 2010, the highest award was $NZ 75,000. As well as an award, applicants could receive an individual apology and access to other services, including limited counselling support and reference to the Confidential Listening and Assistance Service.[47]

Targeted and assessed

In Canada, as well as the non-assessed CEP, an additional, assessable payment to address the sexual and serious physical abuse of former residential school students is available through the Independent Assessment Process (IAP). Claimants applying for the IAP and the CEP received assistance from the Indian Residential Schools Resolution Health Support Program, discussed in Chapter Six. Payments awarded under the IAP are determined according to a matrix that takes into account the nature of the abuse and the consequential harm and loss of opportunity, up to $CDN 275,000, although final sums paid can be more as actual income losses can also be compensated.[48] By the end of 2013, two thirds of IAP claims had been resolved.[49]

Good practice in implementing redress programmes

Having established the nature of redress and various models, we turn now to its implementation. Key attributes include how it is advertised, the support provided to those seeking redress and the expertise of those administering the programme.

Advertising redress programmes

It is vitally important to ensure that those who are likely to apply for redress are aware of its existence. Given the range of circumstances of adult care-leavers, diverse means of advertisement need to be employed to reach the targeted groups. Time needs to be allowed for adult care-leavers to find out about the programmes, and to apply for them. To apply for redress can be a process of major emotional and psychological significance as adult care-leavers confront their past.[50]

In Canada, for example, there was a four-pronged plan of ensuring that former students of residential schools were aware of the settlement agreement. Part of the plan was to send letters to those known to be party to the settlement. There were also advertisements in Aboriginal and mainstream media on television and radio and in newspapers. Information was available in multiple languages, including English, French and Indigenous languages. A dedicated website and a toll-free call centre provided further information. A third aspect of the plan was community outreach activities conducted by a range of organisations, including Aboriginal Affairs and Northern Development Canada, the Truth and Reconciliation Commission and Health Canada. In addition, the Assembly of First Nations worked with over 600 First Nations communities across Canada to impart the information. Finally, the Advocacy and Public Information Program funded grassroots Aboriginal organisations to disseminate information about the settlement agreement, particularly to those who were incarcerated, homeless or living in remote locations.[51]

Advertising redress programmes is not just about informing the community as widely as possible; those who may not be able to apply on their own behalf also need to be taken into account.

For example, in Western Australia, the Public Advocate made applications to Redress WA in 2009 on behalf of those who could not do so. She worked with people who 'have been haunted by their lost childhood throughout their lives. For the majority of this group, they have literally "drowned their sorrows" in alcohol and as a consequence these people now have diminished capacity'.[52] The Public Advocate is the guardian 'of last resort' and was empowered to make decisions on behalf of these adult care-leavers, in accordance with the State Administrative Tribunal's guardianship order.[53]

Supporting adult care-leavers during redress processes

As noted by the Law Commission of Canada:

> confronting a difficult, in some cases traumatic, past is never an easy experience. Survivors seeking personal redress ... may need psychological and emotional support so that their participation in a process does not unduly exacerbate the harm they have already suffered.[54]

In particular, 'every effort must be made to minimise the potential harm of redress processes themselves'.[55] However, re-traumatisation can be integral to redress processes, as was found in Western Australia, Ireland and the UK.[56] For example, during Redress WA:

> Telling their story, often for the first time, sometimes for yet another time, was deeply re-traumatising for many applicants ... almost daily reporting of people who had been abused, on radio, television or other media stirred up memories and feelings and many repeatedly re-experienced their trauma at this time.[57]

In Ireland, for those who had not previously attended counselling at the time of seeking redress, 'The experience of telling your story for the first time to a panel of strangers with whom you had built up no rapport, and who were only interested in the facts of your case, was a terrible ordeal'.[58] While in these situations, adult care-leavers could access 'emergency counselling' but then 'go home in an anxious state without professional support'.[59] It is imperative, then, that emotional support is built into redress schemes to avoid re-traumatisation.

Although not necessarily intended as such, some who were contracted by the Western Australian Government to assist adult care-leavers to apply to Redress WA used this process as an opportunity for therapeutic interventions. The capacity to take on this therapeutic role was reliant on staff having an understanding of the history of care in Australia and knowledge of trauma-informed strategies. Such an approach was characterised by the validation of the applicant's account and the offer of an apology.[60] In contrast, the Indian Residential Schools Resolution Health Support Program was set up with the specific intention of providing therapeutic and other support to applicants to the CEP and IAP, discussed in Chapter Seven.

An example whereby the redress process caused harm was in the case of Redress WA, when it changed the maximum payment figure. As noted earlier, with a change of government, this amount was reduced. As explained by Gail Green and her colleagues, who were involved in assisting applicants:

> Applicants, many of whom had experienced significant trauma, expressed high levels of anger and frustration toward the Government at the reduction in ex-gratia payments. Many applicants stated the reduction perpetuated thoughts and feelings of distrust and anger towards the Government. For some the changes maintained feelings of worthlessness, hopelessness, of being tricked and then being betrayed.[61]

Part of the process of providing support concerns managing the expectations of applicants. According to Green et al, Redress WA produced:

> many people who were very grateful for the personal assistance, the ex-gratia payments and the letters

of apology they received. Many applicants used the money wisely and felt believed and validated. However an implicit expectation was created that simply telling their story would change their daily lives. It was deeply saddening that some woke up at the end of the process with their lives still broken and deeply impacted by trauma.[62]

Expertise of redress programme staff

As noted by Gail Green and her colleagues when reflecting on their experiences in assisting adult care-leavers to apply to Redress WA: 'inquiries [and redress] can become a turning point for positive change however, if the process is not conducted with skill and empathy a vulnerable population is at risk of re-traumatisation and even of suicide and self-harm.'[63] They note the importance of paying attention to such matters as 'how questions are asked ... and even how phones are answered'.[64] Reflecting these concerns, the Law Commission of Canada advises that 'Those involved in conducting or administering different processes must have sufficient training to ensure that they understand the circumstances of survivors of institutional child abuse'.[65] More than this, though, clinical supervision is required for all staff, as well as access to employee assistance programmes.[66]

Conclusion

This chapter has outlined the nature of redress and provided justification for the inclusion of cash payments, as well as other means of addressing the needs of adult care-leavers. Across the five countries, four different models were identified that varied according to who the redress programme targeted and whether claims were assessed or not. While there have been comprehensive redress schemes in place in Ireland for all who grew up in care and for former students of residential schools and for some particular institutions in Canada, elsewhere, such redress programmes have been less than robust. Central to redress programmes is the need to provide support to claimants. Other elements are identified in Box 5.1.

Box 5.1: Key elements of redress schemes for adult care-leavers

- Seek input from adult care-leavers on the design and implementation of redress schemes.
- Consult with adult care-leavers on what they consider to be the necessary components of a redress package.
- Cash payments are a widely recognised means of reparation for harms and should be considered as part of a redress programme for adult care-leavers.
- Support adult care-leavers through the process.
- Avoid further harm and minimise re-traumatisation.
- Advertise redress widely in multiple media and through personal networks to make contact with all those likely to be eligible.
- Allow sufficient time for claimants to apply, bearing in mind that redress processes are likely to be emotionally challenging to undertake, relying as they do on remembering and documenting confronting childhood experiences.
- Ensure that staff are equipped with the skills and knowledge to carry out redress programmes.

SIX

Specialist support

The scale of the atrocity is appalling. It happened in institutions respected by the community. The community is today bearing the cost of this treatment; in ruined lives and in expensive tertiary treatments, for example prisons and homeless and mental health services. The cost to the individual is almost unbearable to contemplate. (Caroline Carroll, adult care-leaver and advocate, 2014[1])

Caroline Carroll, President of the Alliance of Forgotten Australians, quoted above, highlights the scale of the abuse, the consequences for those worst affected and the need for support services. In this chapter, we consider the specialist support needs of adult care-leavers, and how attempts are made to meet these needs through the provision of services. In Chapter Two, key areas of support for adult care-leavers were identified, including: mental health; others areas such as education, employment and social engagement; and cultural reconnection. As we have seen in Chapter Five, these are sometimes provided as part of a redress package targeting individuals or groups or they are available universally to all adult care-leavers in a jurisdiction. These are programmes available to adult care-leavers at no cost, as a form of in-kind recognition of the harms experienced. There is also, of course, a range of specialist support that could be available for payment, or as part of wider support service systems that do not specifically target adult care-leavers, such as a community mental health clinic.

Specialist support as part of a redress programme or otherwise available to this group is what some adult care-leavers want most, rather than compensation in the form of cash payments, or as well as cash. In this way, funds are available to specifically address their needs. In addition, there are risks in handing over large sums of money. Overspending may be considered a person's choice as to how to use these funds, but there is also a duty of care to those for whom risky behaviours such as problematic drug and alcohol use could lead to overdose or injury through accidents. Cash payment by instalment is a way that these difficulties have been managed in some jurisdictions.[2] Regardless, some express concern about the removal of agency in the provision of services to adult care-leavers rather than cash payments – adult care-leavers may not be given the opportunity to say what it is that they actually want, or whether what is provided is sufficient to make a difference to their lives, especially in circumstances of universal provision. In providing high-quality services, these concerns need to be taken into account, and, indeed, should be central to the provision of such support. Evaluation of such service provision is, then, an important component of these initiatives in order to test whether these are the most effective means of providing support and to consider ways in which improvements could be made.

As suggested, specialist support services sit alongside others that are provided for all members of the community – generic or mainstream health and welfare services. In addition, generic criminal injuries compensation schemes provide support to victims (even though the difficulties in gaining criminal convictions are acknowledged in this area). It could be asked: why do adult care-leavers need more and different services to what other members of the community receive? Importantly, these mainstream services are not sufficient because adult care-leavers may seek support without identifying themselves as adult care-leavers, so those who they contact are not aware of the harms experienced during their childhood. Due to the stigma of care, some may never disclose this as a key reason that they are seeking support from these services; they may also not realise that the cause of their troubles is their childhood experiences. This alerts us to a key issue: the professional expertise of health and welfare practitioners to identify adult care-leavers, and to offer specialist support, discussed later in this chapter. Unlike generic services, specialist services typically employ workers who are qualified to work with adult care-leavers and have the skills and background knowledge to be most effective in this work. Sometimes, such services employ adult care-leavers themselves because of this expertise. There are also likely to be elements of their location, setting or layout that take into account what is most comfortable and effective for adult care-leavers, as discussed later.

To some extent, the availability of support specifically for adult care-leavers could be related to the nature and extent of the wider health and welfare services in each country, available to all through generic or mainstream services. There is, however, no obvious correlation between those countries that provide specialist services and the extent of their welfare systems, at least partly due to the complexities of such systems. It may be the case that those countries that have an extensive welfare system are more likely to provide specialist services. For example, Australia has a relatively well-developed health and welfare system – albeit overstretched. Community health centres and other forms of the public health system offer mental health support. Local community centres provide opportunities to learn vocational skills or meet others in a friendly environment. Telephone crisis lines provide support and refer on to other services. While adult care-leavers can also access all these services, as we will see, there is also a network of specialist services in each Australian state that provide referral and a range of programmes specifically to adult care-leavers.

There are certainly cautions in the provision of specialist support services. For example, criticism has been levelled at the provision solely of individualistic responses that do not recognise the 'systemic and pervasive nature' of the harms wrought against children in care. As noted by Pamela O'Connor in the Canadian context, and applicable elsewhere: 'instead of proposing measures for compensation, justice and redress, those harmed by the system are to be assisted in their individual healing and recovery by the provision of therapeutic services'.[3] It is possible, however, to provide both responses that address the systemic nature of harm (through financial compensation schemes, apologies and other acknowledgements) and also programmes that provide therapeutic and other support to individuals. As acknowledged in Chapter Two, there are individual harms that demand responses and, as discussed in Chapter Five, redress can be more than financial compensation. Redress can include acknowledgement of 'the multiple ways in which these harms impact on a person.[4] Thus, for some, individualistic responses are needed. This point is illustrated in one of the few evaluations of specialist support services, where it was found that adult care-leavers sought assistance from the In Care Survivors Service Scotland because of:

> a composite of interacting psychological, behavioural, emotional, relational, practical and life events which had aggravated their difficulties.... Further, an overwhelming number of clients referred to being at a critical stage of need of support where most experienced emotional and psychological difficulties that had left them feeling powerless to continue to attempt to contain their trauma.[5]

In this chapter, an overview of the specialist support offered is first discussed, with a range of examples demonstrating the diversity of social policy programmes and models. Then, key features of good practice in service provision are highlighted. Finally, attention is paid to the area of professional education in an effort to highlight the need for greater work in this area.

Provision of specialist support

Chapter Two outlined five key areas where research suggests that adult care-leavers experience difficulties: mental health; education and employment; interpersonal relationships; cultural connection; and identity and family relationships. The latter is addressed in Chapter Seven as a specialist area of work that has developed in this field. Forms of specialist support are in place that respond to the first four areas just listed, and the organisation of the following discussion is guided by the ways in which this support is delivered.

Mental health

In research for the Law Commission of Canada, it was found that 'counselling is seen by survivors and others as the most critical service to be available through the process of addressing institutional abuse'.[6] The need for mental health support may be immediate and crisis-oriented, or longer-term. These, of course, may overlap, but their responses have been provided differently, and for different reasons. Mental health support may be available universally to an adult care-leaver population or be targeted at individuals through a redress package. There is also the range of services that refer adult care-leavers for mental health support, and may provide short-term counselling in doing so. These are typically among those initiatives that are engaged in the provision of educational and social activities, and are thus discussed in the next section. In addition, counselling support is provided in the context of releasing records and family reunification, discussed in Chapter Seven. In this discussion, I distinguish between counselling and therapy, whereby the latter is a range of approaches that is intensive and long-term. Counselling, on the other hand, is less intensive and responds to more immediate issues than therapy.[7] A key element that informs this work today is that adult care-leavers have experienced trauma in their childhood through abuse and separation from their family.

Typically, public inquiries have included or instigated the establishment of some form of counselling support initiative to provide immediate emotional assistance to those who become aware of the inquiry and may react adversely, and for those who participate in them. Such services are imperative to support adult care-leavers through the process. In some instances, these telephone lines or other initiatives have continued after the conclusion of the inquiry. Longer-term mental health support has been provided in a number of ways. Psychotherapy is usually provided on an individual basis and by a qualified psychiatrist, psychologist, nurse or social worker. For some, very long-term mental health support, delivered over numbers of years, could be described as outpatient psychotherapy. Such therapy may commence as a result of the awareness of a public inquiry, participation in it or a life crisis. Advocates may also set up self-help groups, or existing adult care-leavers' services may establish specialist group programmes to provide ongoing mental health support, which are both other ways of providing longer-term support. Mental health support may also be provided by a traditional Aboriginal healer, as is evident particularly in the Canadian context. It is worth noting that the other initiatives discussed in the following may also contribute to mental health improvements.

There are a number of examples of shorter-term mental health support initiatives. In Canada, the Indian Residential School crisis line was established to support former residential school students, and is available all hours. Both through accessing material on the website and engaging in the redress processes, the Canadian government acknowledges that former residents may experience 'trauma invoked by memories of past abuse'.[8] The crisis line is part of a wider initiative supporting the health needs of former residential school students, the Indian Residential Schools Resolution Health Support Program, discussed in the next section.

In Northern Ireland, a similar understanding ensured the provision of support from the establishment the inquiry, with 'every effort … made to ensure that sufficient emotional support is available for victims and survivors while they recount their experiences to the Acknowledgement Forum or give evidence to the Inquiry'.[9] In this case, the support is in the form of witness support officers for those participating in the statutory inquiry, an emotionally supportive environment when speaking at the Acknowledgment Forum and access to dedicated counsellors from the newly established Victim Support Service. This agency provides 'support and advice to victims and survivors before, during and after the Inquiry'.[10] In Australia, there has been similar acknowledgement of the difficulties in engaging with the Royal Commission into Institutional Responses to Child Sexual Abuse, and additional funding has been provided to existing specialist services to support those involved or affected.[11]

In relation to long-term psychotherapeutic support, there are fewer examples, at least partly because of the cost involved where therapy may involve years of engagement. As the Law Commission of Canada has noted: 'The trauma of child abuse often has profound consequences for survivors.... Coming to understand the connections between one's experience of abuse as a child and one's behaviour as an adult can be a lengthy and complex process'.[12] In contrast, in some jurisdictions, including much of Australia and New Zealand, state-funded programmes typically provide only for a time-limited number of sessions, which is unlikely to deal with such complex consequences. The Royal Commission into Institutional Responses to Child Sexual Abuse has found that 'counselling should be available throughout a survivor's life'; whether this eventuates is yet to be seen.[13]

Ireland has a highly developed service system in relation to short- and longer-term mental health services for adult care-leavers. There are two state-funded services: the National Counselling Service (NCS) and Connect. While both are available to any adults who have experienced trauma and abuse during childhood, their priority is to those who were harmed in care. The NCS provides face-to-face individual counselling and psychotherapy and group therapy. Connect functions as a provider of both short-term support and longer-term therapy (or 'counselling', as Connect refers to it), both provided on the telephone.

Established in 2000 following the Irish Prime Minister's apology, the NCS forms one of the measures to address the needs of adults who were abused in care as children. The NCS identifies accessibility, high quality and client-centredness as its three most important principles of service delivery. Overseen by directors of counselling, more than 70 counsellors or therapists are employed across the 10 regional health boards in Ireland. A range of therapeutic approaches is used, including family therapy, cognitive behavioural therapy and psychodynamic therapy.[14] In the first years of operation until 2003, more than 6,500 people sought counselling from the NCS, with most receiving weekly sessions of one hour for up to 20 sessions. Others were involved in long-term therapy for more than a year.[15] In two internal reviews and a formal evaluation during these first three years of the NCS's operation, clients revealed high levels of satisfaction but there were some concerns about the length of time to receive services. While an initial assessment interview had occurred, there was then a wait for some before ongoing counselling or therapy commenced. As explained by the evaluators, the Health Service Research Centre: 'they felt distressed, exposed and vulnerable at the time of assessment and felt they needed to be seen straight away'.[16] At the same time, while the NCS has a telephone referral line, it does not provide counselling support. Such telephone support was being provided by other adult care-leavers' organisations, such as Right of Place and Aislinn (discussed later). Advocacy from survivor support groups to address this gap in the service system resulted in the establishment of Connect (initially known as the NOVA Helpline) in 2004.

While the NCS is a government service, Connect is a government-funded charitable organisation. Connect provides 20 hours per week of out-of-hours telephone and counselling support services, available to those in Ireland, as well as Northern Ireland and the UK. Counselling is either of a 'supportive' nature, involving 'emotional containment' and 'a listening ear', which can be short-term or ongoing, or 'therapeutic', which is more similar to face-to-face therapy in that it is 'in-depth work with an allocated counsellor and working at scheduled times'.[17] There are various benefits of telephone counselling, such as the potential for greater accessibility of services and increased client autonomy and anonymity, which can facilitate engagement with therapeutic services.[18] Over the period 2006–10, there were over 31,000 calls to Connect, with an increase around the time of the release of the *Ryan Report*. However, around a fifth of these calls were unanswered or abandoned, reflecting a level of unmet demand.[19]

A third element of the provision of mental health support in Ireland is through the Catholic Church's Towards Healing programme. While some do not want to receive support from a Church-funded agency, others argue that using this service is a way in which the Church is taking responsibility by responding to the harms suffered. Funded by the dioceses and congregations and using a brokerage model, Towards Healing pays for the services of therapists. Like the other programmes providing therapeutic support to adult care-leavers in Ireland, counsellors and therapists are accredited with the Irish Association for Counselling and Psychotherapy, or its equivalent where adult care-leavers reside outside Ireland.[20] Reviews of progress are conducted routinely across the period of therapeutic intervention. In addition to this face-to-face counselling, Towards Healing runs a number of other initiatives, including a helpline, life skills workshops and psycho-educational group work.[21] In 2012, Towards Healing provided nearly 30,000 counselling sessions and the telephone helpline dealt with over 18,000 calls.[22]

The amount of mental health support provided across these three Irish services suggests a high level of need, and this level of provision is not replicated elsewhere in such comprehensive ways. Unlike Ireland, in Canada, there is very little specialist mental health support for their adult care-leaver population provided universally to this group. One example is British Columbia's Residential Historic Abuse Program (RHAP), established in 1992 as a provincial programme in response to emerging civil litigation concerned with abuse in care. Since then, the initiative has diversified, with the various health authorities that now manage it taking different approaches. In Vancouver's Coastal Health Authority, for example, RHAP funds counselling for adults who were sexually abused in care as children using a brokerage model. Counsellors or therapists must meet minimum professional standards. Clients are allocated up to 85 hours of individual and or family services each year, and up to 90 hours of group counselling, and this support can be ongoing subject to regular reviews.[23] In contrast to this universal approach, as an outcome of Ontario's Grandview Agreement, claimants received long-term therapy for up to around 12 months, which had been identified in its evaluation as 'the cornerstone' of the Agreement.[24]

As part of the Indian Residential Schools Settlement Agreement, the Indian Residential Schools Resolution Health Support Program (IRSRHSP) provides mental health and emotional support for former students and their families. The IRSRHSP comprises four elements: cultural support, emotional support, professional counselling and transportation to access services. Local Aboriginal organisations across Canada are involved in provision and coordination. Drawing on the expertise of elders and traditional healers, support can be offered in the form of ceremonies, traditional medicines and therapies, and cultural and spiritual activities such as sweat lodges and smudging. In addition to these, a wide range of healing initiatives was established through the Aboriginal Healing Foundation. Resolution Health Support Workers, employed by local Aboriginal organisations, provide support during the Settlement Agreement process.[25]

In Australia, there is largely time-limited access to mental health support for adult care-leavers through the universal services discussed later. A more comprehensive mental health support system is in place for members of the Stolen Generations. The Australian government's Social and Emotional Wellbeing Program includes counselling to members of the Stolen Generations. (It also supports family tracing and reunion services, discussed in Chapter Seven.) These services are provided through the network of Link-Up agencies, as well as other Indigenous organisations.[26] This work is underpinned by cultural respect, which involves 'the recognition, protection and continued advancement of the inherent rights, cultures and traditions of Aboriginal and Torres Strait Islander peoples'.[27]

In Scotland, where wider social policy responses to adult care-leavers are still in development, a telephone helpline set up and run by the advocacy group In Care Abuse Survivors has provided support since 2000. The In Care Survivors Service Scotland (ICSSS) is an initiative derived from the Scottish government's National Strategy for Survivors of Childhood Abuse. Commencing in 2008, ICSSS was developed to 'highlight and address the long-term effects, as well as current and future needs of those survivors subjected to neglect, physical, emotional and sexual abuse whilst in care'.[28] More recently, the scope of the service has been widened to include adult care-leavers whose experience of abuse occurred as children and while not in care. ICSSS is under the auspices of the community-based organisation Open Secret, which works with individuals and their families affected by child abuse. ICSSS provides a range of short- and longer-term mental health (and other) support to adult care-leavers and their families through its 'trauma informed counselling and advocacy'. This includes individual counselling, group work and a telephone helpline that offers advice and information.[29] In a service evaluation, the value of ICSSS was identified by a client:

> The counselling is really important.... People still think that because it's historical that it is over but it is a life-long legacy that takes that length of time to deal with at different points in your life. The fact [the counselling] is open-ended and not restricted to a certain number of sessions like the NHS [National Health Service] makes the world of difference.[30]

An additional element of ICSSS is their befriending service, which aims to build the confidence of adult care-leavers in managing new experiences, and to assist in accessing social, educational and recreational opportunities, all part of supporting mental health. As an adult care-leaver reported: 'I have been institutionalised all my life so life in the community is very hard to cope with. My befriender helps me make this easier'. Another said: 'I feel like a person. I went to the cinema for the first time in my life with my befriender'.[31]

Education, social engagement and other support

There are a number of examples of 'one-stop shop' initiatives that provide a range of health, welfare, social and educational programmes to adult care-leavers, and provide information and referral to other services as needed. Typically, these specialist support services operate from a social model of health and consider a holistic approach as key to working with adult care-leavers. Life skills and educational, social and vocational activities are universally provided to adult care-leavers through these specialist community centres. These centres usually provide advice and referral for a range of matters, such as income support, mental health services and housing. To gain access, there is typically a requirement for evidence of having been in care. An alternative model to this is that whereby specific support has been targeted at individuals in the form of a funded package or as a result of engagement in a redress process.

In Ireland, the Aislinn Education and Support Centre in Dublin was established in 1999 by adult care-leavers advocates Christine Buckley and Carmel McDonnell-Byrne, with Irish government funding subsequent to the apology to survivors of institutional abuse. Lack of education is one of the key impacts of a childhood in care, and Aislinn's goal is to provide education in its various forms, including formally recognised courses, as well as therapeutic and recreational activities. Educational activities include those in art, cookery, literacy, numeracy and computer skills. Aislinn also has a social focus, with the centre providing 'a supportive meeting place' and a source of information and referral for survivors and their families.[32] Outside of Dublin, Right of Place has centres in Cork, Galway and Waterford. It operates with a focus on information, advocacy and referral, with outreach being a focus of its approach.[33]

As well as services in Ireland, there are also organisations in the UK that provide support to Irish adult care-leavers due to their migration there. For example, the Irish Survivors Advice and Support Service (ISASS), based in London, is a self-help organisation established by survivors of Irish institutions. ISASS provides information regarding matters such as housing, pensions and health and welfare benefits. They also supported claimants during the redress application process and provided referrals to lawyers and counsellors. A women's group, running for over 10 years, both advocates for survivors to the Irish government and functions as a self-help support group for its members.[34]

In Australia, a network of services across all states and territories is in place to provide support to adult care-leavers through community centre-style initiatives. Only three Australian governments (and not the federal government) have put in place financial compensation schemes, and the existence of these specialist support services could be considered an in-kind expression of redress. The individual services have varying histories – some long-standing and others more recent. Some were initiated by advocates and have developed into stand-alone services; others are under the auspices of larger community organisations. The way in which they operate and the programmes that they run vary from centre to centre. Typically, centre activities include: social outings and events; life skills and other workshops; educational short courses; and assistance with health and welfare matters. They also offer counselling and referral to brokerage counselling. Many operate as drop-in centres and have established support groups in other locations in that state. Some have received additional resourcing through the Australian government's Find and Connect programme to assist adult care-leavers to access their records (discussed in Chapter Six).[35]

In contrast to these community centre initiatives, individually targeted support is also provided via redress and other schemes. For example, in New Zealand, through the process of attending the Confidential Listening and Assistance Service, counselling and other support is available, with referral and advocacy to other agencies as needed. In two instances, adult care-leavers apply for grants to support them in their daily living and related activities. In Queensland, Australia, the Forde Foundation, an outcome of the Forde Inquiry, provides funding for a range of purposes, including personal development, health and wellness, and dental care.[36] Similarly, in Ireland, adult care-leavers can apply to Caranua (an outcome of the Commission of Inquiry into Child Abuse, and formerly known as the Residential Institutions Statutory Fund) to seek funding for services or equipment for health or medical purposes, personal well-being, housing assistance, and education and personal development.[37]

Cultural support

In Canada and Australia, there are programmes in place to support cultural reconnection and cultural revitalisation, needed as a result of policies of child removal and the subsequent long-term intergenerational impacts on families and communities. This support has been noted in relation to the Indian Residential Schools Resolution Health Support Program in Canada; other ways in which this occurs in Canada are through the programmes of the Truth and Reconciliation Commission and the Aboriginal Healing Foundation. In Australia, the Healing Foundation funds a range of programmes specifically targeting members of the

Stolen Generations, including cultural renewal activities such as bush trips, healing camps on country and events that involve traditional dance, song, arts and ceremonies.[38]

An example of a model of cultural support is the Australian Marumali programme, developed by Lorraine Peeters, a member of the Stolen Generations. Marumali draws on the Kamilaroi word meaning to 'to heal' or 'put back together'. Peeters argues that 'the pathway to recovery involves mind, body and spirit and is holistic in that culture, identity and reconnecting with family, community and country are central to the healing journey'.[39] Moreover, 'the Marumali Circle of Healing model acknowledges that reconnecting with Aboriginal spirituality is a core healing tool to overcome the grief and loss experienced by Aboriginal people from past government removal practices'.[40]

Models of support services

In summary, it is evident that there is a range of models of service provision, including:

- stand-alone counselling or therapy services, including face-to-face and telephone counselling;
- brokerage therapy and other services;
- cultural reconnection and revitalisation programmes;
- community support centres, offering a range of educational, vocational, personal development, social, life skills and other activities;
- self-help groups; and
- targeted individual support that is provided through a redress process or via application to a redress fund.

Key features of good practice

Having established the range of models and considered a number of examples from across the five countries, we now turn to some elements of good practice in service provision. Attention is paid to four features: values and principles; accessibility; governance; and evaluation. A fifth element – that of professional expertise – is addressed in the next section.

Values and principles of service provision

An environment that is non-judgemental and engenders trust is integral to good practice service provision to adult care-leavers. Part of this is giving 'a clear message that they are believed about their abuse, that their truth is accepted'.[41] Underpinning service provision is respect and this involves acknowledging and encouraging strengths.[42] It is also about fully engaging adult care-leavers in all processes, as identified by the Law Commission of Canada:

> This experience of profound powerlessness is what makes it so important to fully engage former residents of institutions for children in any process aimed at overcoming the consequences of abuse they have suffered.... Imposing 'solutions' on survivors without consulting them as to their needs or taking account of those needs can be as offensive as refusing to offer redress altogether. In such cases, once again, others who have more power are making important decisions affecting their lives.[43]

Codes of practice for professional groups such as social workers are likely to be helpful in providing guidance for the ways in which this work with adult care-leavers is conducted. Values can be embedded in practice through identifying principles of service. For example, Anish Corporation, an Indigenous organisation based in Winnipeg, Canada, that is funded to provide emotional support to former students of the residential schools through the Indian Residential Schools Resolution Health Support Program, has 'core values and principles' that 'guide us in our everyday interactions'. They include 'being responsive and encouraging, nurturing and supportive ... patient ... empowering ... and [having] compassion'.[44] In a similar way, Open Place, a government-funded community centre for adult care-leavers in Melbourne, Australia, identifies its principles as 'showing humility and courage, being respectful and strength oriented, committing to flexibility and integration, demonstrating accountability, working together and being inclusive, and honouring diversity and being culturally sensitive'.[45]

New Zealand's Confidential Listening and Assistance Service intentionally put in place processes to demonstrate care, respect and acknowledgement through various symbolic and practical measures. For example, the judge and panel members stand to greet adult care-leavers as they arrive, there are food and drinks provided, and they sit together in a formal setting at a table with flowers and a tablecloth as a mark of respect.[46]

Accessibility

There are several elements to accessibility. One is concerned with advertisement of the service; another is to do with physical location; and another is about the welcoming nature of the site. First, a range of ways needs to be employed to produce widespread knowledge about the specialist support. While websites can be a very useful means of providing information and publicising available services, some adult care-leavers do not have the necessary skills or resources to access such websites. It is important, then, to use a range of methods to advertise, such as through community papers and leaflets in a range of locations likely to be frequented by adult care-leavers, including medical clinics and welfare support services. Second, as noted, a 'physical' location may not be necessary, as telephone counselling is known to provide levels of autonomy, anonymity and flexibility likely to appeal to some. In addition, for those with computer skills and resources, web-based counselling and other support may work well. Where physical locations exist, ensuring access across a country or region can be difficult. Offering support to enable adult care-leavers to visit from distant communities is an important consideration. Transportation is a key element of the Indian Residential Schools Resolution Health Support Program – an acknowledgement of the distances to be covered to receive services in some parts of Canada. Elsewhere, in Ireland, Right of Place has three offices across the country, and in Scotland, ICSSS has partnered with organisations to provide a countrywide service.

The nature of the physical site is also a consideration because the building itself can be troubling for some adult care-leavers. A building in which a children's home once existed can be a place to return to remember a childhood, but it can also be a place that invokes great distress for those harmed there. Some services choose to situate themselves in residential house-style settings, rather than being part of a larger institution or office block. Another way of managing this possible concern is to provide information about the building and its space in advance. Open Place in Melbourne, Australia, has photos of all the spaces in its office on its website so that visitors know what to expect. Including photos of staff and an explanation of who they are and the work they do again provides information in advance and attempts to reassure that it is a place that will welcome them. Providing meals, a kitchen where people can prepare a hot drink and a relaxed space with comfortable chairs are also ways that adult care-leavers can feel welcomed and valued.

Governance

The means of establishment of these specialist supports varies considerably, from the initiative of advocates and their supporters to a government response to a public inquiry. While some agencies have been initiated and are run by advocates, ensuring input from adult care-leavers, others have less engagement with their client group in their governance structure. There are various models to include adult care-leavers in governance. Boards can include a minimum number of adult care-leavers, as is the case with organisations such as Caranua. Another model, in place at ICSSS, is an adult care-leavers' user group, where clients meet regularly to provide feedback to the management of the service. As noted by the Alliance of Forgotten Australians: 'involving Forgotten Australians and their families in the design of programs aimed at assisting them will show respect, reassure and not re-victimise them'.[47]

Evaluation

While a number of the initiatives discussed in this chapter have had some form of evaluation, according to the Health Service Research Centre, there is 'a dearth of evidence on service experience from users of abuse counseling services'.[48] In relation to psychotherapeutic interventions, some agencies used or were seeking to employ benchmarking mechanisms to measure psychological change with individuals. Others, instead, used feedback forms to provide an indication of satisfaction levels with the service provided, either for a specific review or in an ongoing manner. Others had undertaken external reviews of their services, sometimes as a result of funding requirements, and largely incorporating feedback gathered from their clients. Some organisations produced and made available annual reports, another mechanism to collate, analyse and review both the usage and response to services provided. It did not seem, however, to be routine across the range of specialist support agencies to evaluate in an ongoing way; this would be very beneficial, both for local improvements and also to gain a better understanding more broadly about the needs of adult care-leavers.

Professional education

Psychologist Alan Carr and his colleagues noted that in relation to survivors of institutional abuse, 'Clinicians providing [psychological] services should be trained to assess and treat the range of anxiety, mood, substance use and personality disorders, trauma symptoms, adult attachment problems, and significant life problems with which such cases present'.[49] In particular, good practice is informed by an understanding of the impact on care-leavers of complex trauma.[50] In the area of psychotherapy and counselling, there is evidence that professional education occurred locally through regular workshops and staff conferences. Beyond this, while there is a body of research that is concerned with the training of those who work with survivors of sexual abuse, less attention has been paid to survivors who were abused in care or are seeking support as a result of other care experiences.[51] Three examples of work that has been done to skill professionals come from the UK and Australia. Two of these examples have been developed or established by adult care-leavers themselves. Further work could be done in this area, informed by those for whom the support would be provided.

Specialist training for front-line welfare staff and an online guide

The London Irish Centre and Immigrant Counselling and Psychotherapy (ICAP) ran a two-day training programme for front-line welfare professionals in mainstream organisations whose staff work with Irish adult care-leavers in the UK. The London Irish Centre is a provider of a range of welfare services, including those targeting Irish survivors of institutional abuse. ICAP is a specialist psychotherapy and counselling service that also works with Irish adult care-leavers.[52] Funded for three years from 2012 by the Irish philanthropic organisation, St Stephen's Green, through its Survivors of Abuse Grant Scheme, the initiative aimed to address, in particular, the impact of care and childhood abuse, managing disclosures of abuse with adult survivors and effective referrals to mental health services. As well as the training workshop, an online guide has been developed. The guide, *Open Hearts and Open Minds: A Toolkit of Sensitive Practice for Professionals Working with Survivors of Institutional Child Abuse*, is very useful, providing background to institutional abuse in Ireland, information about care experiences and its impact, and guidance on sensitive practice, handling disclosures and enhancing resilience.[53]

Cultural support specialist training

In Australia, the Marumali programmes, mentioned earlier, include a five-day nationally accredited workshop for Aboriginal and Torres Strait Islander service providers that aims to educate about:

> safe, appropriate and effective support to survivors of removal and assimilation policies. Participants are equipped with strategies to deal with the complex

issues of trauma associated with removal practices in a variety of settings, strategies which respect the rights of survivors to control the pace, direction and outcome of their own healing journey.[54]

The workshop is based on a model of healing developed by Lorraine Peeters for members of the Stolen Generations. Other workshops are run for non-Aboriginal workers and for settings such as jails and other correctional facilities. Since its inception in 2000, over 2,200 workers have participated in the workshops.[55] The Marumali programme has been used extensively as a means of providing training to Link-Up workers, counsellors and other Aboriginal staff in community-based organisations that provide support to members of the Stolen Generations. The programme was identified as 'best practice' in an evaluation of Indigenous mental health support.[56]

Guide and DVD for welfare and health-care professionals

While not professional education programmes, a guide and DVD developed by the Alliance of Forgotten Australians (AFA) and funded by the Australian government through its Department of Social Services are useful and practical aids in assisting health-care and other social welfare personnel in working with adult care-leavers.[57] The DVD, presenting six life stories, is an educational resource to promote understanding of the experiences of adult care-leavers. First produced in 2008, 175,000 copies of the guide have been distributed.[58] It aims to provide 'the background information [these personnel] need to recognise, relate to and assist people who are experiencing long term trauma because of a childhood spent in orphanages or Homes'.[59] The guide explains that, while many adult care-leavers are already engaging with mainstream health and welfare systems, seeking support for such matters as mental ill-health, substance abuse, family violence, homelessness or unemployment, importantly, they may never have disclosed that they experienced a childhood in care. As childhood abuse may be the 'root cause of their problems', they may need 'understanding and assistance to help them acknowledge and speak of their experiences'.[60] Key guidance includes: the need to develop trust and convey belief; appreciating a likely sense of fear of authority; taking an approach that is based in respect, consultation and a focus on strengths; ensuring the involvement of family; and being aware of possible poor literacy.

Conclusion

Three key elements of specialist support are in place across the five countries. While there are overlaps in the activities of the various services that provide them, these key elements can be identified as support for: mental health; education and social engagement; and cultural reconnection. Across the countries surveyed, varying degrees of attention have been paid to the different areas. There is increasing recognition that adult care-leavers may have experienced complex trauma as children – and it is particularly significant because trauma was ongoing during childhood. Not enough has been done to address these specific mental health concerns and there has not been the resourcing of long-term psychotherapeutic support elsewhere to the extent that there has been in Ireland. In Australia and Ireland, the funding of services that provide a range of educational and social support has provided opportunities for community engagement, as well as a means of enhancing life skills and improving mental health. These are also initiatives that could be further developed in other locations that currently have limited support in place for adult care-leavers.

Professional education about adult care-leavers is an emerging area and one that, if implemented successfully, could reap considerable benefits. There are other areas, though, that are, as yet, little researched. In particular, as adult care-leavers age, the possibility of the need for care in later life arises. For some, the need for aged care raises major concerns about their welfare and well-being, such as their willingness to reside in an institution as an older person after a childhood in which other institutions have caused great distress and harm. Compounding this situation is that adult care-leavers may not have family to care for them in old age. Thus, the social policy implications of the aged care of adult care-leavers need attention.

Box 6.1: Key features of specialist services for adult care-leavers

• Seek input from adult care-leavers into the design and operation of support services.
• Ensure ongoing engagement with adult care-leavers through their membership of boards of management and/or consultative committees.
• Provide multiple points of access to support services – an online presence, as well as other means to engage those that are not computer-literate or have these resources.
• Employ staff who have specialist expertise in working with adult care-leavers.
• Regularly review programmes to ensure that they are meeting the needs of adult care-leavers.

SEVEN

Access to records and family reunification

> I didn't know anything about the system, the foster family wouldn't help me whatsoever.... It was hard enough just to live life on an everyday level with the obstacles that I got hit with to just be sort of normal in society. (Roseanne, adult care-leaver, 2011[1])

In the opening quotation, Roseanne, a member of the Stolen Generations now aged in her 50s, refers to the challenges that she experienced over many years as she searched for information about herself and her family. Only more recently have services been available to assist her to do this, as well as to offer assistance for the range of other 'obstacles' she endured. Roseanne's is an extraordinary story where, through accessing her personal records, she was to discover that she was Aboriginal, that she had grown up in a foster home with another young woman who was her sister although she did not know this until many years later, and that she had many other siblings. She was also reunited with her father, with whom she had last had contact when she was two years old. When she was still only an infant, he had returned to England believing that he was no longer able to have any contact with his daughter. While acknowledging the different circumstances, the importance of this need to have a sense of identity is similarly illustrated in relation to child migrants:

> just as much as adults, [former child migrants] have their own unique histories, however brief and fragmentary, that remain a crucial part of their sense

of identity. Their knowledge and understanding of their past may be incomplete because they have 'not been told', or have been given confusing, false or contradictory accounts of what happened to them. Nonetheless, what they do know or believe is not easily forgotten, be it people, places, experiences or possessions. Although movement – especially from one culture to another – ruptures a past, it does not extinguish it; indeed, it is likely to intensify the desire to know and to remember the details of that past.[2]

Moreover:

there is a great sense of the deep need to know about family and friends and to have a significant 'connection' with someone. It belies the widespread belief at the time that once in Canada children would find a 'new life' in a 'new family' and put the past behind them.[3]

Access to personal records can be enormously significant in making sense of childhood and assisting in the reunification of families. As Roseanne's account demonstrates, accessing records can be a powerful means of finding out much about ourselves and our family. Its importance is due to the centrality of identity to health and well-being, and is recognised today through the use of life-story books and other strategies to ensure that children in care have access to information about themselves and their families.

Personal records may reveal information about family members that they did not know existed. The practices of institutions themselves encouraged the breaking up of families through the separation of children by age and gender, with sometimes little encouragement to remain in contact. Children may also have had little or no contact with their parents, or been told that they were not alive and then have been shocked to discover upon reading their records that this was not the case. Accessing records, then, can be a stepping stone to finding or mending these fractured relationships, but it is a process that is not always without difficulties and that may produce other harms for those concerned, as discussed later. As noted by Julia Feast:

> accessing information can help people build a stronger sense of identity by answering fundamental and significant questions about self and family history. Information can help people develop a coherent account of the main events and significant figures in their life.[4]

For those who grew up in care in past decades, personal records, where they exist, may be the only artefacts that remain of their childhood. Adult care-leavers may never have had the opportunity to have reminders of their childhood, such as photos or mementos, or engage in family storytelling. While the quality and quantity of records varies, collections could include such items as social work reports, court records and school certificates, as well as remnants of contact with their family, such as letters that were never passed on or a folder of receipts for payments of their care; or there may be an entry in a register and little else. Even the most minimal information can be meaningful, if not also disappointing, because it is evidence of a lost childhood. Records, then, can 'assist in resolving questions of identity from a lack of knowledge about some or all of their family of origin and they can help make sense of childhood memories and experiences'.[5]

There are also other very practical reasons why an adult care-leaver might access their records – to find out about childhood illnesses, or those of other family members, that may impact on them in adulthood. Thus, access may be triggered by the need to know about their medical history. Wider social events, such as a public inquiry into child abuse or an apology to former residents of children's homes, may cause them to think about their childhood. Not uncommonly, adult care-leavers access their records in middle to older age as they reflect on their lives, have more time to do so or are asked about their childhood by family members.[6] Thus, finding out about family history by those other than the adult care-leavers themselves, is another reason why records might be sought, and is an emerging area of research for the descendants of adult care-leavers (but not one that is addressed directly in this book).

In this chapter, we consider the services available to support adult care-leavers to access their personal records and find and reunite with their families. This is an area that has received some attention, although practice varies within and across countries and less attention has been paid to family reunification than to access to records. In particular, advocates have worked to make improvements, which we will consider in more detail in Chapter Eight. In contrast, internationally, considerably more attention has been paid to adoptees' access to records.[7] This chapter surveys the provision of records, considering their archiving and records management, accessibility, processes of release, family contact, and support. It provides examples of good practice in this area and suggests principles for undertaking this work. In addition, finding aids and guides are discussed. First, we turn to four key aspects of this work: recognising the importance of the records, and what this then means in terms of storage, records management and their accessibility; the concept of supported release and its application to accessing records; the value of photographs; and, finally, the work of facilitating family reunions.

Key aspects of access to records and family reunification

Recognising the importance of personal records

Before helpful work can begin in the area of releasing records to adult care-leavers, there must be a recognition of the importance of the records. The preceding discussion outlined why records might be important. For adult care-leavers, they can be central, or, at least, a starting point, to understanding aspects of their childhood, finding family and making sense of who they were as a child, and who they have become. Appreciating their significance can change the way an organisation works with these records. In a workshop held several years ago, I saw these 'light bulb' moments when staff who had responsibility for managing and releasing records listened to adult care-leavers speak about the importance of these records. Their approach shifted from the release of records being an 'administrative task' (if the records were there or if they could find them) to a situation of care and support for people who were looking for important answers about their childhood and their families. A similar 'light bulb' moment had occurred for me when I read Frank Golding's biography and he explained that he was in care for 10 years as a child *and did not know why*. It was only when he read his records that he began to have some understanding of his family circumstances at the time and what had therefore prevented him returning to his family.[8]

Having established that the records are important, then, the questions are: are the records there? Can they be found? Can adult care-leavers access them? What is the most appropriate way for people to access their records? If records are considered important, they will be kept, and kept in ways in which they can be found, and accessed. My own experience of seeking organisations, or the part of an organisation, to speak to about their processes of releasing records is instructive.[9] In seeking such programmes, I was directed and redirected within organisations on a number of occasions, which is indicative of the difficulties that adult care-leavers may also experience in tracing their records. On one occasion (and to demonstrate the issue of whether records have been kept and stored appropriately), my enquiry to staff at Agency X's archive, where I had been told by another part of the organisation that the records were held, resulted in the following response:

> Thank you for your enquiry. The primary [organisation] responsible for orphanages etc is [Agency X]. Although a national body, each major region maintains its own records. *The [Southern] records are lost, [Western] misplaced and [Eastern] records are thin on the ground.*[10]

So, if an adult care-leaver was seeking records from one of these three parts of the agency, it seemed likely that they were going to be unsuccessful. This is not uncommon, as many adult care-leavers will attest, as do other researchers. Tom Shaw, in his review of residential schools and children's homes in Scotland, found that 'many aspects of records – from their accessibility to their very existence – proved extremely challenging'; both record-keeping and their availability, he reported, were 'very patchy indeed'.[11]

Returning to my own experience of tracking down access to records services for the purposes of this research, unlike other parts of Agency X, 'Northern' held 'extensive' records, but there was confusion about where the records were held – in an archive or with the agency – again creating more potential roadblocks for an adult care-leaver seeking their records:

> [Archive] is meant to be holding [Northern] records which are extensive, since their beginnings, but [Archive] only have been given the more recent records. The exception to this is the photos of which we have a number of albums, which go right back to the establishment of the homes.[12]

My direct contact with 'Northern' resulted in contact with their records officer, who was very helpful and advised that they did, indeed, have a substantial collection of records. To the extent that resources allowed, she also described a process of supported release of records to her clients. So, having got there, if they had resided in a 'Northern' home, it was likely that an adult care-leaver would have received a positive outcome to their request for records.

While it is sometimes the case that an adult care-leaver knows to make direct contact with the institution in which they grew up, it is also possible that they lived in a number of homes, that they no longer remembered the name of the institution where they lived as a child or that the home no longer exists (as many do not). Hence, they may initially attempt to make contact through a government office or the Church, rather than the home itself. In all these cases, the road to successfully finding their records gets bumpier when records are not archived and managed in ways that allow them to be readily accessible, and information about this process is not made available. Information could be made available through internet-based sources from the organisation's webpage, as well as a range of other non-digital means in order to ensure that those without computer access can find this information.

So, appropriate, long-term and secure storage to ensure that these invaluable records are protected from floods, fire and other hazards must be in place, and their archiving and records management are vital.[13] Clear information about how adult care-leavers access their records must be provided.

These matters can be major resourcing issues for organisations and means that they must place priority on funding for what could be, for a large, long-established, organisation, a major undertaking. In Victoria, Australia, for example, the need for such attention is apparent for the records of state wards, held by the Department of Human Services (DHS). In a report by the Victorian auditor-general, while acknowledging that there had been attempts to improve practice, he concluded that:

> DHS needs to address deficiencies in their record keeping practices as a priority. Records are being lost, disposed of incorrectly or rendered inaccessible. DHS's record management facility has inappropriate physical storage conditions – causing records to deteriorate – and inefficient indexing systems. As a result, information cannot be found when needed.[14]

In contrast to this, while admittedly of much smaller volume, a Victorian non-government organisation, MacKillop Family Services, prioritised the resourcing of a substantial state-of-the-art archive, which has now secured the long-term survival of its 170,000 adult care-leaver records. Following its lead, other similar Church-based organisations in Victoria have investigated ways of archiving their records, as well as setting up access to records services modelled on MacKillop's.

Another wider consideration in the recognition of the importance of records is the existence and use of relevant legislation. While legislation in many jurisdictions ensures that some records will be kept (eg those of government, for a set period of time), it does not necessarily provide guidance on how this occurs or how they are released (unlike in relation to adoption, in some instances), or, indeed, whether they will be released at all on request.[15] These are matters that bear directly on the experience of those seeking their records, and most fundamental is the concern that records may not have been kept in the past. Legislation, then, can play an important role in improving access to records, and discussion has occurred in the UK and Australia about the need for adult care-leaver-specific legislation regarding access to records, in the same way that adoptees have.[16] In the absence of such legislation, it is a seemingly unintended consequence of privacy legislation (known as the Privacy Act in Australia [and similarly in Australian states] and the Data Protection Act in the UK) that has been the most helpful. While the intention of privacy legislation is to restrict others gaining access to personal information, it also includes the ability for a person to review information held about themselves. This has been used by adult care-leavers to access information about themselves from both government and non-government sources, and retrospectively. This aspect is not necessarily well known, and some organisations wrongly assume that privacy legislation is intended to protect the organisation from the need to release records. In these situations of misunderstanding, the release of records will be driven by the needs of the organisation rather than those of the adult care-leaver. Privacy legislation is a powerful tool that can be used by adult care-leavers to facilitate access to their records. This 'legislative tool', however, is not without its difficulties (which might otherwise be overcome with adult care-leaver-specific legislation), as discussed in the next section.

Supported release

In the five countries under study in this book, there were examples of agencies for which access to records was either not something that had been considered before or was done with very little appreciation of its importance; hence, 'unsupported' release was standard practice. 'Unsupported release' means that an adult care-leaver would apply for their records and they would be sent to them without any engagement with them about the content of the records, their impact or any further actions that arise from receiving this information. Counselling support may be offered, but its provision is not directly part of the process of releasing the records. In contrast, 'supported release' involves a process whereby adult care-leavers are offered assistance in understanding the records, typically through face-to-face meetings, ongoing support to deal with the impact of the records and, sometimes, further assistance to gather information from other sources, possibly with the goal of family reunification. Supported release is characteristic of an approach that has a well-developed appreciation of the significance of the records.

Across the five countries, there were a number of examples that clearly demonstrated regard for the importance of the records and a commitment to supported release. Such examples include Barnardo Ireland Origins, a government-funded service that was put in place at the time of the Irish Commission to Inquire into Child Abuse to assist people to access their records and reunite with family, and Quarriers in Scotland, which has a long history of providing such support to their former residents, including former child migrants. Barnardo Ireland and Quarriers characterise two different types of organisation that undertake supported release. Quarriers is a care provider and record-holder and releases its own records; in addition, it also supports adult care-leavers to access other relevant information. Barnardo's Origins did not provide care in Ireland and hence does not hold records. It is a support service that works with adult care-leavers to gain access to records from other organisations. Three further examples from Australia and England – two are support services, the third is a record-holder – are discussed in some detail later in this chapter.

What, then, does supported release entail and why is this process important? Reflecting on her experiences as manager of MacKillop Family Services' newly established Heritage and Information Service in 1998, Jenny Glare explained:

> Former clients appear keen to try and reconstruct the daily routines of their life in institutional care, to match their memories with recorded information and to question particular procedures and practices. Most are very keen to try and understand the social history of the times, the involvement of the church

in the placement of children, to talk about the shame and secrecy associated with becoming pregnant when not married [as may have been the case for their birth mother].... For others who were made state wards, much of their focus is on trying to understand the reasons why they were placed in care, how their circumstances came to the attention of the child welfare authorities and why they remained in care for so long.[17]

Supported release, then, can be the provision of records in the context of a detailed conversation with the adult care-leaver, responding to their questions and providing additional information to help explain their childhood circumstances, at times taking up a number of hours. Such contacts can occur over long periods of time – as long as decades – with re-contact with further questions or requesting other information. This, then, begins to present a picture of what supported release may entail.

However, while records may be helpful in assisting a person to make sense of their childhood and their life since, they can also be:

disturbing and disruptive to their sense of self-identity. Alternatively, records may offer little towards providing an explanation for their childhood, either because the records have been lost, destroyed or withheld or because the information was never documented in the first place.[18]

Circumstances such as these suggest the need not just for a conversation about the records, but also to take into account the emotional impact of the records (or lack of the records), and to ensure the availability of emotional support or counselling. Not all adult care-leavers will take up such an offer, but it is important that the agency providing the records does so, or provides a referral to a suitable service. However, approaches that assume the need for support and a relationship of dependency to the record-holder may be experienced as 'disrespectful and patronizing'.[19]

Adult care-leavers might find records 'disturbing and disruptive to their sense of self-identity' for a range of reasons. As suggested, records may reveal the existence of parents, siblings and other family members previously unknown. They can explain why a child went into care, also previously unknown, such as their mother's mental ill-health or their father's violence, or that they had been deemed to be neglected by the child welfare authorities. As well as the information itself causing distress, the way in which it is presented can be concerning. This information can be 'incomplete, insulting, incorrect and incomprehensible'.[20] Incompleteness can be because the records could not be found. In this instance, other information, while not filling in the most personal details, can provide some understanding of this period of their life. Documents such as orphanage annual reports or organisational histories will provide some context, and those undertaking supported release can provide this material and discuss it with the adult care-leaver seeking information. Incompleteness can also be because of a lack of understanding of how records are constructed. A 'record' is 'typically a composite of a variety of information kept for a range of purposes ... it is likely that there is not "one record", but rather a number of "files" in a range of locations'.[21] Thus, it is important to be aware of this fragmentation of record-holdings and for those engaged in supported release to seek all possible sources across the organisation.

Incompleteness is also related to redaction, or the removal of third-party information, which is consistently one of the most concerning elements of receiving records experienced by adult care-leavers. As noted, privacy legislation provides for an entitlement for adult care-leavers to access their records, but it does not mean that all information therein can be released to them. Where records contain information about others (sometimes called 'third parties'), decisions are made by the record-holders about what is reasonable to release given the impact of disclosure of this information on these other parties. Consent can also be sought from the affected parties for this information to be released. Unfortunately, at times, this legislation does not sit well with the needs of adult care-leavers. Seeking information about their mother, why they came into care or whether there is any evidence of abuse that they experienced as a child in the institution in an effort to make claims for compensation deals with third parties, this very information may then be redacted. Typically, organisations have erred on the side of caution and redacted more rather than less in an effort to avoid perceived risks of litigation, or to protect their own interests. So, while the legislation is useful in providing access, it is complicated by the real or perceived restrictions that it imposes on what can be released. As noted by Derek Kirton, Julia Feast and Jim Goddard, 'the crucial tension is that between the identity needs and rights of post-care adults and the rights of other family members to privacy and confidentiality'.[22] Supported release takes into account these competing interests, aiming for full disclosure and the maximum release of information while redacting as little as possible to protect others' privacy. In instances where information is redacted, explanation is given. Central to this process is open communication.[23]

The issue of redaction draws our attention to an issue that is of deep concern to some adult care-leavers. Some argue that because the records are about them, they are their records and they should therefore be given the records. Typically, organisations take the view that the records belong to them, but the information is accessible to adult care-leavers (or at least that which relates to them, as according to privacy legislation). There are, however, instances where materials found in the records would be given to adult care-leavers, such as undelivered letters from their mother or father. Other documents, such as the entry in a register or a social work report, would be considered organisational records to which they were entitled copies. To make them as authentic as possible, MacKillop Family Services colour photocopies such documents – being able to see a likeness to the original blue ink that signed a report can hold great meaning.

With older records in particular, the language used to describe children and their families can be highly insulting and can cause great distress. Derogatory and racist terms, for example, can be experienced as hurtful and disrespectful. While acknowledging the harm caused, supported release of records may entail a conversation about the social context in which these records were written. Records can also be incorrect – again experienced as hurtful and symbolising 'a complete disregard for them as individuals and a lack of care'.[24] In undertaking supported release, it is important to give the adult care-leaver the opportunity to set the record straight, both by telling the support worker and by suggesting that they amend the record, as is possible under privacy legislation. Finally, handwritten records may be incomprehensible and experienced as highly frustrating, but a situation that can be improved if given assistance at the time of the records' release.

In providing personal records to adult care-leavers, other sources can be used to provide background, such as annual reports and organisational histories, as well as wider sources such as contemporary newspaper articles and social histories of the time. In addition, further sources may reveal personal or family information, such as their father's military records or births, deaths and marriage certificates. These sources are discussed in relation to searching for family and family reunification, but we first turn to the topic of photos, one of the most important items that adult care-leavers seek.

Photos

When seeking their records, adult care-leavers often request photos from their childhood. For those who spent much or all of their childhood in care, they may have no photos from this period of their life. They may want photos of themselves or others with whom they grew up, or images of special events that occurred during their childhood. They may want photos that are reminders of staff who they remember warmly, the sites where they lived and examples of daily life in the children's home. Finding a photo, and other records, may be the only traces that an adult care-leaver is able to acquire of their childhood.

Not uncommonly, institutions do hold photos, and some hold very large collections. These photos may have been taken by staff or the children themselves over the years in either regular or ad hoc ways, but are not necessarily now organised in ways that make them readily accessible. They may not be catalogued, but rather stored in boxes or albums marked by year but little else. Typically, individuals in the photos are not identified by name, so there are further difficulties in tracing the subject of those photos. To ensure their accessibility, there are also issues, then, concerned with archiving and digitising. Like other records management, there are major resourcing issues in ensuring that photos are looked after for the long term.

Where photo collection databases have yet to be put in place, or where cataloguing and identifying are still a work in progress, a common practice to assist adult care-leavers to find photos is to give them albums to browse of those years when they were in care. This also gives them opportunities to see photos of others they knew, and the circumstances of their life at this time. This work, of course, should be done with care and support, as photos can be powerful triggers of childhood memories, both positive and negative. Where photos are found, copies are made for them to keep. They can also assist in identifying others in the photos for future reference. Sometimes, at reunions of children's homes, photo albums are displayed for former residents to browse.

One concern raised in Australia, at least, is that photos can include information about others (their images) and it may be in contravention of privacy legislation to release such an identifiable image if the photo was taken in a private situation within a children's home (for example in contrast to a school class photo intended for shared ownership). In this private situation, it is argued, the images of others should be redacted by blurring their faces, unless these people give consent for their image to be shared. However, like the matter of redacted written records, this is an action that can cause great distress to adult care-leavers. Again, the redaction represents a loss of access to information about their childhood experience. Another strategy that has been employed is to provide full images on the condition that they are for personal use only, and not to be distributed in public ways, with this information stamped on the back of the photo.

As well as care providers, other organisations hold photos of great interest to adult care-leavers. For example, the Shingwauk Project in Ontario, Canada, in collaboration with Algoma University, the Children of Shingwauk Alumni Association and the National Residential School Survivors' Society, and with support from the Aboriginal Healing Foundation and others, aims to:

research, collect, preserve and display the history
of the Residential Schools; develop and deliver
projects of 'sharing, healing and learning' in relation
to the impacts of the Schools, and of individual and
community cultural restoration and accomplish 'the
true realization of Chief Shingwauk's vision'.[25]

Algoma University has as a special mission 'cross-cultural
Aboriginal education and research', based on Chief Shingwauk's
vision, and is located on the site of the former Shingwauk and
Wawanosh residential schools. A Residential Schools Centre has
been established that, in collaboration with the university library,
manages and displays residential school artefacts, photographs
and other items.

Another example of a photo collection of interest to adult
care-leavers is the Australian Institute of Aboriginal and Torres
Strait Islander Studies' (AIATSIS's) Audiovisual Archive. This
archive holds the world's largest collection of moving images,
recorded sound and photographic materials relating to Australian
Aboriginal and Torres Strait Islander cultures and histories,
having approximately 650,000 photographic images, 40,000
hours of recorded sound, 8,000 video titles and 830 films. The
AIATSIS library also holds an extensive collection of print
materials. AIATSIS has produced a series of guides to family
history research, and has an online catalogue of bibliographic
details of all materials held, as discussed later.[26] While not
specifically developed for members of the Stolen Generations,
these AIATSIS resources are invaluable, especially as they are
catalogued and can be searched online using their Mura finding
aid.[27]

Family reunification

Much of the work in the area of family reunification has been
informed by that with adoptees.[28] A significant difference,
though, is that there are specific legislative frameworks that are
more supportive of adoptees receiving information than what
exists for adult care-leavers. There are two key elements to
family reunification: one is finding family; the other is making

contact and (possibly) establishing a relationship. While many organisations release records, and do this in supported ways, they do not necessarily also assist adult care-leavers to take further steps to find their families in situations where unknown family members are identified in their records and they want to take this information further. To find a person, then, usually requires further research, and this can be laborious and time-consuming, but highly rewarding. Other sources that can be used to find information about family members but about which there can be limits on what information is released to adult care-leavers include: births, deaths and marriages registers; electoral rolls; court and police records; military archives; articles in newspapers and other media; and other specialist resources, such as the AIATSIS library and Residential Schools Centre, mentioned earlier. As with the supported release of records, this process of finding family is done in collaboration with the adult care-leaver, keeping them informed of progress and seeking their guidance on which avenues to pursue.

It may be that a family member cannot be found for a range of reasons, or if they are, that the second step – of making contact – is not undertaken. Sometimes, of course, the person being sought may have died, and a graveside reunion is planned. Whether to make contact in whatever form is always the decision of the adult care-leaver. It is also the case that contact by the family member may be refused and this can be distressing for the adult care-leaver, and support needs to be available. If contact does proceed, there are various ways in which this can occur, which may not involve meeting in person. These processes can also take time as the parties involved come to terms with the emotional significance of reuniting. Initial contact may be facilitated by the support worker, and then followed up over some time by letters, emails or phone contact between the parties prior to meeting in person. The location of this meeting needs to be considered as somewhere that feels safe and comfortable by both the adult care-leaver and their family member.[29] However, reunification may not proceed as hoped, so that it is 'more upsetting than heartwarming' and the adult care-leaver may end up feeling, at worst, 'doubly rejected'.[30] It is important that adult care-leavers are offered counselling or other support during this process.

For Indigenous adult care-leavers, finding family can also be about finding their community of origin and, in Australia, their country. It may be, then, that the goal of accessing records for Indigenous people (and others) is primarily about family reunification. The focus of Link-Up, an Australian Indigenous network of services discussed later, is on 'counseling, family tracing and reunion services to members of the Stolen Generations'.[31] Link-Up services have a detailed guide to conducting family reunions, based around the phases of pre-reunion, reunion and post-reunion activities. These phases acknowledge the planning that goes into such events, as well as the need for ongoing support.[32] Link-Up is involved in family reunions, as well as graveside reunions, and return to community, institution and country reunions.

Good practice examples of supported release and family reunification

Across the five countries, there were several examples of good practice; to illustrate this good practice, case studies are provided from Australia and the UK.

Link-Up

Link-Up provides a good practice example of the work of a support service that is undertaken with the aim of reuniting adult care-leavers with their family. Link-Up has a long history of doing this work. In addition, it is a network of services that has been formally reviewed and evaluated on at least two occasions; this is noteworthy because few services providing support to adult care-leavers have been evaluated, but it may also reflect the government scrutiny not uncommonly imposed on Indigenous organisations.

Initially started in New South Wales, Australia, in 1980, it is now a national organisation with eight services in all Australian states and the Northern Territory. Link-Up was founded by historian Peter Read, who was undertaking oral history research in the late 1970s with the Wiradjuri people of South-Western New South Wales who had grown up in institutions and did not know their families. Together with one of his research participants, Coral Edwards, he went on to form Link-Up to assist others to find their families. Around this time, Read coined the term 'stolen generations' as there was an emerging understanding of the significance of social policy to the removal of Aboriginal children from their families.[33]

Link-Up was first funded by the federal government in 1983, and considerably more funding came after the publication of the *Bringing Them Home* report in 1997.[34] Among the recommendations from the inquiry were several that addressed the need to 'assist Aboriginal and Torres Strait Islander people separated from their families under past laws, practices and policies of Australian governments, to undertake family tracing and reunion initiatives'.[35] While, by this time, all states and the Northern Territory had in place an agency that provided family tracing and reunion services to members of the Stolen Generations, a national Link-Up network was then established, existing services were expanded and others were initiated. A review had been undertaken at this time and a best practice model was developed.[36] More recently, as a result of another evaluation, the funding of Link-Up services has been relocated to programmes aimed at improving mental health and well-being within the Social and Emotional Wellbeing Program of the federal government's Department of Health and Aging (DoHA). The services themselves remain located in Aboriginal community organisations, either stand-alone or part of a larger organisation. The *Handbook for Link Up Service Providers* outlines the current model of practice for all Link-Up services and was developed out of a review of the previous manual used by Link-Up workers and in consultation with the Link-Up workforce.[37]

Link-Up aims to 'assist clients to reunite with their families, culture and community and restore their social and emotional wellbeing wherever possible', and works closely with other Social and Emotional Wellbeing counselling services, discussed in Chapter Six.[38] The issue of identity to health, well-being and social inclusion is highly significant:

> The primary aim of reunions (reuniting family members) is to provide an opportunity for members

of Stolen Generations … to find and re-establish family connections…. Reunions can assist clients to regain a sense of identity and belonging … reunions can often provide a significant step forward in the healing process for a client and their family.[39]

While there is acknowledgement of the intergenerational impacts of family separation, the priority with the current funding programme is to assist first generations to reunite with immediate family. Funding is available for one assisted reunion per client and includes the costs of travel and accommodation. Between 1998 and 2006, there was an average of 5,025 client contacts with Link-Up services per year (where one client may have many contacts recorded, and clients may remain active over more than one year), and for the same period, there was an average of 182 family reunions per year across Australia.[40]

According to current funding arrangements, the work with Link-Up clients is done by caseworkers and counsellors; the former undertake family tracing and reunions and the latter undertake counselling and support throughout the search, reunion and post-reunion processes. A range of records of government and non-government agencies is likely to be sought by caseworkers, as well as enlisting the assistance of the Family History Unit at AIATSIS. Minimum qualifications are required for staff of Link-Up services, who must hold tertiary-level qualifications in counselling, psychology, social work or related areas for counsellors, and family history research, Indigenous studies, records management or related areas for caseworkers. There is acknowledgement that such academic training may not be present for those otherwise qualified, which is addressed in the following manner:

> It can be difficult to find and recruit staff with both cultural and professional experience. It is acknowledged that some employees may be qualified through life experience and other means that is acceptable in the first instance. If a person is employed in a Link Up caseworker or SEWB [Social and Emotional Wellbeing] counseling position

without the minimum qualification required, the Link Up service must ensure that the staff member gains the minimum qualification within one year of commencing their employment.[41]

MacKillop Family Services' Heritage and Information Service

MacKillop Family Services is a good practice example of a record-holding organisation that champions the supported release of records and facilitates family reunions. MacKillop Family Services was formed in the Australian state of Victoria in 1997 as a refounding of seven Catholic welfare agencies sponsored by three religious congregations, Sisters of Mercy, Sisters of St Joseph and the Christian Brothers. These agencies provided an extensive system of babies' homes, orphanages and children's institutions, first established in the 1880s.[42] Today, MacKillop Family Services continues to provide out-of-home care, although no longer in large institutions, as well as other welfare services to children and young people with disabilities and refugees, and educational support services for young people.

MacKillop's Heritage and Information Service is a service dedicated to adult care-leavers and includes a substantial archival repository that holds approximately 170,000 records of the former institutions, dating back to 1854. The records held at the Heritage and Information Service include original client admission registers, admission cards and paper files, educational and medical reports, and photographic and other memorabilia relating to former clients. In 2013, a heritage display was opened that 'tells the story of the history of Catholic child welfare in Victoria with a particular emphasis on the lived experience of residents and staff of the founding agencies of MacKillop Family Services'.[43] Moreover:

> This display also acknowledges that the past always contains lessons for the future. MacKillop Family Services believes that the display is a place of reflection to remember and honour the lives of the children and mothers, to celebrate their diversity of experience and to tell their stories. We hope that it

will bear witness to their place in MacKillop Family Services shared history.[44]

MacKillop developed its Heritage and Information Service in a spirit of reconciliation and healing, and offered an apology to former residents in 2013:

> We acknowledge the trauma of mothers separated from their children. We likewise acknowledge the pain experienced by children who were separated from parents and siblings. In hindsight, we have come to understand the bitter legacy for so many who have grown up apart from their family of origin. This is experienced in a loss of identity and sense of belonging. We acknowledge that such pain and dislocation are ongoing. We apologise unreservedly to those who experienced abuse and neglect while in our care. We express our deep shame and sorrow.[45]

In developing its Heritage and Information Service, MacKillop drew on its long involvement of working with former clients who had been adopted. The service provides supported access to records, facilitates family reunifications and plays a lead role in Australia advocating for and raising community understanding of their experiences. In addition, the Heritage and Information Service supports the establishment and maintenance of networks between former residents through a newsletter and reunions. In 2014, the Heritage and Information Service received approximately 50 new requests for record searches each month. The service is staffed by experienced, specialist social workers.

The Heritage and Information Service is located in the headquarters of MacKillop Family Services in the building of the former St Vincent's Orphanage. While the site may evoke painful memories, for many, returning there is a valued opportunity to visit their childhood home. The building has been recently fully renovated and visitors can see the heritage display as well as other parts, including the chapel (now a meeting space retaining many of its original features) and the dormitories upstairs (now office space). As a way of highlighting the history of the building and the lives of the former residents, quotations from their personal files and reflections on their lives in care are on the walls – poignant memorials of an earlier time. A plaque at the entrance to the building 'commemorates and honours the lives of these children and acknowledges this site is a special and significant place'. An important element of the Heritage and Information Service is the welcome room, a comfortable, private space used for meeting with adult care-leavers to talk with them about their records.

Child Migrants Trust

The Child Migrants Trust is a good practice example of an international support service that works to reunite families. Like Link-Up and MacKillop Family Services, supported release of records is integral to their work. In 2013, on the third anniversary of the UK apology to former child migrants, former Prime Minister Gordon Brown said:

> The work of the Child Migrants Trust over the last 26 years has been instrumental in helping thousands of innocent children come to terms with their ordeal. They were deported, robbed of their childhoods and deprived of contact with their families. As Prime Minister in 2010 I offered an apology on behalf of the nation for the part the UK played in this shameful practice. Today, it remains as important as ever that we are mindful of the mistakes of the past – and that we continue to do all we can to ensure that former child migrants enjoy the same rights and privileges as we all do. I offer my very best wishes and heartfelt thanks to the Trust which continues to carry out its vital work.[46]

The Child Migrants Trust was established in 1987 by a Nottinghamshire social worker, Margaret Humphreys, who came across people in her work who had been taken as children from their families in the UK and sent to Canada, New Zealand, the former Rhodesia and Australia. She was astounded by these practices and the lack of knowledge about them, and support for the people affected. She proceeded to set up a specialist service that became the Child Migrants Trust, based in England and Australia, with offices in Nottingham, Perth and Melbourne.[47] The Child Migrants Trust provides a range of social work services, including counselling and family reunions. This involves 'careful family research, often having first obtained files from the relevant agencies. This enables information to be provided regarding family origins together with sensitive counselling to prepare individuals to reunite with their families after decades of painful, unnecessary separation'.[48] The Child Migrants Trust reports that over a thousand families have been reunited.

The UK and Australian state and federal governments have provided funding to the Child Migrants Trust.[49] The Family Restoration Fund, managed by the Child Migrants Trust, is a means by which families are reunited. The fund aims to 'help to reunite former child migrants with their families so that they can build relationships, be involved in significant family events or urgently visit relatives in times of crisis such as serious illness or death'.[50] The fund is only available to former child migrants, not to their family members or their children or siblings in the instance of a former child migrant's death. The Child Migrants Trust lists the following services to former child migrants: retrieving files and personal documents from both government departments and the migrating agency archives; obtaining full birth certificates; conducting family research worldwide; providing professional counselling services to former child migrants and their family members; assisting former child migrants to apply for citizenship; and providing support around redress schemes.[51]

Finding aids and guides

Finding aids are important not only for finding specific records within a collection, but also for finding collections as it is not uncommon for adult care-leavers to have difficulty locating where their records might be among the various government and non-government institutions involved in their care over their childhood. As AIATSIS helpfully informs us: 'a finding aid is a detailed listing of what is in a collection of papers, sound recordings or moving images or photographs'.[52] There are various examples of such aids, some of which are discussed in this section, with many also including other helpful information about searching for records. These various examples provide models to draw upon in the development of such aids for those enhancing access to records. Guides are another tool for undertaking this work and there are two useful examples from the UK that provide information about how to search for records for adult care-leavers and how to release them for those working in the area.

Finding aids

The most substantial of the finding aids that has been developed specifically for adult care-leavers is known as Find and Connect (formerly known as Pathways in Victoria). Devised by a team at the University of Melbourne and funded by the Australian government, this innovative project has resulted in a comprehensive and detailed database of the records held by orphanages, children's homes and related organisations involved in the out-of-home care of children across Australia, as well as related information.[53] The website does not publish personal records, but provides information about where such collections of records are held. In line with adult care-leavers' interest in photos, it has a database of photos that can also be searched. There are detailed instructions on how to work with the website, as well as a guide on 'what to expect when accessing records' and information about support services. While this project received substantial funding over several years, it is unclear at the time of writing how this valuable resource will be maintained over time.

Library and Archives Canada has several detailed online finding aids to assist in searching records about Canadian Indigenous peoples, their ancestry and residential schools. They include background information on how to conduct the research with explanations of key terms, listings and descriptions of the most relevant records series held by the archives, and suggestions for further research sources.[54] The National Archives of Australia has also undertaken work to assist Indigenous people to seek personal records and other related information. In response to the *Bringing Them Home* report, the federal government funded research to index the names of Indigenous people in Commonwealth records in order to improve accessibility for those wishing to link up with their families and communities, a database now known as the *Bringing Them Home* name index.

The database includes the names of Aboriginal and Torres Strait Islander people, the names of non-Indigenous people associated with or related to Indigenous people, the names of missions and institutions in which they were placed, and the places where they lived.[55] AIATSIS has a similar finding aid for its collection – the Aboriginal and Torres Strait Islander Biographical Index.[56] As well as its Mura finding aid, AIATSIS has a series of 14 very useful fact sheets to provide guidance in seeking records. These fact sheets include the topics of: contact details of key organisations in each state and territory; births, deaths and marriages indexes; and advice on getting started.[57] In some states of Australia, findings aids have been developed to assist searches of records held in these state-based archives, such as that produced by the Public Records Office Victoria, Aboriginal Affairs Victoria and the Koori Heritage Trust.[58]

Some advocacy organisations have developed resources to assist adult care-leavers to search for information. For example, the British Home Children Advocacy and Research Association in Canada has an online finding aid that suggests places to search, such as the Library and Archives Canada Home Child database and various private collections.[59]

Guides

In the UK, the Care Leavers' Association (CLA) has developed a guide for adult care-leavers that has a strong focus on understanding the implications of the Data Protection Act for accessing their records.[60] The CLA has also developed a guide for record-holders with an associated quality mark for those accredited with high-quality access to records processes in place.[61] This quality mark is part of a campaign to improve access to records, and is discussed in Chapter Eight as an example of successful advocacy.

The most comprehensive guide to the release of records has been produced by the British Association for Adoption and Fostering.[62] While framed within the UK's legislative context, it is a very useful model for the development of such guides internationally. The guide proposes values and principles underpinning access to records and support services, as well as detailed directions on how to respond to requests, prepare records for release and facilitate reunions. There are many case-study examples that illustrate common issues in the release of records and a collection of template documents, such as those for application forms, various forms of letters to adult care-leavers and other parties and service evaluations. A comprehensive listing of resources is also provided.

Conclusion

This chapter has highlighted key elements of good practice in the release of records to adult care-leavers. Recognition of the records' importance to identity, emotional health and well-being is essential, and adult care-leavers can play a major role in informing those who work in this area of their importance. Good practice, then, derives from this understanding. Records need to be looked after so that they can survive in good condition and be easily searched and found, hence the need for archiving and records management. Support is offered, but the adult care-leaver has a say in how the release of records occurs. Supported release can involve explanation of the material, as well as providing additional sources of information to provide background or to compensate when records are not available. These sources may reveal personal or family information previously unknown that may lead to family reunion.

Box 7.1: Key elements of access to records services for adult care-leavers

• An appreciation of the importance of the records is essential.

• Ensure proper archiving and records management processes are in place.

• Provide multiple points of access to the records and family reunification service, including an online presence as well as other means.

• Supported release underpins this work.

• Employ staff who have specialist expertise in releasing records to adult care-leavers and providing support for family reunification.

• The purpose of finding records may be family reunification, so assistance needs to be offered for this to occur.

EIGHT

Advocacy and
consumer participation

> Until very recently, no-one would believe the abuse
> and harm that had been done to us! The awfulness
> we experienced as children has cast long shadows over
> our adult lives. (Care Leavers Australia Network[1])

Over the past 15 years, Care Leavers Australia Network (CLAN)
has been instrumental in the development of social policy
responses to adult care-leavers in Australia. CLAN has engaged
in a range of advocacy activities, including regular protests
about the treatment of adult care-leavers in Australia and the
lack of support for them. In their protest brochure, from which
the above quotation is derived, they point to the need for the
wider community to understand their experiences of care and its
aftermath, a change that is occurring at the time of writing due to
publicity surrounding the Royal Commission into Institutional
Responses to Child Sexual Abuse.

This chapter is concerned with the ways in which adult
care-leavers and advocacy organisations such as CLAN have
been involved in bringing about social policy changes. Two
ways are considered: advocacy and consumer participation.
Both involve the engagement of adult care-leavers in social
policy processes to ensure the inclusion of their perspectives,
with the aim of creating 'opportunities for change ... through
active citizenship and participation in decision-making around
the issues that affect them'.[2] With advocacy, adult care-leavers
lead and attempt to influence social policy from 'outside'; in
contrast, consumer participation entails working on the 'inside'

in the social policy processes. Advocates may, of course, also be consumer participants.

Advocacy can involve work with individuals (sometimes known as case advocacy) or collectives (cause advocacy) to bring about change. Case advocacy entails 'collaborating with a client, then going with them to the site of the injustice and assisting them to navigate systems, public servants, and the general public'.[3] Cause advocacy is involved with 'pleading the case of injustice ... to meet the needs of specific groups'.[4] Advocacy operates both in terms of its outcomes and also its process – both the ends and the means. As noted by Andrew Hewett and John Wiseman, 'advocacy work is about achieving change in a policy or practice of targeted public or private sector institutions'; it is also about 'enhancing the capacity and the strength of individuals and communities so that they may shape their own futures'.[5] This chapter focuses on advocacy that occurs by adult care-leavers for adult care-leavers, sometimes known as self-advocacy (rather than that of others who advocate on behalf of adult care-leavers). Self-advocacy is the most direct way in which adult care-leaver perspectives are brought to policy and practice. Some attention is also paid to consumer participation in governance structures and consultation processes – another way in which adult care-leaver perspectives are brought to bear on policy and practice, being means by which they have informed others of their circumstances to bring about change.

Advocacy groups representing the interests of care-leavers exist in each of the countries under consideration in this book, although there is considerable variation across and within the five countries with different population groups. In this chapter, first, there is a discussion of advocacy and what it entails, and the nature of advocacy organisations and their activities. Examples are drawn from across the five countries to illustrate these various attributes. Two examples – Care Leavers' Association (UK) and Care Leavers Australia Network (Australia) – are discussed in more detail to provide evidence of successful advocacy campaigns. Consumer participation is then outlined and a detailed example is provided of an Australian research project.

Self-advocacy

Self-advocacy is a 'process in which an individual, or a group of people, speak or act on their own behalf in pursuit of their own needs and interests'.[6] Self-advocacy organisations (henceforth identified as advocacy organisations in this chapter) include consumer groups who are typically responding to a particular issue, such as a harmful medical procedure, or are seeking active involvement in decision-making about their health care.[7] This is somewhat different to the longer-term and more diffuse experiences of adult care-leavers. However, consumer groups share some common characteristics with adult care-leaver advocacy organisations, as we shall see.

As noted by Neil Bateman, 'it is easy to underestimate the influence that the collective power of groups of otherwise voiceless people can have on the welfare state'.[8] For example, in the fields of physical disability and mental health, there has been successful advocacy.[9] As explained by Susan Arai and her colleagues in relation to people with physical disabilities:

> Consumer-driven disability organizations emerged in recent decades to recognize people's ability and need to be involved in decisions affecting their lives. The shift from more traditional rehabilitation-oriented services to community-based, consumer-driven approaches brought an emphasis on quality of life, consumer choice and control, empowerment, self-determination, and an independent living philosophy.[10]

Similarly, in the area of mental health self-advocacy, there has been 'a history of struggle against the power of the medical profession and a concern to respect the dignity, social rights and autonomy of people living with mental illness'.[11] Strong and successful networks of advocacy organisations may result in the development of a social movement, as in the case of the well-developed self-advocacy of those with mental illness.[12]

As children, adult care-leavers were typically characterised by three features: their vulnerability both as children and often also as members of population groups marginalised on the basis of their Aboriginality, ethnicity or family or socio-economic status; the power imbalance between these children and their carers, often magnified by the authority of the Church or state who were responsible for their care; and their experiences having been largely invisible to the wider community.[13] This 'voicelessness' may well have continued into adulthood as adult care-leavers felt stigmatised and experienced the social and economic disadvantages of the aftermath of care. Despite this, adult care-leavers have been able to achieve successful advocacy, as we will see; there are also related groups who share common causes that are more well-established, such as abuse survivor advocacy organisations.

While adult care-leaver groups are not yet readily identified as social movements, they share common characteristics, as described by Judith Allsop and her colleagues in their discussion of health consumer groups: 'People are drawn into new social movements because they feel marginalized by dominant social practices, and movements gain adherents because a positive sense of identity can develop where perceptions are shared'.[14] Like the adult care-leaver organisations, they 'become political when they approach third parties, and take action in the public arena. This may be concerned with obtaining redress, reshaping services, or by challenging the assumptions underlying policy and practice'.[15] These groups are 'based largely in the belief in the validity of lay experience' and this 'situated knowledge which draws on personal experience' is further legitimated by the breadth of common experience across the membership.[16] Michael DeGagné, from the Aboriginal Healing Foundation, describes what happened in Canada:

> Not long ago, in Canada, speaking of residential school abuse was a universal taboo. Aboriginal people suffered their unmentionable wounds. It was as if a kind of sleep had swallowed a generation. Then one day, a man woke up. Somewhere, a woman told her story. Soon after, three survivors had gathered in a room. That which had once been beyond challenge

was torn from history's dark places and thrown into the light.[17]

Two key activities of advocacy organisations are service provision and political lobbying, which can be understood as 'caring' and 'emancipatory', respectively.[18] As noted by Geoffrey Nelson and his colleagues, advocacy organisations 'vary in terms of the relative emphasis' of these characteristics.[19] Service provision includes providing information and advice to their membership, however defined, and members of the public, as well as helplines and self-help groups. Advocacy organisations may also be involved in facilitating the establishment of professional services as a result of lobbying. The Scottish advocacy organisation In Care Abuse Survivors has run a largely unfunded helpline for many years, as well as their political lobbying. In Dublin, Aislinn Education and Support Centre runs a drop-in centre, as well as providing case (and cause) advocacy and education programmes for adult care-leavers. Other advocacy groups provide support to adult care-leavers in a range of ways, including assistance to access their personal records. In research for the Law Commission of Canada, it was found that 'survivors expressed general satisfaction with mutual aid [self-help], through support groups, where they existed. They were not of interest to all survivors, but clearly offered support, information and a sense of belonging that was important to many'.[20]

The other key aspect of advocacy organisations is their political activities (though, as suggested, these are often entwined with their service provision activities): raising awareness of adult care-leavers' concerns and campaigning for changes to policy and services, or lobbying for an inquiry or an apology. Lobbying can involve petitioning Parliament for an apology, as the British Home Children Research and Advocacy Association has done in Canada, or running a postcard campaign with a key message addressed to Members of Parliament and having regular protests on the steps of Parliament House, as the Care Leavers Australia Network has done (discussed later). Other strategies include writing letters to the editors of newspapers, seeking media publicity through highlighting particular events or anniversaries, and meeting with Members of Parliament to discuss their concerns. The use of 'official channels', such as meeting with government officers about policy issues, membership of advisory committees and submissions to inquiries, are also common lobbying strategies. Some work with mainstream organisations as consumer representatives to influence their policy and practice in order to better address the needs of adult care-leavers – others find this a clash of values as they deal with the dilemma of an insider role and the 'danger of co-optation'.[21] The internet has greatly facilitated the effectiveness and reach of advocacy groups, including those working with adult care-leavers. In addition to making information available and linking adult care-leavers with each other, the internet has also been a way of connecting with wider communities that organisations want to inform and gain their support.[22] All of these activities were present across the range of adult care-leaver advocacy organisations in the five countries.

Clarity of goals is crucial to advocacy organisations as these will determine the type of actions that are undertaken. According to Andrew Hewett and John Wiseman, 'the capacity to think strategically, linking goals and action in ways which remain open to the need for flexibility as circumstances change, is a subtle and valuable skill'.[23] For adult care-leaver advocates, a primary goal has been to get a number of adult care-leaver-related issues onto the political and policy agenda, such as abuse in care, redress and reparation, and access to records. In Australia, for example, their work has focused on 'gaining media coverage, broad public understanding and support from influential commentators', as well as lobbying to bring about change through key people in government and Parliament.[24] Indeed, 'the success of social movements depends on their ability to build public support and momentum for change that they seek. The key is to then translate the growing public support into political, administrative or even legislative change'.[25]

As explained by political scientist Verity Burgmann: 'public expression of grievances ... is a crucial component of effective agitation ... the means by which the oppressed can be heard'.[26] In successfully articulating grievances, advocates are able to create 'new verbal frameworks and vocabularies, thereby converting relations of subordination into perceived relations of oppression';

this reframing occurring through 'strategic effort by groups of people to fashion [new] shared understandings of the world and of themselves that legitimate and motivate collective action'.[27] This reframing occurred in Ireland in a striking manner as a result of the work of advocates and their supporters who brought about a public inquiry and significant changes in Irish society. They were supported in this work by the production of two television programmes that powerfully demonstrated that 'orphans' had not been looked after properly or kindly, and, in many cases, had been harmed in care. This occurred in a context where the Church had been understood to have been charitably supporting children and providing them with the love and care otherwise not available to them. Instead, this early work of advocates, and the public inquiry that followed, demonstrated that the Church had been paid to care for children but had sometimes done so in exploitative ways, and many had been seriously harmed.

In Australia, too, there is a striking way in which an issue was reframed, a combination of the development of a more widely understood social and political history, and the subsequent rejection by the community of the government response to this issue. The reframing involved moving from an understanding of Indigenous children who had grown up in care as being a result of 'neglectful' or otherwise unsuitable parents to an understanding of them as the 'Stolen Generations' removed from their families and communities. The public response urging the Prime Minister to say 'sorry' emerged out of this reframing and was one of the largest Australian political movements of the late 20th and early 21st centuries.

Although presented in relation to health consumer groups, the narratives of their founding members are similar to those of adult care-leaver organisations. This narrative is described as:

> Anger about what happened to them; the perception that the condition [experience] was not well understood; a belief that service provision [and social policy] is inappropriate and a deep concern about the lack of information available for patients [adult care-leavers]. Activists wanted to support others and draw attention to shortcomings at a number of levels, such

as changing the perception of professionals and the public and influencing national and local providers [and policymakers].[28]

Not uncommonly, as with adult care-leavers, advocacy originates in the courageous actions of individuals. In Canada, in 1990, the former National Chief of the Assembly of First Nations, Phil Fontaine, was one of the first to speak publicly about his experiences of physical, psychological and sexual abuse while a student at a residential school. He called for action to be taken in support of students who had been abused in these schools.[29] In 1991, the government convened a Royal Commission on Aboriginal Peoples and many people told the Commission about their residential school experiences. The Commission's 1996 report recommended a separate public inquiry into residential schools. In 1997, the Law Commission of Canada commenced its work investigating ways to address the harm caused by the physical and sexual abuse of children in institutions, including residential schools for Aboriginal children. Fontaine speaking out encouraged others to do so, and ultimately led to bringing about major changes in social policy responses to Canada's Indigenous peoples.

In Ireland, Christine Buckley spoke out about the institutional abuse of children from the early 1990s and was the main subject of the 1996 RTÉ television documentary *Dear Daughter*, which was a catalyst for the Irish Commission to Inquire into Child Abuse. The film told the story of her childhood in Goldenbridge orphanage in Dublin run by the Sisters of Mercy. With Carmel McDonnell-Byrne, Buckley set up the Aislinn Centre, an education and support service for adult care-leavers. At her death in 2014, the Taoiseach (Prime Minister), Enda Kenny, described her as 'a pioneer' in the campaign to highlight the abuse of children in industrial schools. Catholic Archbishop of Dublin Diarmuid Martin said that her 'courage played a major role in exposing problems in both Church and State'. The former chair of the Commission to Inquire into Child Abuse, Seán Ryan, explained that 'at great personal cost, she brought to public attention terrible wrongs done to children with the authority of the State. The nation owes her an enormous debt of gratitude'.[30]

In New Zealand, in 2011, Netta Christian was outraged by the actions of lawyers whom she believed had unfairly represented her over the course of some years when it was very unlikely there would be success with her abuse in care legal claims.[31] She advocated not just to gain proper redress for adult care-leavers who had experienced abuse as children, but also to ensure that they were not exploited in the legal system. She decided to form a lobby group and approached her local newspaper to place an advertisement seeking others to work with her. The newspaper was interested in her story and published a front-page article that led to many people contacting her to seek her advice and support. She was also approached by CLAN, and since then a New Zealand branch has formed.

As well as those who initiate, others, who are sometimes adult-care-leavers or have a personal connection to them, can also be significant to the success of advocates, as in the case of two parliamentarians. Senator Andrew Murray, a former child migrant, has been a champion of adult care-leavers in Australia and has worked closely with CLAN. He was instrumental in the establishment of three of the four public inquiries and is most recently a commissioner with the current Royal Commission into Institutional Responses to Child Sexual Abuse.[32] Another champion is Jim Brownell, a Member of Parliament in the Ontario Parliament, whose grandmother came to Canada as a 14-year-old home child. Brownell successfully advocated for the proclamation of 28 September as British Home Child Day. As another parliamentarian commented: 'British home children were something he'd known nothing about and, but for Brownell's efforts, probably never would have'.[33]

Typically, advocacy organisations have memberships comprised mainly (if not exclusively) of the people on whose behalf the advocacy is directed, as is the case with adult care-leaver groups. These advocacy groups 'often have relatively few formal structures … and there will be a large element of participative democracy in their running'.[34] However, these governance structures do vary, like other organisations, in terms of what being a member entails, who has the authority to speak on behalf of the organisation and the nature of the executive and its powers. Often, those who initiated the organisation take up executive positions. There are also variations in terms of funding sources. Some have gained government funding to provide services to adult care-leavers, which ensures some measure of sustainability, whereas others do not accept government funding in order to retain autonomy. Other sources of funding include membership fees, donations from supporters and larger sums from charities or philanthropists. Adult care-leavers' compensation payments have also been used to support the work of advocacy organisations, and the work of advocates is often unpaid. These resources support lobbying and other political activities, as well as service provision, such as case advocacy, helplines and self-help groups.

Advocacy organisations and their successful campaigns

Having described the nature of advocacy and the range of organisations working in the area of adult care-leavers, we now turn to two examples that have run successful campaigns. The Care Leavers' Association UK (CLA) has successfully advocated for significant changes to practice around the release of records. Its sibling organisation in Australia, CLAN, ran a campaign to establish a Royal Commission into institutional sexual abuse, which is now underway, and follows in the footsteps of a parliamentary inquiry in Victoria that investigated related matters.

Care Leavers' Association UK

CLA, formed in 2000, is a user-led membership organisation that engages in both caring and emancipatory activities. CLA aims:

> to bring together the voices of care leavers of all ages so that we improve the current care system, improve the quality of life of care leavers throughout their lives and change for the better society's perception of people who have been in care as children.[35]

CLA is registered as a charity and has a staffed office in Manchester.

CLA's activities include: establishing networks of care-leavers in the UK; ensuring that support and information to care-leavers is available to those who need it; offering training to organisations who work with care-leavers; and advocating around care-leaver issues. CLA encourages user involvement as a way of ensuring the inclusion of care-leavers' perspectives. As we saw in Chapter Three, in the UK, there has not been a large-scale public inquiry into care, as there has been in Ireland, Canada and Australia. While CLA is not currently campaigning for such an inquiry, they are lobbying for 'an apology from government for historical abuse and the general lack of positive care experienced in the care system over the last 80 years'.[36]

Three elements of CLA distinguish it as a care-leaver organisation. First, their focus is on all care-leavers, not just those who are older. While their sibling organisation CLAN (and some other Australian agencies) differentiates between older and younger care-leavers, at least partly because of significant legislative changes that occurred from the 1990s that impacted on children's welfare, CLA does not do so. Regardless of a changed context, CLA sees its mandate as using the experiences of those who grew up in care in past times to inform those leaving care today. Thus, their work is also with young care-leavers to 'support the transition to adulthood' and to have input into care-leaving policies, such as raising the age of state responsibility.[37]

Second, CLA places great emphasis on the importance of support for care-leavers through social networks. One way that this has occurred is through their very successful Careleavers Reunited website. Care-leavers can make contact with each other, and also with former social workers or foster carers. In 2014, there were over 6,300 registered users from nearly 2,000 homes.[38]

Third, CLA is concerned to change community perceptions of care-leavers. CLA has run a long-standing campaign informing the general public, and care-leavers themselves, about the many people who grew up in care, such as actor Marilyn Monroe, soul singer Seal and journalist and author Paolo Hewitt. Care can be a stigmatising experience for children, and this stigma and the associated shame can remain with a care-leaver over their lifetime. In Ireland, for example:

> One of the most enduring legacies of the industrial schools was the sense of shame they instilled in the minds of many who grew up there. It has dogged the survivors of the system, often for their entire lives. Even some of those now in their eighties continue to feel that society looks down on them because of their upbringing.[39]

To challenge such negative stereotypes of care, and care-leavers, CLA explains:

> Each person from care is unique and has a different experience of life in care. They also go on to lead all kinds of varied lives. The Care Leavers' Association (CLA) recognises that diversity and strives to change negative public perceptions and stereotypes of care leavers ... although care leavers are over-represented amongst some of society's most disadvantaged groups, many of them go on to lead happy and successful lives. We want to celebrate that, as well as recognising that there are still many problems to be addressed.[40]

The most successful campaign that CLA has undertaken is in relation to access to records, and this work has occurred on several fronts since 2002. A campaign titled 'It's our history, it's our right', in place since 2007, has three aims: to increase awareness of care-leavers' rights to access their files; to improve recognition of the importance of these personal records to care-leavers; and to promote best practice in the release of care-leavers' records. In an effort to better understand current practice, in 2007, CLA contacted 100 local authorities to find out about their records release practices, which were highly variable. Some received many requests for records, others none. This research inspired their aim to improve knowledge about care-leavers' rights to access their records.[41] As discussed in Chapter Seven, CLA has developed a guide for adult care-leavers that has a strong focus on understanding the implications of the Data Protection Act to accessing records.[42] To promote best practice, CLA developed the associated quality mark for those accredited with high-quality access to records processes in place.[43] More recently, CLA joined forces with a number of other organisations, including Barnardo and the British Association for Adoption and Fostering, and gained the collaboration of a care-leaver and champion, member of the House of Lords, Baroness Margaret Young of Hornsey.[44] In Parliament, during debates on amendments to the Children and Families Bill, Baroness Young explained:

> Several thousand people ask to see their records and many of these requests come from people in their middle or later years. The lifelong needs of adult care leavers are at least as pressing as those of adults who have been adopted, although this is rarely recognised in respect of access to care records and the aftermath. The DPA [Data Protection Act] enables care leavers to see personal information about them on their care files. The problem is that when asking a local authority to see these files, care leavers' experiences range from a response which is at best enabling and supportive and at worst bureaucratic, restrictive and inconsistent with the corporate parenting role. There are some examples of good practice but we want the Government to ensure that local authorities work with the Information Commissioner's Office to enable care leavers to have all the personal information they are entitled to, and to exercise their discretion regarding third-party information in a less restrictive way.[45]

There was considerable support and subsequently 'a government commitment to produce statutory guidance for local authorities clearly setting out their obligation to provide comprehensive information and proper support'; within this guidance, 'any redactions must be fully explained, and that the applicant's needs are kept at the heart of the request'.[46] This commitment has been a major win for CLA and presents a significant opportunity to improve adult care-leavers' access to their records. It may also serve as a useful model internationally.

Care Leavers Australia Network

Like CLA, CLAN commenced in 2000. The two founding members, Joanna Penglase and Leonie Sheedy, met when Penglase was conducting research for her doctoral thesis, which became the book *Orphans of the Living* and was 'an attempt to understand her own experience of growing up in a children's home'.[47] They describe how they came to establish CLAN:

> The formation of CLAN was the culmination of a long journey for both of us. For some years, we had both been attempting, though in different ways, to raise awareness of issues about our childhood in 'care' which we felt to be unacknowledged, and even invisible.[48]

They identified that while the experiences of some groups of children had been recognised, for others like themselves, this had not occurred.

> In Australia over recent decades, we have become increasingly aware, as a society, of other groups of people who as children had experiences which caused them trauma and suffering and which had severely detrimental effects on their life outcomes. Some examples are adoptees, the Aboriginal stolen generations, and the child migrants sent to Australia from Britain particularly in the postwar years. Care Leavers – people who as children grew up in Children's Homes and orphanages or were fostered – have had childhood experiences that were similar, and in many cases identical, to those suffered by these groups. Nevertheless, we seem to have been invisible as a group of citizens entitled to similar recognition, support and assistance to that available to other groups.[49]

Thus, Penglase and Sheedy set about doing something about this lack of understanding and recognition of their plight. They took the name 'Care Leavers Australia Network' with the intention of being linked to the Care Leavers' Association and in recognition that they are 'united worldwide by our past'.[50] In addition, like CLA, they were interested in pursuing both caring and emancipatory goals. While Penglase has since stood down from an active role in CLAN, Sheedy continues to be very involved as CLAN's executive officer and a board member.

At CLAN's first public meeting, several hundred people turned up; their membership now stands at around 1,000 from across Australia. CLAN is an incorporated, non-profit organisation funded by membership fees, donations and small grants, with offices in Sydney and Melbourne and an impressive and informative website. Their objectives include: providing a network through which adult care-leavers can have contact with each other; raising awareness of care and its impacts; and lobbying governments to provide acknowledgement and support for adult care-leavers. In particular, CLAN has worked towards the establishment of dedicated support services to assist people to find lost family members and make contact with them, and to provide life skills and other educational courses. They have also sought dedicated therapy and counselling services for adult care-leavers.

CLAN has, in fact, been remarkably successful in achieving its aims. There are now support services in each Australian state and territory, and they have been instrumental in the establishment of three public inquiries and the issuing of national and state apologies. CLAN has also facilitated many reunions of former residents of children's homes, held numerous social events, hosted a number of conferences, run a national survey of adult care-leavers, published a regular newsletter and established a museum. In addition, they continue to provide a counselling service to adult care-leavers (including receiving funding to support those involved with the Royal Commission into Institutional Responses to Child Sexual Abuse), offer guidance on accessing personal records and assist with a range of individual welfare and other issues.[51] One area that CLAN continues to lobby for is a national redress scheme, as discussed later.

CLAN has been very effective in engaging the media and the wider public. For example, in 2010, Australia's SBS television broadcaster showed *The Forgotten Australians*, a documentary that 'follows the extraordinary efforts' of Penglase and Sheedy 'to bring the [adult care-leaver] scandal out of the shadows'.[52] CLAN provided much information and photographs that informed the National Museum of Australia's 'Inside' touring exhibition and the teaching kit that accompanies the exhibition. CLAN routinely gains press coverage through newspaper, television and radio interviews and operates a Twitter account.[53]

CLAN has also been very successful in working with politicians, a number of whom are patrons of CLAN, including from each of the three main Australian political parties. CLAN has had various campaigns, one of which was to send hundreds of cards to politicians on their birthday. As well as wishing them a happy birthday, the card informed them that 'Australian children in orphanages, children's homes and foster care did not receive a card or have their birthday celebrated'. Most did not respond but one heartfelt acknowledgement came from a New South Wales Greens Member of Parliament, David Shoebridge:

> Sincere thanks for the card I received for my birthday, I was delighted to receive it, and moved by the reminder that so many Australian children in Orphanages and Homes did not receive any kind of recognition on their birthdays. I also acknowledge the emotional distress and physical pain that so many former residents of Orphanages and Homes continue to experience as a result of their time in NSW [New South Wales] institutions. Please let me know what I can do to advance the work of CLAN in calling for redress schemes for Australian Care Leavers. My very best wishes for the ongoing campaign.[54]

The political lobbying work that CLAN has done that has been most effective is the dozens of silent protests that have been conducted since 2007. The first protest, in Melbourne, came out of frustration at the lack of 'real commitments to justice, redress and the provision of services' – 50 people met on the steps of the Victorian Parliament House and held a silent vigil.[55] The messages they wanted to convey were on hand-written signs and banners, and inscribed on their clothes. Over time, they also protested for the establishment of state-based and national inquiries, resulting in the Victorian Parliamentary Inquiry into the Handling of Child Abuse by Religious and other Non-government Organisations and the Royal Commission into Institutional Responses to Child Sexual Abuse.[56] At the same time, CLAN ran a campaign through which thousands of postcards were sent to politicians urging them to support the setting up of the Royal Commission. CLAN continues to hold silent protests at significant sites, including outside parliament houses and churches. For example, in April and May 2014, CLAN held a fortnight of rallies outside where the Royal Commission was holding its hearings in Perth, Western Australia, in an attempt to 'make the general public aware of the criminal treatment' that children had experienced in care in that state. CLAN also continues to protest for a national redress scheme. As their protest brochure demands:

> While CLAN commends the holding of a Royal Commission into Child Sexual Abuse, many thousands of us who were, as innocent children, brutally used and abused while in Orphanages, Children's Homes, foster care and other government Institutions, have had our lives ruined because of what was done to us. The nightmares, the poverty and the disadvantage continue to this day.... THE ROYAL COMMISSION IS NOT ENOUGH! CLAN is calling for a National Independent Compensation Scheme that all Churches, Charities and State Governments must contribute to in order to start to address the gross harm done to all Australian Care Leavers.[57]

In the same way that CLAN has been a key part of shifting Australian understandings of what it meant for children to grow up in care in past decades, they are also endeavouring to change perceptions about the need for reparations to those who were harmed in an effort to gain social justice for this group.

Consumer participation

Consumer participation is another means by which adult care-leavers' perspectives are brought to bear on policy and practice. According to Suzie Braye, this approach 'promotes the social inclusion of those traditionally marginalised within the power structures of society'.[58] However, it is acknowledged that 'this is contested territory'.[59] How participation occurs can vary from minimal involvement through to partnerships; thus, the extent to which consumers are actually able to have an impact is the subject of some debate.[60]

The Law Commission of Canada suggests two underpinning values of consumer participation. First:

> A primary value is to respect and engage survivors. This might seem self-evident. In practice it is difficult to put this value into practice. In the desire to help, there is a temptation to tell people what is best for them, ignoring or overriding their own wishes and needs. Professionals are particularly susceptible to such behaviour.[61]

On this point, social worker Donna McIntosh provides a timely reminder in discussing the membership of a state-wide task force: 'Although social workers may represent a consumer perspective in such venues, we must not come to accept that we are the consumer voice. We are not, and we must advocate for the consumer's right to have a voice'.[62] We should also not assume that a social worker could not also be a 'consumer', in this case, an adult care-leaver. A further difficulty in adult care-leavers taking up such invited positions on boards and task forces is their ability to represent (all) the views of their constituents, as there are likely to be many such views; a problem common to those who are representatives of their constituency.

The second value underpinning the consumer participation of adult care-leavers is thus ensuring that they have assistance to carry out these activities. Effective consumer participation requires:

> the information and support to express the needs they feel and to make considered choices about how they wish to deal with those needs.... Survivors need comprehensive information from disinterested parties in order to understand and assess the professional advice being presented. This disinterested information must be followed by support from professionals and from those who have themselves experienced abuse.[63]

Consumer participation can occur in a range of ways, including having identified adult care-leaver positions on committees of management or other forms of governance structures of services that work with this group. Alternatively, a group of adult care-leavers could be routinely consulted on service provision or in the course of policy development or their evaluation. While consumer participation has occurred in relation to service provision and policy development and their evaluation, to date, there has been less engagement of adult care-leavers in the design and conduct of research concerned with adult care-leavers. (There has, however, been involvement of children in care and adult care-leavers in research regarding children in care.[64]) This is an area requiring further attention because increased consumer participation in research is likely to enhance our capacity to gain knowledge about the life course of adults who grew up in care.[65] An example is the Australian research project 'Who Am I?', which is discussed next as a good practice example of consumer participation.

'Who Am I?' research project

The 'Who Am I?' research project, undertaken over the period 2009–12, investigated the role played by archiving and record-keeping practices in the construction of identity for people who experienced out-of-home care as children (including members of the Stolen Generations and Forgotten Australians). Inspired by the recommendations from *Forgotten Australians*, the interdisciplinary research team from social work, history and archival studies explored the issues of creating, storing and accessing records. The project, based at the University of Melbourne and funded by the Australian Research Council, worked collaboratively with a number of partner organisations, such as the Salvation Army, Wesley Mission Victoria, Anglicare Victoria, Berry Street Family Welfare, Child and Family Services Ballarat, the Victorian Department of Human Services, Kildonan Uniting Care and MacKillop Family Services, and adult care-leavers organisations including CLAN and the Aboriginal Child Care Agency.[66]

There were four strands to the research project. The first was concerned with the development of a web resource that provides information about the historical context of care; initially known as Pathways, this is now the national Find and Connect website, discussed in Chapter Seven. The second strand was concerned with archiving policy and practice, and an archival self-assessment tool was developed to support the work of record-keeping organisations.[67] A third strand of the research involved interviews with adult care-leavers and record-holding organisations to gain a better understanding of both the experiences of accessing records and organisational records' release policies and practices. In particular, the concept of supported release was explored in this aspect of the research.[68] The final strand was concerned with the implications of record-keeping for children in care today, ensuring that records are portable and that recording practice takes into account long-term identity needs.[69]

Reference groups that included adult care-leaver participation oversaw the research. Each strand held workshops with members of the partner organisations over the course of the research, with each workshop commencing with presentations from adult care-leavers reflecting on their experiences in relation to the topic of the workshop. These were powerful reminders of the purpose of the research, and all present invariably found these presentations very moving and informative.

The 'Who Am I?' research used an action research methodology and was underpinned by the 'knowledge diamond', developed by social work academic Cathy Humphreys, lead researcher of 'Who Am I?'. As explained in Chapter One, the knowledge diamond draws from four sources: 'service user/consumer [adult care-leaver] experience, practitioner wisdom, policy perspectives and research evidence' (see Figure 1.1).[70] Consistent with this approach, the researchers in the archiving strand of the project worked closely with an adult care-leaver, Vlad Selakovic, in understanding his records from his perspective. Now aged in his 50s and a member of CLAN, Selakovic spent many years of his childhood in care. He introduced a 'Who Am I?' archiving workshop, and a research collaboration grew out of that.[71] At the archiving workshop, Selakovic described how it felt to access his state ward file from the Department of Human Services (DHS):

> Page after page ... that [file] there reminded me that I was once upon a time society's reject ... it reminded me of all the loneliness, of all the horror and shame that I carried with me my whole life.[72]

After the presentation, the archiving team spoke with him, and he agreed to give them access to his files 'to see what sense [they] could make of them, and study the processes by which they were made available to him'.[73] Selakovic found the records not only distressing because of their contents, but also confusing in the way they were presented and released. The researchers concluded that:

> some of the significant distress and confusion experienced by Vlad could have been alleviated by changes to DHS's administrative and archival procedures. Vlad's story demonstrated how an organisation's 'routine' practices and language can contribute to a negative experience of records access.[74]

Compounding this confusion is the need to change processes to take into account that 'many Forgotten Australians mistrust authority figures, have low literacy levels, lack confidence and self-esteem, and will experience great apprehension when approaching a service provider'.[75] This research collaboration resulted in Selakovic providing important insights into archiving and records release in Victoria that subsequently informed changes to the policies and practices of the government record-holder. Having adult care-leavers as consumer participants involved in the 'Who Am I?' research made a significant difference to the outcomes of the research.

Conclusion

A central theme of this book has been the importance of adult care-leaver perspectives to the development and implementation of social policy responses, consistent with an approach guided by the 'knowledge diamond'. In this chapter, we have considered two ways in which this has been undertaken; first, through the self-advocacy of adult care-leavers themselves; and, second, through their engagement as consumer participants. Advocates have been very successful in bringing about changes, including the establishment of inquiries and improvements in service provision, as the examples of CLA and CLAN illustrate. Consumer participants have the potential to significantly influence policy, practice and research.

Having surveyed social policy responses to adult care-leavers across Australia, Canada, Ireland, New Zealand and the UK, what, then, can we draw from this to inform good practice? This is the focus of Chapter Nine.

NINE

Good practice in supporting adult care-leavers

> In Canada, our history of institutional abuse has been a tragedy of enormous proportion. It is not, sadly, only an issue of the past. (Law Commission of Canada, 2000[1])

Harmful experiences in care are not unique to Canada. In every country where inquiries have been held, there has been shocking evidence of how poorly many children have been treated. What is more, this abuse, inadequate care and separation from family has typically resulted in long-term impacts. Furthermore, while not all of the countries under review in this book have undertaken public inquiries, there is no reason to think that the findings would be that different as three key factors were likely to have been in place: the children were vulnerable, they were relatively powerless in relation to those who cared for them and wider society was unaware of their plight or unwilling to act. At the same time, we know that some children had positive experiences in care.

Having established that some children had received poor treatment, this book set out to outline what had been done about the long-term harmful effects of a childhood in care. In doing so, it sought an answer to the question: how can we best support adult care-leavers? So, when I started the research for this book, I wanted to know how the five countries of Australia, Canada, Ireland, New Zealand and the UK have responded to adult care-leavers, and what is good practice. I had begun to know something about this from my previous research doing life-history interviews with people who grew up in care in Australia and researching access to personal records about time in care. I knew already, generally, that there had been different social policy responses to adult care-leavers internationally. However, what became quickly apparent was that there are striking differences across countries, as well as within countries. So, while the focus of my enquiry was on how countries have responded and what is good practice, in the back of my mind, I was also thinking about why. Why are there different responses among these countries? Why have some countries provided responses to some groups, but not others? This, then, could explain the differences, the examples of good practice and how they might be replicated elsewhere.

Early on, I had been told that cost was one of the key reasons that social policies had not been implemented in certain contexts. Particularly in England, with the largest population of the countries discussed here, this explanation made some sense as it has done less than others and has many who grew up in care. 'It would cost too much to do anything' was the argument suggested. In contrast, other smaller jurisdictions in the UK – Northern Ireland and Scotland – have taken various social policy steps, costing less, according to this argument. However, other jurisdictions, such as some provinces of Canada, which have considerably smaller populations than England and are more similar to Northern Ireland and Scotland in size, have not taken action universally for their non-Indigenous adult care-leaver populations, although there have been major federal social policy responses to their Indigenous peoples. In Australia, there has been some support provided for all three groups of their adult care-leaver populations but not in the same comprehensive way as in Ireland. So, having a smaller population (and presumably less cost) does not mean that social policy responses occur.

Financial cost is not a sufficient explanation, especially when not acting produces costs as well, such as those expended in mental health care, income support and other social services for those for whom the long-term harms have been the greatest. Furthermore, as I have argued, harms typically result in compensation, resulting in costs. This is a common tenet of the civil law in the jurisdictions studied in this book, so for adults who as children were harmed in the care of the state, it should be unremarkable that they are entitled to financial and other compensation. So, another cost when nothing (else) is done is that of the cost of litigation, as has occurred in a number of countries. However, for all concerned, in some instances, it has been more financially effective to produce some form of negotiated agreement rather than defend these claims against the state (and other parties) in the courts, particularly as there are emotional costs to claimants in such adversarial environments. Indeed, where there have been significant claims against the state, there have been social policy responses, as discussed later.

There is, of course, an assumption that when we talk about cost, it refers largely to financial compensation. However, it is not uncommon to hear from adult care-leavers and their advocates that monetary compensation is not what is wanted by all, or, indeed, many. Rather, they would prefer to be asked how they might be compensated – whether in cash or in-kind in the various ways possible. This book has described some of these other ways, in the form of apologies, memorials, therapeutic counselling and other support services that assist with practical, social and emotional legacies, and initiatives that promote adult care-leavers' involvement with cultural practices and facilitate re-engagement with their communities of origin. Summaries of these responses follow in the next sections of this chapter. In addition, awareness of the cost to adult care-leavers raises the issue that there are ongoing costs due to the impact of policies and practices affecting children in care today. A desire by adult care-leavers to address long-term concerns is typically coupled with a willingness to bring about improvements for children currently in care or leaving care.

Costs are not only monetary and practical because there are also social and moral benefits in responding to adult care-leavers. Where one group has been victimised, putting in place social policy responses prevents the re-victimisation from not acting, and the social consequences that can result. Acknowledging the harm done can bring a country together, as apologies have done in the countries where they have occurred. The reconsideration of national histories that are more inclusive of all, even when the accounts are hard for some to hear, is important. Morally, responding to harm in care acknowledges that this was wrong, that it should never have occurred and that as a society, we are sorry that we did not act to prevent it occurring or to intervene. Such actions aim for reconciliation with those individuals and groups who were harmed and hope for a better future characterised by fairness and healing.

So, if financial costs are not a full explanation, and if by acting there are moral and social benefits, why have there not been the consistent responses across countries and population groups? At least part of the answer to this question is related to the existence of advocacy organisations, and their ability to engage effectively in political processes. Those countries where advocates have worked most effectively are where they have gained the support of key parliamentarians. Ireland is an example of where adult care-leaver advocates did not stop knocking on doors until they were listened to and, around the same time, national attention was drawn to the issue through television programmes that powerfully depicted the worst elements of the care system and the harms that they had wrought. Sometimes, these advocates, or champions, are parliamentarians themselves, or parliamentarians are family members, or they hold other key positions. Examples include National Chief Phil Fontaine of the Assembly of First Nations in Canada and Senator Andrew Murray in Australia. Through this process of advocacy, increased understanding and awareness of the legacies of a childhood in care occurs, and this legitimated knowledge is brought to the attention of others due to the influence of these key political figures. At other times, an issue is so striking that it captures the attention of the public, as it did in Australia in relation to the apology to members of the Stolen Generations. Due to these shifts in understanding, political will drives change based on a broad-based agreement that action must be taken.

A second reason that responses are put in place is that alluded to earlier, and is a somewhat more mercenary reason but, regardless, a means of achieving change. Here, governments recognise the need to circumvent logjams in the courts, and save money through not having to defend hundreds (or sometimes thousands) of cases brought by those who were harmed while in the care of the state. Furthermore, where cases are won by claimants, the potential costs are significant. Putting in place redress initiatives and related support services can be cost-effective measures. There are striking examples of where this has occurred, including in New Zealand and Ireland, and in Canada in relation to their Indigenous people through the Indian Residential Schools Settlement Agreement, as well as redress schemes put in place in relation to specific Canadian children's homes.

These examples draw our attention to the differential treatment within nations. Among those countries where there is more than one population group who experienced care, Canada is a striking example of where there has been differential treatment. This is not in any way to discount the need for responses to their Indigenous population, but rather to point out that for non-Indigenous people, there is virtually no targeted support provided universally across Canada or within provinces and territories. Unlike the universal social policy responses to the former residents of residential schools, what has occurred are largely targeted responses to those who resided in specific homes, which included both Indigenous and non-Indigenous children. There has not been a strong national advocacy movement in Canada for non-Indigenous adult care-leavers and these responses have largely derived from the outcomes of specific court cases. (This may be at least partly due to responsibility for these matters being held exclusively by provincial and territorial governments without federal government involvement.) In Australia, for example, where there are similar adult care-leavers' groups to those in Canada, with similar policy histories but a federal government with interests in such social policy, the responses in place are much more evenly distributed and available universally to these groups, with the responses to Indigenous people having first been put in place.

A third reason, and often occurring because of the presence of either or both effective advocates and high volumes of litigation, is the provision of detailed, rigorous and exhaustive evidence acquired through public inquiries. While public inquiries do not necessarily result in comprehensive social policy responses to adult care-leavers, they do typically result in the establishment of some support services and forms of acknowledgement. Some, though, have cautioned about the necessity of public inquiries due to the potential for the re-traumatisation of those who participate, and their cost, and that there may be better ways to access this evidence. If public inquiries are in place, support must be provided to those giving evidence.

Having discussed 'why', let us turn now to 'how' – a summary of the social policy responses discussed in this book. So, how can we best support adult care-leavers?

Summary of social policy responses

Provide opportunities to tell their story

From the 1990s, adult care-leavers brought their personal accounts to the wider public through their willingness to speak at inquiries. The focus of these public inquiries has varied according to population group, time period, forms of care and whether they were specifically care-related. When not about care specifically, a typical focus has been on one or more forms of child abuse in a range of settings, including abuse against children in care. Public inquiries have been a powerful means of changing understandings about care and its aftermath, playing a major role in producing an alternative historical narrative. While not all countries surveyed in this book have conducted inquiries, among those that have, the evidence reflects consistent patterns internationally. Where children have been marginalised by their age, ethnicity or family or socio-economic status, as well as by their relative powerlessness to the state or Church authority figures caring for them, plus the invisibility of their circumstances to the wider community, situations arose where poor – and harmful – practices of care flourished. A lack of documented histories of life in care and its aftermath, and widespread misunderstanding of childhood experiences, contributed to feelings of stigmatisation into adulthood.

Acknowledge experiences of care and its aftermath

Invariably, inquiries have recommended a variety of acknowledgements, including apology, memorials and other forms of remembrance. While also a form of acknowledgement, museum exhibitions and oral history collections have brought information about the lives of adult care-leavers to a wider audience. Apologies are a central feature of social policy responses to adult care-leavers but not all countries reviewed in this book have delivered them, or in a timely manner. A mature apology includes acknowledgement of the harms and taking responsibility for them, as well as reparations.

Compensate for harm

Public inquiries have informed us that there is much evidence to suggest that many children in care have been harmed. Yet, in some jurisdictions, reparations for adult care-leavers are controversial. In particular, financial compensation for harm is contested. Challenging this reluctance to compensate for harm is a matter about which advocates continue to lobby.

Reparation is not just about cash payments, and many adult care-leavers say that they do not want money and that it would never compensate for the harms they experienced. Others feel entitled to the money, and that cash payments are important symbolically, but other forms of support, such as dental care or counselling, would also be useful. Others are concerned for their fellow adult care-leavers because of their vulnerability to exploitation or misuse of the large sums of money granted as compensation. Engaging adult care-leavers in a process of negotiation to determine what is likely to best meet their needs is a central element of providing reparations.

Redress schemes in place across all five countries have typically included financial compensation, but not always. Other practical measures, such as access to therapeutic support, educational or vocational resourcing, and assistance to access records, can all be part of redress programmes. Models vary according to what elements are included, who is targeted as recipients and on what grounds redress is granted. Good practice in implementing redress programmes includes: advertising widely; providing support to adult care-leavers throughout the process; and ensuring that all staff have the skills and knowledge to work with this group. Avoiding further harm and minimisation are crucial.

Provide specialist support

What we know about care and its aftermath is that there can be the need for specialist support in relation to mental health, education, life skills and other areas, and cultural reconnection. Abuse in care can produce long-term mental ill-health. Loss of family can exacerbate the lack of social support and limit the existence of networks of care that might otherwise be available. Access to education in care may have been restricted or a child's ability to engage may have been reduced due to the effects of abuse or their involvement in work activities. Institutional settings may have provided few opportunities to gain independent living skills, such as managing money or basic cooking skills. For Indigenous adult care-leavers, reconnecting with their cultural heritage is an important area of specialist support.

To date, specialist support has been provided in a range of ways across the countries surveyed, with recognition that such support is needed to varying degrees across these countries. For example, in relation to psychotherapy, there is much greater resourcing in some jurisdictions than others. This may reflect a greater willingness to acknowledge the long-term, complex trauma that has been experienced by adult care-leavers. Another form of initiative evident in a number of countries is a specialist community centre that includes a range of services, such as welfare support, counselling, educational programmes and social outings. For those working directly with adult care-leavers, there is the need for professional development, and also the integration of this knowledge and expertise into wider health and social services.

Support identity formation and family reunification

While inquiries into care have typically paid attention to physical and sexual abuse, sometimes loss of identity and family relationships have not been given due prominence. For many adult care-leavers, a lack of knowledge of family, or a loss of connection to them, has been central to the harms they experienced as children. For Indigenous people, a loss of connection to their community and country has been devastating to themselves and to their families and communities left behind. Adult care-leavers may have questions such as: who is my family? Why was I in care? What happened when I was a child in care? Their personal records, and other contextual information such as institutional documents and wider social histories, can help make sense of who they are and what happened. Thus, at the heart of releasing personal records is an appreciation of their importance to adult care-leavers. Sometimes, there is little information held about a person; even this is valuable as it is evidence of their childhood. Records can reveal unknown family members and can be sought as a stepping stone to find family. Supported release underpins work in this area, and it requires staff who have specialist knowledge in this area of practice, and in family reunification.

Good practice principles

Based on the findings of these initiatives and in an effort to facilitate good practice, the following guiding principles are put forward.

Consult with adult care-leavers in the development of social policy responses

In speaking with an Aboriginal elder, I began to better understand the importance of consultation, engagement and negotiation. Receiving money as compensation was not his preferred response, but it had been offered to him as a former student of a residential school in the outcome of the settlement agreement where payments were applied universally. He wanted to have been asked what he wanted, and, for him, it was not financial compensation that would repair the damage that had been caused to himself, his family and community. Instead, he and his family wanted to ensure the ongoing survival and prosperity of their community. Programmes that provided opportunities for language revival and its teaching, the revitalisation of cultural practices, ceremonies, curriculum development, and the research and recording of community histories, were all alternative ways that meaningful compensation could have been provided. For others, access to long-term psychotherapy or dental care could be the preferred support, and a more effective way of promoting a healthier and more satisfying life for them. In a more positive example of consultation and engagement, in developing the apology to the members of the Stolen Generations, Minister Jenny Macklin and her staff worked closely with Aboriginal advocates and organisations to write an apology that would be most meaningful to them.

Engage adult care-leavers as consumer participants

Those who experienced care – and its aftermath – are the experts in understanding what has happened and what is needed. As reiterated by the Law Commission of Canada:

> Engaging survivors as much as possible in any approach to redress [or any other social policy initiative] is a clear way to demonstrate respect for them. It is a public acknowledgement that they know what is needed in order to undo the harm done to them. Engagement may also mean full consultation on the design and implementation of any programs of redress directed to particular groups of survivors.[2]

In Ireland, Caranua resources daily living support and is overseen by a board of trustees, including half who are former residents of industrial schools, all of whom are long-term advocates for improved responses to those who were harmed in the care of the state.

Support the work of advocates

Adult care-leaver advocates are involved in both caring and emancipatory activities. In caring, they provide support to other adult care-leavers through self-help groups and helplines. Emancipatory work involves increasing the awareness and understanding of the wider public about the harms of care and its aftermath, and what can be done about it. Over the past

25 years, advocates, and their champions, have been successful political lobbyists in gaining support for public inquiries and a range of initiatives. More remains to be done, and advocates are leading the way.

Build in support to adult care-leavers as part of any social policy initiative

Social policy initiatives for adult care-leavers are designed to respond to harms in care. These are matters that are likely to evoke responses that impact on an adult care-leaver's emotional health and well-being. Speaking at a public inquiry, applying for redress, seeking personal records or attending a commemorative event are all situations that may trigger painful memories. For this reason, support mechanisms must be built into any social policy initiative. This may include providing access to counselling or a telephone helpline. It also assumes that those working most closely with adult care-leavers are skilled in recognising the need for support and are able to refer as needed, as well as such services being available more widely. The promotion of these support mechanisms needs to be advertised in a variety of forms and media. An underlying principle is the minimisation of harm and the avoidance of re-victimisation.

Ensure staff have the skills and knowledge to work with adult care-leavers

Understanding the circumstances of care and the likely impacts of harm is a prerequisite to working with adult care-leavers. While there are some examples of emerging good practice, to date, little attention has been paid to professional development. There is a lack of recognition of the specialist skills and knowledge that would enhance this work, reflective of the limited understanding of care and its aftermath for those harmed. Several innovative resources, such as the DVD and guide produced by the Alliance of Forgotten Australians, are important additions to this area of work but much more could be done. One initiative would be to ensure that the educational curricula of social work, health personnel and other professions working with adult care-leavers includes relevant material and that professional development training is available for existing staff. An essential element of such training is the input of adult care-leavers themselves.

Embed principles of respect and dignity in all programmes for adult care-leavers

Adult care-leavers may feel stigmatised by having grown up in care and by the harms that they experienced there. They may feel that society at large does not believe what happened during their childhood or understand the impact that it has had on their life. Treating adult care-leavers with respect and dignity, being compassionate and believing them, with the aim of facilitating their empowerment, are all principles to guide work in this area.

With knowledge comes responsibility?

In this book, we have examined the range of responses to adult care-leavers across five countries. So, in conclusion, we can ask: have the programmes in place addressed the needs that have been identified? What else could be in place to support adult care-leavers? What else do we need to know, and how might we find out? In answer to the first question, to some extent, in some places (Ireland), for some groups (Canada), the initiatives are addressing identified needs. Here, we could say, as Helen Holland noted, knowledge has resulted in (some level of) responsibility. However, in some places, there are groups whose needs are not yet addressed fully, or it is still very much a work in progress (Northern Ireland and Scotland). In other places, responses are minimal (England) or present but not comprehensive (New Zealand, Australia and Canada).

In relation to the need for other initiatives, three matters are particularly pressing. First, as adult care-leavers age, the possibility of the need for care in later life arises. For some, the need for aged care raises major concerns about their welfare and well-being, such as their willingness to reside in an institution as an older person after a childhood in which other institutions have caused great distress and harm. Compounding this situation is that adult care-leavers may not have family to care for them in old age. Thus, the social policy implications of the aged care of adult care-leavers need attention.

Second, some adult care-leavers have experienced severe socio-economic disadvantage. For example, in those jurisdictions where financial compensation for harm has not been provided, as well as in other circumstances, such as that for those who received a poor education or an education blighted by the effects of abuse or childhood labour, with the resulting loss of vocational opportunities, lifetime low incomes have produced poverty. At the very least, financial compensation for harm must be offered. To further compensate for these disadvantages, giving adult care-leavers priority access to medical, dental and housing services would be a step in the right direction. Third, the mental health consequences of abuse in care are yet to be fully recognised in some jurisdictions, and this is another area that requires improved responses.

Finally, we do not know enough about the specific long-term effects of care across the life course to know what the range of needs might be. While we know that there is a diversity of outcomes among adult care-leavers, we do not know what produces the best outcomes across the life course. Research involving and directed by adult care-leavers could throw further light on what these needs might be and how we might act on them, as well as finding out about how effective the current initiatives are. Knowing more about what is supportive for adult care-leavers will inform current work in this area. Understanding what facilitates success in adulthood, according to adult care-leavers themselves, can also inform policy and practice for children in care today.

Throughout this book, there has been encouragement to listen to adult care-leavers. However, what is needed is more than this. Like Helen Holland's exhortation that with knowledge comes responsibility, 20 years ago, the Canadian Assembly of First Nations' study *Breaking the Silence* concluded by stating: 'My story is a gift. If I give you a gift and you accept that gift, then you don't go and throw that gift in the waste basket. You do something with it'.[3] So, having heard accounts of care and its aftermath, and being aware of the range of social policy responses, and other possibilities, there is an obligation to take action.

Notes and references

Chapter One

[1] Brian, interviewed by Suellen Murray, 21 January 2011. Some of the quotations that head each chapter are drawn from participants in previous research I have conducted with adult care-leavers, with their consent; others are derived from interviews with care-leaver advocates gained through my research for this book, also with their consent; others are from published sources.

[2] See, for example, Commission to Inquire into Child Abuse (CICA), *Commission to Inquire into Child Abuse Report (Ryan Report)*, Government of Ireland, Dublin, 2009; Senate Community Affairs References Committee (SCARC), *Forgotten Australians: A Report on Australians who Experienced Institutional or Out-of-Home Care as Children*, Commonwealth of Australia, Canberra, 2004.

[3] For a summary of the long-term adverse effects of child abuse, see Alan Carr, Barbara Dooley, Mark Fitzpatrick, Edel Flanagan, Roisin Flanagan-Howard, Kevin Tierney, Megan White, Margaret Daly and Jonathan Egan, 'Adult adjustment of survivors of institutional abuse in Ireland', *Child Abuse and Neglect*, vol 34, no 7, 2010, pp 477–89, 478.

[4] Another way in which these questions could be asked is: 'In what ways have the human rights of people who grew up in care as children been violated, what have been the long-term impacts, and what can be done about this?' To date, such a human rights framework has not typically been used in relation to adult care-leavers by governments, the exception is Scotland; see Scottish Human Rights Commission (SHRC), *A Human Rights Framework for the Design and Implementation of the Proposed 'Acknowledgement and Accountability Forum' and Other Remedies for Historic Child Abuse in Scotland*, SHRC, Edinburgh, 2010; Andrew Kendrick, Moyra Hawthorn, Samina Karim and Julie Shaw, 'Scotland: abuse in care and human rights', in Johanna Sköld and Shurlee Swain (eds), *Apologies and the Legacies of Abuse of Children in 'Care'*, Palgrave Macmillan, Basingstoke, 2015; see also Chapter Three of this book.

[5] Other relevant social policy responses are the investigation of allegations of abuse and the criminal prosecution of offenders. While acknowledging that such processes can be part of a public inquiry (or otherwise) and that they

can hold great significance to adult care-leavers, they are beyond the scope of this book.

[6] Law Commission of Canada, *Restoring Dignity: Responding to Child Abuse in Canadian Institutions*, Minister of Public Works and Government Services, Ottawa, 2000. There have been criticisms of this report, one being that it does not pay due attention to ensuring 'fairness to alleged abusers' through attention to due process, or acknowledging this limitation of redress programmes; Margaret Hall, 'Book review: Law Commission of Canada, *Restoring Dignity: Responding to Child Abuse in Canadian Institutions*', *International Journal of Children's Rights*, vol 10, no 3, pp 295–302, 298. For more discussion, see Chapters Three and Five.

[7] Law Commission of Canada, *Restoring Dignity*, p 2.

[8] Law Commission of Canada, *Restoring Dignity*, p 2.

[9] Lesley Laing, Cathy Humphreys and Kate Cavanagh, *Social Work and Domestic Violence: Developing Critical and Reflective Practice*, Sage, London, 2013, p 9; see also Cathy Humphreys and Margaret Kertesz, '"Putting the heart back into the record": personal records to support young people in care', *Adoption and Fostering*, vol 36, no 1, pp 27–39, 31.

[10] Laing, Humphreys and Cavanagh, *Social Work and Domestic Violence*, p 10.

[11] Laing, Humphreys and Cavanagh, *Social Work and Domestic Violence*, p 9.

[12] What is known as 'care' in Australia is more likely to be called 'childcare' (or, more recently, the care of 'looked-after children') in the UK. I have chosen not to use the term 'childcare' because in Australia, 'childcare' more commonly means the 'day care' of young children, but not in a residential setting. I do not include adoption in my discussion, although some adult care-leavers were adopted either before or after their time in care.

[13] Stephen Winter, *Transitional Justice in Established Democracies: A Political Theory*, Palgrave Macmillan, Basingstoke, 2014, p 185.

[14] Johanna Sköld, 'Historical abuse – a contemporary issue: compiling inquiries into abuse and neglect of children in out-of-home care worldwide', *Journal of Scandinavian Studies in Criminology and Crime Prevention*, vol 14, sup 1, 2013, pp 5–23, 13.

[15] SCARC, *Forgotten Australians*, p xv.

[16] Fred Powell and Margaret Scanlon, *Dark Secrets of Childhood: Media Power, Child Abuse and Public Scandals*, Policy Press, Bristol, 2015, p 128.

[17] According to Australian advocacy group Care Leavers Australia Network (CLAN), a 'Care Leaver' is 'a person who was in institutional care or other form of out-of-home care, including foster care, as a child or youth (or both) at some time during the 20th century'; CLAN, 'Constitution of Care Leavers Australia Network (CLAN) Incorporated', 2011, p 5, available at: http://www.clan.org.

au/perch/resources/clan-constitution-2011.pdf (accessed 14 October 2015). Eligibility for the Victorian support service Open Place is that people 'spent all or part of their childhood in a Children's Home or Orphanage during the last Century prior to 1990'; Open Place, 'Am I eligible?', available at: http://www.openplace.org.au/NeedHelp (accessed 26 May 2014). The UK advocacy group Care Leavers' Association works with all care-leavers, regardless of age.

[18] Mike Stein, *Young People Leaving Care: Supporting Pathways to Adulthood*, Jessica Kingsley Publishing, London, 2012; Mike Stein and Emily Munro (eds), *Young People's Transitions from Care to Adulthood: International Research and Practice*, Jessica Kingsley Publishing, London, 2008.

[19] In relation to Canadian Indigenous children, see, for example, Erin Hanson, 'Sixties scoop', available at: http://Indigenousfoundations.arts.ubc.ca/home/government-policy/sixties-scoop.html (accessed 14 November 2014).

[20] For a discussion of 'female delinquency', see, for example, Nell Musgrove, *The Scars Remain: A Long History of Forgotten Australians and Children's Institutions*, Australian Scholarly Publishing, Melbourne, 2013, pp 86–7.

[21] However, I acknowledge that the central governments of three of these countries are not responsible for the initiatives discussed in this book; rather, they are either undertaken by the governments of their constituent states or in a shared arrangement between the central and these other governments.

[22] Office for National Statistics, 'Population estimates for UK, England and Wales, Scotland and Northern Ireland, mid-2011 and mid-2012', available at: http://www.ons.gov.uk/ons/rel/pop-estimate/population-estimates-for-uk--england-and-wales--scotland-and-northern-ireland/mid-2011-and-mid-2012/index.html (accessed 26 May 2014); World Bank, 'Population, total – 2012', available at: http://data.worldbank.org/indicator/SP.POP.TOT (accessed 26 May 2014).

Chapter Two

[1] Commission to Inquire into Child Abuse (CICA), *Commission to Inquire into Child Abuse Report (Ryan Report), Executive Summary*, Government of Ireland, Dublin, 2009, p 15.

[2] CICA, *Executive Summary*, p 13.

[3] Jeff Hearn, Tarja Pösö, Carole Smith, Sue White and Joanna Korpinen, 'What is child protection? Historical and methodological issues in comparative research on *lastensuojelu*/child protection', *International Journal of Social Welfare*, vol 13, 2004, pp 28–41, 28; their research was concerned with England and Finland.

[4] Nell Musgrove, *The Scars Remain: A Long History of Forgotten Australians and Children's Institutions*, Australian Scholarly Publishing, Melbourne, 2013, p xvii.

[5] For histories of the provision of care in the UK, see, for example: Brian Corby, Alan Doig and Vicky Roberts, *Public Inquiries into Residential Abuse of Children*, Jessica Kingsley Publishers, London, 2001; Robin Sen, Andrew Kendrick, Ian Milligan and Moyra Hawthorn, 'Lessons learnt? Abuse in residential care in Scotland', *Child and Family Social Work*, vol 13, no 4, 2008, pp 411–22. For New Zealand, see Bronwyn Dalley, *Family Matters: Child Welfare in Twentieth-Century New Zealand*, Auckland University Press, Auckland, 1998. For Australia, see: Anna Haebich, *Broken Circles: Fragmenting Indigenous Families, 1800–2000*, Fremantle Arts Centre Press, Fremantle, 2000; Musgrove, *The Scars Remain*; Shurlee Swain, 'The state and the child', *Australian Journal of Legal History*, vol 4, 1998, pp 57–77. For Ireland, see: Mary Raftery and Eoin O'Sullivan, *Suffer the Little Children: The Inside Story of Ireland's Industrial Schools*, New Island, Dublin, 1999; Eoin O'Sullivan, *Residential Child Welfare in Ireland, 1965–2008: An Outline of Policy, Legislation and Practice*, CICA, Dublin, 2009. For Canada, see: Margaret Jacobs, *A Generation Removed: The Fostering and Adoption of Indigenous Children in the Postwar World*, University of Nebraska Press, Lincoln, 2014; Truth and Reconciliation Commission of Canada (TRCC), *They Came for the Children: Canada, Aboriginal Peoples and Residential Schools*, TRCC, Winnipeg, 2012.

[6] Hearn et al, 'What is child protection?', p 30.

[7] Raftery and O'Sullivan, *Suffer the Little Children*, pp 105–7.

[8] Kathleen Murray and Malcolm Hill, 'The recent history of Scottish child welfare', *Children and Society*, vol 5, no 3, 1991, pp 266–81, 268.

[9] See, for example, Dalley, *Family Matters*, pp 336–7; O'Donnell and O'Sullivan, 'Setting the scene', p 7; Shurlee Swain and Renate Howe, *Single Mothers and their Children: Disposal, Punishment and Survival in Australia*, Cambridge University Press, Melbourne, 1995.

[10] Dalley, *Family Matters*, p 5; see also Swain, 'The state and the child'.

[11] Shurlee Swain, *History of Child Protection Legislation*, Australian Catholic University, Melbourne, 2014, p 6.

[12] Raftery and O'Sullivan, *Suffer the Little Children*, p 64.

[13] Swain, *History of Child Protection Legislation*, p 7; see also 'Child Welfare', available at: http://www.thecanadianencyclopedia.ca/en/article/child-welfare/ (accessed 16 November 2014); Maria Luddy, 'The early years of the NSPCC in Ireland', in Maria Luddy and James M. Smith (eds), *Children, Childhood and Irish Society*, Four Courts Press, Dublin, 2014, pp 100–20; Murray and Hill, 'The recent history of Scottish child welfare'; Fred Powell and Margaret Scanlon, *Dark Secrets of Childhood: Media Power, Child Abuse and Public Scandals*, Policy

Press, Bristol, 2015, pp 28–31; Swain, 'The state and the child'; Tomison, 'A history of child protection'.

[14] Tomison, 'A history of child protection', p 50.

[15] Murray and Hill, 'The recent history of Scottish child welfare', p 267.

[16] O'Sullivan, *Residential Child Welfare in Ireland, 1965–2008*, p 56.

[17] Maria Luddy and James M. Smith, 'Introduction', in Maria Luddy and James M. Smith (eds), *Children, Childhood and Irish Society*, Four Courts Press, Dublin, 2014, p 18; see also Robbie Gilligan, 'The "public child" and the reluctant state?', in Maria Luddy and James M. Smith (eds), *Children, Childhood and Irish Society*, Four Courts Press, Dublin, 2014, p 148.

[18] Raftery and O'Sullivan, *Suffer the Little Children*, pp 69–71.

[19] Adam M. Tomison, 'A history of child protection: back to the future?', *Family Matters*, no 60, 2001, pp 46–57, 47–8, 50; Corby et al, *Public Inquiries into Residential Abuse of Children*, p 40; Dalley, *Family Matters*, pp 342–61; Powell and Scanlon, *Dark Secrets of Childhood*, pp 33–8.

[20] Tomison, 'A history of child protection', p 46.

[21] Tomison, 'A history of child protection', p 50.

[22] J. Heywood, *Children in Care*, London, Routledge and Kegan Paul, 1978, cited in Murray and Hill, 'The recent history of Scottish child welfare', p 267.

[23] Tomison 'A history of child protection', p 51.

[24] Dalley, *Family Matters*, p 361.

[25] Tomison, 'A history of child protection', p 52.

[26] Tomison, 'A history of child protection', p 53.

[27] Hearn et al, 'What is child protection?', p 35.

[28] For discussion of the United Nations Convention on the Rights of the Child, see Kate Cregan and Denise Cuthbert, *Global Childhoods: Issues and Debates*, Sage, London, 2014.

[29] Ontario Association of Children Aid Societies, 'History of child welfare', available at: http://www.oacas.org/childwelfare/history.htm (accessed 2 December 2014); see also John McCullagh, *A Legacy of Caring: A History of the Children's Aid Society of Toronto*, Dundurn, Toronto, 2002.

[30] Dalley, *Family Matters*; O'Sullivan, *Residential Child Welfare in Ireland, 1965–2008*; Gilligan, 'The "public child" and the reluctant state?', pp 147, 150.

[31] Tomison, 'A history of child protection', p 49; Dalley, *Family Matters*, p 3.

[32] Kerryn Pollock, 'Children's homes and fostering – Church institutions and charitable aid', Te Ara – The Encyclopedia of New Zealand, available

at: http://www.teara.govt.nz/en/childrens-homes-and-fostering/page-1 (accessed 26 May 2014).

[33] CICA, *Ryan Report, Executive Summary*, p 16; see also Ian O'Donnell and Eoin O'Sullivan, 'Setting the scene', in Eoin O'Sullivan and Ian O'Donnell (eds), *Coercive Confinement in Ireland: Patients, Prisoners and Penitents*, Manchester University Press, Manchester, 2012, pp 24–5.

[34] The potential isolation of children in foster care and the instability of multiple placements can be concerns. While residential care presents greater difficulties regarding attachment, it can be a more stable environment to grow up in, with friendships with other children in the home, as reported by some adult care-leavers; see, for example, Duncalf, *Listen Up!*; see also Pecora et al, *What Works in Foster Care?*, p 10; Dalley, *Family Matters*, pp 322–36.

[35] Tomison, 'A history of child protection', p 51.

[36] Vandna Sinha and Anna Kozlowski, 'The structure of Aboriginal child welfare in Canada', *International Indigenous Policy Journal*, vol 4, no 2, 2013, pp 1–21, 5.

[37] That such responses for adult care-leavers are not provided through child welfare services is entirely appropriate. After all, they are no longer children.

[38] Child Migrants Trust, 'Child migration: history', available at: http://www.childmigrantstrust.com/our-work/child-migration-history (accessed 26 May 2014); Terry Hearn, 'English – special groups', Te Ara – the Encyclopedia of New Zealand, available at: http://www.teara.govt.nz/en/photograph/1931/child-migrants-1949 (accessed 26 May 2014); see also Ellen Boucher, *Empire's Children: Child Emigration, Welfare and the Decline of the British World, 1869–1967*, Cambridge University Press, New York, 2014; 'On their own – Britain's child migrants', an exhibition jointly produced by the Australian Maritime Museum and the National Museums Liverpool; Dugald McDonald and Suzanne de Joux, *British Child Migrants in New Zealand, 1949–1999*, Social Work Press, Christchurch, 2000; Cregan and Cuthbert, *Global Childhoods*, pp 122–5. The number of child migrants varies across sources partly because there was a range of migration programmes, some of which were for older teenagers – sometimes considered independent young adults rather than children – who may or may not be included in the count.

[39] Child Migrants Trust, 'Child migration: history'; Barry Coldrey, *Good British Stock: Child and Youth Migration to Australia*, National Archives of Australia, Canberra, 1999; National Archives of Australia, 'Child migration to Australia – fact sheet 124', available at: http://www.naa.gov.au/collection/fact-sheets/fs124.aspx (accessed 26 May 2014).

[40] See, for example, Roy Parker, *Uprooted: The Shipment of Poor Children to Canada, 1867–1917*, The Policy Press, Bristol, 2010; Boucher, *Empire's Children*; Phyllis Harrison (ed), *The Home Children: Their Personal Stories*, J. Gordon Shillingford Publishing, Winnipeg, 2003 [1979]; Kenneth Bagnell,

The Little Immigrants: The Orphans Who Came to Canada, Dundurn Press, Toronto, 2001.

[41] See, for example, British Home Children Advocacy and Research Association, 'British Home Children Advocacy and Research Association', available at: http://britishhomechildrenadvocacy.weebly.com/ (accessed 12 November 2014).

[42] Parker, *Uprooted*, p 16.

[43] Parker, *Uprooted*, p 134; for descriptions of the hard work that many child migrants undertook on Canadian farms, see Harrison, *The Home Children*.

[44] Parker, *Uprooted*, p 136.

[45] Child Migrants Trust, 'Child migration: history'; see also Boucher, *Empire's Children*, ch 3. The 2010 film *Oranges and Sunshine*, directed by Jim Loach, portrays the foundational work of the Child Migrants Trust. It is based on the book by Margaret Humphreys, *Empty Cradles*, Doubleday, London, 1994.

[46] National Archives of Australia, 'Child migration to Australia – fact sheet 124'; see also Boucher, *Empire's Children*, p 193.

[47] Child Migrants Trust, 'Child migration: history'.

[48] Boucher, *Empire's Children*; National Archives of Australia, 'Child migration to Australia – fact sheet 124'.

[49] See, for example, David Hill, *The Forgotten Children: Fairbridge Farm School and its Betrayal of British Child Migrants to Australia*, Random House, Sydney, 2007.

[50] Dalley, *Family Matters*, p 176.

[51] Barnardos, 'Child migration – history', available at: http://www.barnardos. org.au/barnardos/html/child_migration.cfm (accessed 21 May 2013).

[52] See, Human Rights and Equal Opportunity Commission (HREOC), *Bringing Them Home: National Inquiry into the Separation of Aboriginal and Torres Strait Islander Children from their Families*, Commonwealth of Australia, Sydney, 1997; Royal Commission on Aboriginal Peoples (RACP), *Report of the Royal Commission on Aboriginal Peoples*, Government of Canada, Ottawa, 1996. In both Canada and Australia, Indigenous peoples are small minorities of the total populations. In 2006, in Australia, Indigenous peoples were 2.5% of the total population, and in Canada, they comprised 3.8%; Australian Bureau of Statistics, 'Population distribution, Aboriginal and Torres Strait Islanders, 2006', Cat No 4705.0, available at: http://www.abs.gov.au/ausstats/abs@.nsf/ mf/4705.0 (accessed 24 June 2014); Statistics Canada, 'Aboriginal peoples in Canada in 2006: Inuit, Métis and First Nations, 2006 Census', Cat No 97-558-XIE, available at: http://www12.statcan.ca/census-recensement/2006/ as-sa/97-558/pdf/97-558-XIE2006001.pdf (accessed 24 June 2014).

[53] Australian Human Rights Commission, 'International review of Indigenous issues in 2000: Australia – 6. Indigenous children as victims of racism', available at: http://www.humanrights.gov.au/publications/international-review-Indigenous-issues-2000-australia-6-Indigenous-children-victims (accessed 26 May 2014); see also HREOC, *Bringing Them Home*; Haebich, *Broken Circles*.

[54] This change was to occur after a referendum in 1967 that overwhelmingly handed responsibility to the federal government.

[55] Margaret D. Jacobs, *A Generation Removed: The Fostering and Adoption of Indigenous Children in the Postwar World*, University of Nebraska Press, Lincoln, 2014, p 215 (emphasis in original).

[56] Australian Government, 'Documentation of forced removal of children', available at: http://australia.gov.au/about-australia/australian-story/sorry-day-stolen-generations (accessed 26 May 2014).

[57] Jacobs, *A Generation Removed*, pp 215–16. Musgrove, *The Scars Remain*, pp 29–31; Haebich, *Broken Circles*, ch 6.

[58] Commonwealth of Australia, Aboriginal Welfare, 'Initial conference of Commonwealth and State Aboriginal Authorities', Canberra, 21–23 April 1937, p 21, available at: http://www.aiatsis.gov.au/_files/archive/referendum/20663.pdf (accessed 26 May 2014); see also Cassidy, 'The best interests of the child?', p 131.

[59] HREOC, *Bringing Them Home*; Cassidy, 'The best interests of the child?'.

[60] Australian Government, 'Documentation of forced removal of children'.

[61] CBC News, 'A history of residential schools in Canada', available at: http://www.cbc.ca/news/canada/a-history-of-residential-schools-in-canada-1.702280 (accessed 26 May 2014); see also Pamela O'Connor, 'Squaring the circle: how Canada is dealing with the legacy of its Indian residential schools experiment', *Australian Journal of Human Rights*, vol 6, no 1, 2000, pp 188–211; TRCC, *They Came for the Children*.

[62] RACP, *Report*.

[63] O'Connor, 'Squaring the circle', p 191. This economic motivation has also been suggested as a reason for the removal of children in Australia; see Julie Cassidy, 'The best interests of the child: the Stolen Generations in Canada and Australia', *Griffith Law Review*, vol 15, no 1, 2006, pp 111–52.

[64] Jacobs, *A Generation Removed*; Raven Sinclair, 'Identity lost and found: lessons from the Sixties Scoop', *First Peoples Child and Family Review*, vol 3, no 1, 2007, pp 65–82; Sinha and Kozlowski, 'The structure of Aboriginal child welfare in Canada'; Laurence J. Kirmayer, Caroline L. Tait and Cori Simpson, 'The mental health of Aboriginal peoples in Canada: transformations of identity and community', in Laurence J. Kirmayer and Gail Guthrie Valakakis (eds),

Healing Traditions: The Mental Health of Aboriginal Peoples in Canada, UBC Press, Vancouver, 2009, pp 3–35.

[65] Sinha and Kozlowski, 'The structure of Aboriginal child welfare in Canada', p 4.

[66] TRCC, 'Residential schools', available at: http://www.trc.ca/websites/trcinstitution/index.php?p=4 (accessed 26 May 2014).

[67] Families Commission, 'Safety of subsequent children: Māori children and Whānau. A review of selected literature', available at: http://www.familiescommission.org.nz/web/m%C4%81ori-children-wh%C4%81nau/mauri-ora_cultural-identity.html (accessed 26 May 2014); Kerryn Pollock, 'Children's homes and fostering – government institutions', Te Ara – the Encyclopedia of New Zealand, available at: http://www.teara.govt.nz/en/childrens-homes-and-fostering/page-2 (accessed 26 May 2014); see also Stephen Winter, *Transitional Justice in Established Democracies: A Political Theory*, Palgrave Macmillan, Basingstoke, 2014, pp 85–6.

[68] However, this is not to say that Māori themselves have not acted in relation to their experiences in care. In 2008, a claim was made to the Waitangi Tribunal 'on behalf of all Māori who were adopted, fostered or made wards of the state through government welfare systems'. The claim stated that 'the Crown, in breach of its Treaty of Waitangi obligations, prejudicially affected Māori by passing and enforcing the Adoption Act 1955'; Anne Else, 'Adoption – Māori and colonial adoption', Te Ara – the Encyclopedia of New Zealand, at: http://www.teara.govt.nz/en/adoption/page-1 (accessed 26 May 2014); see also Melissa Nobles, *The Politics of Official Apologies*, Cambridge University Press, Melbourne, 2008, pp 80–5.

[67] See, for example, Raftery and O'Sullivan, *Suffer the Little Children*, pp 241–2; Senate Community Affairs References Committee (SCARC), *Forgotten Australians: A Report on Australians who Experienced Institutional or Out-of-Home Care as Children*, Commonwealth of Australia, Canberra, 2004, p 125; TRCC, *They Came for the Children*, pp 45–9. This was also the case in the Swedish inquiry, see Johanna Sköld, Emma Foberg and Johanna Hedström, 'Conflicting or complementing narratives? Interviewees' stories compared to their documentary records in the Swedish Commission to Inquire into Child Abuse and Neglect in Institutions and Foster Homes', *Archives and Manuscripts*, vol 40, no 1, pp 15–28, 16. Some children prefer to be in care than with their families of origin; see, for example, Jim Wade, Nina Biehal, Nicola Farrelly and Ian Sinclair, *Caring for Abused and Neglected Children: Making the Right Decisions for Reunification or Long-term Care*, Jessica Kingsley Publishers, London, 2011; Nina Biehal, 'A sense of belonging: meanings of family and home in the long-term foster care', *British Journal of Social Work*, vol 44, 2014, pp 955–71.

[70] CICA, *Ryan Report, Executive Summary*, p 14.

[71] HREOC, *Bringing Them Home*; RACP, *Report*.

[72] As this book is concerned with adult care-leavers (ie people who grew up in care and are aged over 25 years), research concerned with children in care or leaving care and immediate post-care is not discussed.

[73] Parker, *Uprooted*, p xii.

[74] Parts of this section are derived from Suellen Murray and Jim Goddard, 'Adult care-leavers: informing policy and practice through research', *Australian Social Work*, vol 67, no 1, 2014, pp 102–17; I acknowledge Jim Goddard's contributions.

[75] Peter J. Pecora, Ronald C. Kessler, Jason Williams, A. Chris Downs, Diana J. English, James White and Kirk O'Brien, *What Works in Foster Care? Key Components of Success from the Northwest Foster Care Alumni Study*, Oxford University Press, Oxford, 2010, p 14. This study focuses on so-called 'long-term outcomes' and is concerned with those up to age 33 years only. In the study, 'foster care' was understood to include both 'family foster care' and care in 'group homes and residential settings' (p 6).

[76] Parker, *Uprooted*, p xii.

[77] Kirmayer et al, 'The mental health of Aboriginal peoples in Canada', pp 18–19.

[78] Murray and Goddard, 'Adult care-leavers: informing policy and practice through research'.

[79] See, for example, Paddy Doyle, *The God Squad: The Bestselling Story of One Child's Triumph Over Adversity*, Corgi, London, 1989; Netta England, *Stolen Lives: A New Zealand Foster Child's Story from the '40s and '50s*, Netta Christian, Hamilton, 2014; Frank Golding, *An Orphan's Escape: Memories of a Lost Childhood*, Lothian Books, Melbourne, 2005; James MacVeigh, *Gaskin*, Jonathan Cape, London, 1982; Bruce Oldfield, *Rootless*, Hutchinson, London, 2004; Ryszard Szablicki, *Orphanage Boy: Through the Eyes of innocence*, New Holland Publishers, Sydney, 2010.

[80] For example, Paolo Hewitt, *The Looked After Kid*, Mainstream Publishing, Edinburgh, 2002.

[81] Examples include Doris Pilkington, *Follow the Rabbit-Proof Fence*, University of Queensland Press, Brisbane, 1996; Theodore Fontaine, *Broken Circle: The Dark Legacy of Indian Residential Schools*, Heritage House, Victoria, 2010; see also Rhonda Claes and Deborah Clifton, *Needs and Expectations for Redress of Victims of Abuse at Residential Schools*, Law Commission of Canada, Ottawa, 1998, where they refer to a number of other autobiographical accounts of Canadian residential schools.

[82] Murray and Goddard, 'Adult care-leavers: informing policy and practice through research'.

[83] Johanna Sköld, 'Historical abuse – a contemporary issue: compiling inquiries into abuse and neglect of children in out-of-home care worldwide', *Journal of Scandinavian Studies in Criminology and Crime Prevention*, vol 14, sup 1, 2013, pp 5–23, 13.

[84] See, for example, Health Service Research Centre, *SENCS: Survivors' Experiences of the National Counselling Service*, Health Boards Executive, Dublin, 2003; Thanos Karatzias, *In Care Survivors Service Scotland (ICSSS) Evaluation*, Napier University, Edinburgh, 2011.

[85] Care Leavers Australia Network (CLAN), *A Terrible Way to Grow Up: The Experience of Institutional Care and its Outcomes for Care Leavers in Australia*, CLAN, Sydney, 2008; Zachari Duncalf, *Listen Up! Adult Care Leavers Speak Out. Research Gathered from 310 Care Leavers aged 17–78*, Care Leavers' Association, Manchester, 2010. In 2014, the advocacy and support service Right of Place undertook a survey of Irish adult care-leavers to find out more about their needs and the kinds of services required; see Right of Place, 'Biggest survey of survivors needs in Ireland', available at: http://www.rightofplace.com/component/content/article/10-news/171-the-biggest-survey-of-survivors-needs-in-ireland (accessed 30 May 2014).

[86] Alan Carr, Barbara Dooley, Mark Fitzpatrick, Edel Flanagan, Roisin Flanagan-Howard, Kevin Tierney, Megan White, Margaret Daly and Jonathan Egan, 'Adult adjustment of survivors of institutional abuse in Ireland', *Child Abuse and Neglect*, vol 34, no 7, 2010, pp 477–89, 478; Pecora et al, *What Works in Foster Care?*; J. Christopher Perry, John J. Sigal, Sophie Boucher, Nikolas Paré, Marie Ouimet, Julie Normand and Melissa Henry, 'Personal strengths and traumatic experiences among institutionalised children given up at birth (Les enfants de Duplessis – Duplessis' children), II: adaptation in late adulthood', *Journal of Nervous and Mental Disorders*, vol 193, no 12, 2005, pp 783–9; Kirmayer et al, 'The mental health of Aboriginal peoples in Canada'; Aliya Saied-Tessier, *Estimating the Costs of Child Sexual Abuse in the UK*, National Society for the Prevention of Cruelty to Children, London, 2014, p 12; David A. Wolfe, Karen J. Francis and Anna-Lee Straatman, 'Child abuse in religiously affiliated institutions: long-term impact on men's mental health', *Child Abuse and Neglect*, vol 30, 2006, pp 205–12; see also Sunitha Raman and Catherine Forbes, *It's Not Too Late to Care: Report on the Research into Life Outcomes for People Brought Up in Institutional Care in Victoria*, Centre for Excellence in Child and Family Welfare, Melbourne, 2008; CLAN, *A Terrible Way to Grow Up*; Duncalf, *Listen Up*.

[87] Bozena Spila, Marta Makara, Gustaw Kozak and Anna Urbanska, 'Abuse in childhood and mental disorder in adult life', *Child Abuse Review*, vol 17, no 2, 2008, pp 133–8; Carr et al, 'Adult adjustment of survivors of institutional abuse in Ireland', p 478; Saied-Tessier, *Estimating the Costs of Child Sexual Abuse in the UK*, p 12; Wolfe et al, 'Child abuse in religiously-affiliated institutions'; see also Pecora et al, *What Works in Foster Care?*, ch 6.

[88] Brian Draper, Jon J. Pfaff, Jane Pirkis, John Snowdon, Nicola T. Lautenschlager, Ian Wilson and Osvaldo P. Almeida, 'Long-term effects of childhood abuse on the quality of life and health of older people: results from the depression and early prevention of suicide in general practice project', *Journal of the American Geriatrics Society*, vol 56, no 2, 2008, pp 262–71, 270.

[89] Laurence Kirmayer, Cori Simpson and Margaret Cargo, 'Healing traditions: culture, community and mental health promotion with Canadian Aboriginal people', *Australasian Psychiatry*, vol 11(S), 2013, pp 15–23, 18; see also Mason Durie, Helen Milroy and Ernest Hunter, 'Mental health and the Indigenous peoples of Australia and New Zealand', in Laurence J. Kirmayer and Gail Guthrie Valakakis (eds), *Healing Traditions: The Mental Health of Aboriginal Peoples in Canada*, UBC Press, Vancouver, 2009, pp 36–55; Jacqui Kidd, Kerri Butler and Reina Harris, 'Māori mental health', in Nicholas Procter, Terry Froggatt, Denise McGarry, Helen P. Hamer and Rhonda L Wilson (eds), *Mental Health: A Person-Centred Approach*, Cambridge University Press, Melbourne, 2014, pp 72–91; Debra Hocking, 'The social and emotional well-being of Aboriginal Australians and the collaborative consumer narrative', in Nicholas Procter, Terry Froggatt, Denise McGarry, Helen P. Hamer and Rhonda L. Wilson (eds), *Mental Health: A Person-Centred Approach*, Cambridge University Press, Melbourne, 2014, pp 52–71.

[90] Matthew Colton, Maurice Vanstone and Christine Walby, 'Victimization, care and justice: reflections on the experiences of victims/survivors involved in large-scale historical investigations of child sexual abuse in residential institutions', *British Journal of Social Work*, vol 32, 2002, pp 541–51.

[91] Moyra Hawthorn, 'Historic abuse in residential care: sharing good practice', *In Residence*, no 4, 2006, pp 1–4.

[92] Carr et al, 'Adult adjustment of survivors of institutional abuse in Ireland', p 488.

[93] Wolfe, 'Child abuse in religiously-affiliated institutions', p 210.

[94] Jeff Moore, Christine Thornton, Mary Hughes and Eugene Waters, *Open Hearts and Open Minds: A Toolkit of Sensitive Practice for Professionals Working with Survivors of Institutional Child Abuse*, London Irish Centre and Immigrant Counselling and Psychotherapy, London, 2014, available at: http://www.icap.org.uk/wp-content/uploads/2014/10/Appendix-3-Open-Hearts-and-Open-Minds.pdf (accessed 7 December 2014).

[95] Durie et al, 'Mental health and the Indigenous peoples of Australia and New Zealand', p 47.

[96] Durie et al, 'Mental health and the Indigenous peoples of Australia and New Zealand', p 47.

[97] Joseph P. Gone, 'A community-based treatment for Native American historical trauma: prospects for evidence-based practice', *Spirituality in Clinical*

Practice, vol 1(S), 2013, pp 78–94, 81, citing J.P. Gone and C. Alcántara, 'Identifying effective mental health interventions for American Indians and Alaska Natives: a review of the literature', *Culture Diversity and Ethnic Minority Psychology*, vol 13, 2007, pp 356–63.

[98] Gone, 'A community based treatment for Native American historical trauma'.

[99] Rod McCormick, 'Aboriginal approaches to counselling', in Laurence J. Kirmayer and Gail Guthrie Valaskakis (eds), *Healing Traditions: The Mental Health of Aboriginal Peoples in Canada*, UBC Press, Vancouver, 2009, pp 337–54, 337.

[100] For a summary of this research, see Pecora et al, *What Works in Foster Care?*, ch 7.

[101] Public inquiries provide evidence of the poor provision of education in institutional care; see, for example, SCARC, *Forgotten Australians*, pp 109–11.

[102] Duncalf, *Listen Up!*; Murray et al, *After the Orphanage*.

[103] Cheryl Buehler, John G. Orme, James Post and David A. Patterson, 'The long-term correlates of family foster care', *Children and Youth Services Review*, vol 22, no 8, 2000, pp 595–625; Pecora et al, *What Works in Foster Care?*, ch 8; Raman and Forbes, *It's Not Too Late to Care*, p 19; Saied-Tessier, *Estimating the Costs of Child Sexual Abuse in the UK*, pp 12, 18.

[104] Russell M. Viner and Brent Taylor, 'Adult health and social outcomes of children who have been in public care: population-based study', *Pediatrics*, vol 115, no 4, 2005, pp 894–9; SCARC, *Forgotten Australians*, p 160.

[105] See, for example, Antonio Buti, 'The removal of Aboriginal children: Canada and Australia compared', *University of Western Sydney Law Review*, no 6, 2002, pp 25–37; Antonio Buti, 'Bridge over troubled Australian waters: reparations for Aboriginal child removals and British child migrants', *E Law Murdoch University Electronic Journal of Law*, vol 10, no 4, 2003, pp 5–20; Cassidy, 'The best interests of the child?'.

[106] SCARC, *Forgotten Australians*, p xv; see also CLAN, *A Terrible Way to Grow Up*; J. Christopher Perry, John J. Sigal, Sophie Boucher and Nikolas Paré, 'Seven institutionalized children and their adaptation in late adulthood; the Children of Duplessis (Les Enfants de Duplessis)', *Psychiatry*, vol 69, no 4, 2006, pp 283–301; Colton et al, 'Victimization, care and justice', p 545.

[107] See, for example, SCARC, *Forgotten Australians*, pp 149–52.

[108] Kirmayer et al, 'Healing traditions', p 18.

[109] See, for example, David Quinton and Michael Rutter, 'Parents with children in care – I. Current circumstances and parenting', *Journal of Child Psychology and Psychiatry*, vol 25, no 2, 1984, pp 211–29; Dawn Smith, Colleen Varcoe and Nancy Edwards, 'Turning around the intergenerational impact of residential schools on Aboriginal people: implications for health policy and practice',

Canadian Journal of Nursing Research, vol 37, no 4, 2005, pp 38–60; Roberta Stout and Sheryl Peters, *Intergenerational Effects on Professional Women Whose Mothers Are Residential School Survivors*, Prairie Women's Health Centre of Excellence, Winnipeg, 2011; in relation to age at parenting, see Jo Dixon, 'Young people leaving care: health, well-being and outcomes', *Child and Family Social Work*, vol 13, no 2, 2008, pp 207–17.

[110] Gill Pugh, *Unlocking the Past: The Impact of Access to Barnardo's Childcare Records*, Ashgate, Aldershot, 1999; Karen Winter and Olivia Cohen, 'Identity issues for looked after children with no knowledge of their origins', *Adoption and Fostering*, vol 29, no 2, 2005, pp 44–52.

[111] See, for example, Christine Horrocks and Jim Goddard, 'Adults who grew up in care: constructing the self and accessing care files', *Child and Family Social Work*, vol 11, no 2, 2006, pp 264–72; Suellen Murray, Jenny Malone and Jenny Glare, 'Building a life story: providing records and support to former residents of children's homes', *Australian Social Work*, vol 61, no 3, 2008, pp 239–55.

[112] See, for example: Michael Jones and Cate O'Neill, 'Identity, records and archival evidence: exploring the needs of Forgotten Australians and former child migrants', *Archives and Records*, vol 35, no 2, 2014, pp 110–25; Derek Kirton, Julia Feast and Jim Goddard, 'The use of discretion in a "Cinderella" service: data protection and access to child-care files for post-care adults', *British Journal of Social Work*, vol 41, no 5, 2011, pp 912–30; Suellen Murray and Cathy Humphreys, '"My life's been a total disaster but I feel privileged": care-leavers' access to personal records and their implications for social work practice', *Child and Family Social Work*, vol 19, no 2, 2014, pp 215–24.

[113] Julia Feast, *Access to Information for Post-care Adults: A Guide for Social Workers and Access to Records Officers (AROs)*, British Association for Adoption and Fostering, London, 2009.

[114] See, for example, public inquiries, including HREOC, *Bringing Them Home*, and TRCC, *They Came for the Children*; see also Jacobs, *A Generation Removed*; Haebich, *Broken Circles*.

[115] Law Commission of Canada, *Restoring Dignity: Responding to Child Abuse in Canadian Institutions: Executive Summary*, Minister of Public Works and Government Services, Ottawa, 2000, p 2.

[116] Kirmayer et al, 'Healing traditions', p 18.

[117] Laurence J. Kirmayer, 'Cultural competence and evidence-based practice in mental health: epistemic communities and the politics of pluralism', *Social Science and Medicine*, vol 75, 2012, pp 249–56, 253.

[118] Access to healing practices is an integral part of the process of applying for redress within the Indian Residential Schools Settlement Agreement (see Chapter Five).

[119] While acknowledging the significance of accountability in a criminal justice sense, this is not pursued here.

[120] Some public inquiries have focused on how institutions responded when children spoke out against their carers; see, for example, two Australian inquiries; the Inquiry into the Handling of Child Abuse by Religious and Other Non-government Organisations, which reported to the Parliament of Victoria in 2013; and the Royal Commission into Institutional Responses to Child Sexual Abuse, currently ongoing in 2014.

[121] Wolfe et al, 'Child abuse in religiously-affiliated institutions', p 208.

[122] Alliance for Forgotten Australians (AFA), *Forgotten Australians: Life Stories*, DVD, AFA, Canberra, 2011, inside sleeve.

[123] CICA, *Ryan Report, Executive Summary*, p 12; see also Reg Graycar and Jane Wangmann, 'Redress packages for institutional abuse: exploring the Grandview Agreement as a case study in "alternative" dispute resolution', Legal Studies Research Paper No 07/50, University of Sydney Law School, Sydney, 2007, pp 1–53, 19; Tom Shaw, *Historical Abuse Systemic Review: Residential Schools and Children's Homes in Scotland, 1950–1995*, Scottish Government, Edinburgh, 2007, p 155.

[124] CICA, *Ryan Report, Executive Summary*, p 12.

Chapter Three

[1] Helen Holland, interviewed by Suellen Murray, 22 September 2013, Glasgow.

[2] At least five other countries have held inquiries into out-of-home care or foster care since the 1990s. These other countries include Norway, Sweden, Germany, Iceland and Denmark; see Johanna Sköld, 'Historical abuse – a contemporary issue: compiling inquiries into abuse and neglect of children in out-of-home care worldwide', *Journal of Scandinavian Studies in Criminology and Crime Prevention*, vol 14, sup 1, 2013, pp 5–23, 6.

[3] For a discussion of the range of scope of these inquiries, see Sköld, 'Historical abuse – a contemporary issue', pp 12–16.

[4] Law Commission of Canada, *Restoring Dignity: Responding to Child Abuse in Canadian Institutions*, Minister of Public Works and Government Services, Ottawa, 2000, p 249.

[5] Law Commission of Canada, *Restoring Dignity*, p 251.

[6] Law Commission of Canada, *Restoring Dignity*, pp 249, 386.

[7] Law Commission of Canada, *Restoring Dignity*, p 87.

[8] Shurlee Swain, *History of Australian Inquiries Reviewing Institutions Providing Care for Children*, Australian Catholic University, Melbourne, 2014, p 3. For

a discussion of the significance of this oral testimony, see Sköld, 'Historical abuse – a contemporary issue', p 7; for a critique, see Mark Smith, 'Victim narratives of historical abuse in residential child care: do we really know what we think we know?', *Qualitative Social Work*, vol 9, no 3, 2010, pp 303–20.

[9] In New Zealand and Australia, evidence of violations of human rights has been used in efforts to gain support for adult care-leavers. Scotland is notable in that it has developed a right-based framework, see Scottish Human Rights Commission (SHRC), *A Human Rights Framework for the Design and Implementation of the Proposed 'Acknowledgement and Accountability Forum' and Other Remedies for Historic Child Abuse in Scotland*, SHRC, Edinburgh, 2010 (discussed later).

[10] For an overview of Australian enquiries since 1854, see Swain, *History of Australian Inquiries Reviewing Institutions Providing Care for Children*.

[11] Senate Community Affairs References Committee (SCARC), *Lost Innocents: Righting the Record, Report on Child Migration*, Commonwealth of Australia, Canberra, 2001; SCARC, *Forgotten Australians: A Report on Australians Who Experienced Institutional or Out-of-Home Care as Children*, Commonwealth of Australia, Canberra, 2004. A third inquiry looked into the plight of children in care today: SCARC, *Protecting Vulnerable Children: A National Challenge*, Commonwealth of Australia, Canberra, 2005.

[12] Human Rights and Equal Opportunity Commission (HREOC), *Bringing Them Home: The Report of the National Inquiry into the Separation of Aboriginal and Torres Strait Islander Children from their Families*, HREOC, Sydney, 1997.

[13] Shurlee Swain, Leonie Sheedy and Cate O'Neill, 'Responding to "Forgotten Australians": historians and the legacy of out-of-home care', *Journal of Australian Studies*, vol 36, no 1, 2012, pp 17–28, 25.

[14] See Royal Commission into Institutional Responses to Child Sexual Abuse (RCIRCSA), *Interim Report, Volumes 1 and 2*, Commonwealth of Australia, Canberra, 2014.

[15] RCIRCSA, 'Royal Commission marks its one year anniversary', available at: http://www.childabuseroyalcommission.gov.au/media-release/709/royal-commission-marks-its-one-year-anniversary (accessed 28 May 2014); RCIRCSA, 'Royal Commission first anniversary fact sheet'.

[16] RCIRCSA, *Consultation Paper: Redress and Civil Litigation*, RCIRCSA, Sydney, 2015, p 38.

[17] William Budiselik, Frances Crawford and Donna Chung, 'The Australian Royal Commission into Institutional Responses to Child Sexual Abuse: dreaming of child safe organisations?' *Social Science*, vol 3, no 3, 2014, pp 565–83, 566–7. Others are more enthusiastic about what the Royal Commission can achieve, see, for example, Warwick Middleton, Pam Stavropolous, Martin J. Dorahy, Christa Krüger, Roberto Lewis-Fernández, Alfonso Martínez-

Taboas, Vedat Sar and Bethany Brand, 'The Australian Royal Commission into Institutional Responses to Child Sexual Abuse', *Australian and New Zealand Journal of Psychiatry*, vol 48, no 1, 2014, pp 17–21; Mary Hood, 'Feminism and the Royal Commission into Institutional Responses to Child Sexual Abuse', *AASW National Bulletin*, Spring 2014, p 29.

[18] HREOC, *Bringing Them Home*, p 14.

[19] Denise Cuthbert and Marian Quartly, '"Forced adoption" in the Australian story of national regret and apology', *Australian Journal of Politics and History*, vol 58, no 1, 2012, pp 82–96, 85; see also Indigenous Law Resources, 'Royal Commission into Aboriginal Deaths in Custody', available at: http://www.austlii.edu.au/au/other/IndigLRes/rciadic/ (accessed 28 May 2014).

[20] Aboriginal Legal Service of Western Australia (ALSWA), *Telling Our Story: A Report of the Aboriginal Legal Service of Western Australia on the Removal of Aboriginal Children from their Families in Western Australia*, ALSWA, Perth, 1995.

[21] HREOC, *Bringing Them Home*, p 1.

[22] HREOC, *Bringing Them Home*, pp 15–16.

[23] Leneen Forde, Jane Thomason and Hans Heilpern, *Commission of Inquiry into Child Abuse in Queensland Institutions: Final Report*, Queensland Government, Brisbane, 1999; Ted Mullighan, *Children in State Care Commission of Inquiry: Allegations of Sexual Abuse and Death from Criminal Conduct*, South Australian Parliament, Adelaide, 2008; Tasmanian Ombudsman, *Review of Claims of Abuse from Adults in State Care as Children: Final Report*, Tasmanian Ombudsman, Hobart, 2006; Family and Community Development Committee, *Inquiry into the Handling of Child Abuse by Religious and Other Organisations*, Parliament of Victoria, Melbourne, 2013; see also Ben Mathews, 'Queensland government actions to compensate survivors of institutional abuse: a critical and comparative evaluation', *QUT Law and Justice Journal*, vol 4, no 1, 2004, pp 23–45.

[24] RCIRCSA, 'Share your story', available at: http://www.childabuseroyalcommission.gov.au/tell-us-your-story/ (accessed 28 May 2014); see also RCIRCSA, *Interim Report*, vols 1 and 2.

[25] RCIRCSA, 'Support services', available at: http://www.childabuseroyalcommission.gov.au/support/support-services/ (accessed 8 January 2014).

[26] See Goldie Shea, *Redress Programs Relating to Institutional Child Abuse in Canada*, Law Commission of Canada, Ottawa, 1999.

[27] Royal Commission on Aboriginal Peoples (RACP), *Report of the Royal Commission on Aboriginal Peoples*, Government of Canada, Ottawa, 1996; see also Michael DeGagné, 'Implementing reparations: international perspectives', paper presented at 'Moving Forward: Achieving Reparations for the Stolen Generations', 15 August 2011, Australian Human Rights Commission, Sydney,

available at: http://www.humanrights.gov.au/implementing-reparations-international-perspectives (accessed 28 May 2014).

[28] Margaret Hall, 'Book review: Law Commission of Canada, *Restoring Dignity: Responding to Child Abuse in Canadian Institutions*', *International Journal of Children's Rights*, vol 10, no 3, 2002, pp 295–302, 295; see also Jennifer J. Llewellyn, 'Dealing with the legacy of native residential school abuse in Canada: litigation, ADR, and restorative justice', *University of Toronto Law Journal*, no 52, 2002, pp 253–300.

[29] Law Commission of Canada, *Restoring Dignity*, p 2.

[30] Law Commission of Canada, *Restoring Dignity*, p 2.

[31] See Rhonda Claes and Deborah Clifton, *Needs and Expectations for Redress of Victims of Abuse at Residential Schools*, Law Commission of Canada, Ottawa, 1998; Institute for Human Resource Development, *Review of 'The Needs of Victims of Institutional Abuse'*, Law Commission of Canada, Ottawa, 1998.

[32] Law Commission of Canada, *Restoring Dignity*, pp 74–99, 106–73.

[33] Truth and Reconciliation Commission of Canada (TRCC), 'Residential schools', available at: http://www.trc.ca/websites/trcinstitution/index.php?p=4 (accessed 27 May 2014).

[34] For a critical analysis of the work of the Truth and Reconciliation Commission, see Ronald Niezen, *Truth and Indignation: Canada's Truth and Reconciliation Commission on Indian Residential Schools*, University of Toronto Press, Toronto, 2013.

[35] Commission to Inquire into Child Abuse (CICA), *Report of the Commission to Inquire into Child Abuse (Ryan Report)*, Government of Ireland, Dublin, 2009; see also Fred Powell, Martin Geoghegan, Margaret Scanlon and Katharina Swirak, 'The Irish charity myth, child abuse and human rights: contextualising the Ryan Report into care institutions', *British Journal of Social Work*, vol 43, no 1, 2012, pp 7–23; Carol Brennan, 'Facing what cannot be changed: the Irish experience of confronting institutional child abuse', *Journal of Social Welfare and Family Law*, vol 29, nos 3/4, 2007, pp 245–63.

[36] Barry Andrews, TD, Minister for Children and Youth Affairs, 'Foreword', in Office of the Minister for Children and Youth Affairs, *Report of the Commission to Inquire into Child Abuse, 2009: Implementation Plan*, Minister for Health and Children, Dublin, 2009, p xi.

[37] Fred Powell and Margaret Scanlon, *Dark Secrets of Childhood: Media Power, Child Abuse and Public Scandals*, Policy Press, Bristol, 2015, pp 136–40; see also Eoin O'Sullivan, 'Residential child welfare in Ireland: from Kennedy to the Task Force', in Maria Luddy and James M. Smith (eds), *Children, Childhood and Irish Society*, Four Courts Press, Dublin, 2014, pp 121–44.

[38] Irish Film Board, *Dear Daughter*, directed by Louis Lentin, 1996, available at: http://directory.irishfilmboard.ie/films/168-dear-daughter (accessed 27 May 2014).

[39] *States of Fear*, directed by Mary Rafferty, 1999; see also Mary Rafferty and Eion O'Sullivan, *Suffer the Little Children: The Inside Story of Ireland's Industrial Schools*, New Island, Dublin, 1999. For a discussion of these programmes, see Emily Pine, *The Politics of Memory: Performing Remembrance in Contemporary Irish Culture*, Palgrave Macmillan, Basingstoke, 2011.

[40] Powell et al, 'The Irish charity myth'; Powell and Scanlon, *Dark Secrets of Childhood*, pp 140–1.

[41] Powell et al, 'The Irish charity myth', p 12.

[42] Section 4(1) of the Principal Act of 2000 and as amended by Section 4 of the 2005 Act, cited in CICA, *Ryan Report*, vol I, p 1.

[43] CICA, *Ryan Report*, vol I, p 3.

[44] CICA, *Ryan Report*, vol I, p 3.

[45] Section 12 of the Principal Act of 2000 and as amended by Section 7 of the 2005 Act, cited in CICA, *Ryan Report*, vol I, p 3.

[46] Hall, 'Book review', p 300.

[47] See, for example, Carol Brennan, 'Trials and contestations: Ireland's Ryan Commission', in J. Sköld and S. Swain (eds), *Apologies and the Legacies of Abuse of Children in "Care"*, Palgrave Macmillan, Basingstoke, 2015; Hall, 'Book review', pp 300–1; Powell and Scanlon, *Dark Secrets of Childhood*, p 127.

[48] See, for example, Eoin O'Sullivan, 'Residential child welfare in Ireland, 1965–2008: an outline of policy, legislation and practice: a paper prepared for the Commission to Inquire into Child Abuse', in CICA, *Ryan Report*, vol IV, ch 4.

[49] Dublin Opinion, press release from Survivors of Institutional Abuse Ireland, 'March of solidarity – June 10th', available at: http://dublinopinion.com/2009/06/09/march-of-solidarity-june-10th/ (accessed 27 May 2014); see also Eoin O'Sullivan and Ian O'Donnell, 'Explaining coercive confinement: why was the past such a different place?', in Eoin O'Sullivan and Ian O'Donnell (eds), *Patients, Prisoners and Penitents: Coercive Confinement in Ireland*, Manchester University Press, Manchester, 2012, p 256.

[50] RTÉ News, 'Solidarity march for abuse victims', 10 June 2009, available at: http://www.rte.ie/news/2009/0610/118254-abuse/ (accessed 27 May 2014).

[51] Dublin Opinion, press release.

[52] Male Survivors of Sexual Abuse, 'Campaign to launch a Royal Commission into Institutional Historical Child Abuse', available at: http://survivor.org.nz/

campaign-to-launch-a-royal-commission-into-institutional-historical-child-abuse/campaigns/ (accessed 13 July 2015).

[53] Cited in United Nations, 'Convention against Torture and Other Cruel, Inhuman or Degrading Treatment or Punishment, Consideration of reports submitted by states parties under article 19 of the Convention, Follow-up responses by New Zealand to the concluding observations of the Committee against Torture', (CAT/C/NZL/CO/5) [19 May 2010], 2011, p 7.

[54] Cited in United Nations, 'Convention against Torture – follow-up responses', p 7.

[55] Cited in United Nations, 'Convention against Torture – follow-up responses', p 7.

[56] The 'Understanding Kohitere' research project was commissioned by the Care Claims and Resolution Team in order to provide information to assist in considering claims from the former residents of Kohitere Boy's Training Centre; see also Wendy Parker, *Social Welfare Residential Care 1950–1994*, Ministry of Social Development, Wellington, 2006.

[57] See Confidential Listening and Assistance Service, 'Terms of reference', available at: http://www.listening.govt.nz/web/RCCMS_cla.nsf/vwluResources/terms%20of%20reference/$file/Amended%20Terms%20of%20Reference%20pdf%20.pdf (accessed 9 January 2014).

[58] While there has been no public inquiry into child migration to New Zealand, or an apology to child migrants, there has been state acknowledgement of their plight. During the late 1990s, in response to the UK's *Health Report – An Inquiry into the Welfare of Former British Child Migrants*, a New Zealand social welfare programme was established to contact all of the former child migrants in an effort to advise them of funding that was available to assist them to find and make contact with their family and for them to return to the UK to reunite with family; see TVNZ, 'NZ govt statement regarding child migrants', One News, 16 November 2009, available at: http://tvnz.co.nz/national-news/nz-govt-statement-regarding-child-migrants-3148096 (accessed 27 May 2014).

[59] For discussion of these local inquiries, see Brian Corby, Alan Doig and Vicky Roberts, *Public Inquiries into Residential Abuse of Children*, Jessica Kingsley Publishers, London, 2001; Powell and Scanlon, *Dark Secrets of Childhood*, pp 38–41. That there has been no national enquiry is at least partly because responsibility for social welfare is devolved to constituent states.

[60] National Crime Agency, 'North Wales Police, Operation Pallial: public report on progress', available at: http://www.north-wales.police.uk/pdf/PEnglishfinal.pdf (accessed 27 May 2014).

[61] Independent Panel Inquiry into Child Sexual Abuse, 'Independent Panel Inquiry into Child Sexual Abuse', available at: https://childsexualabuseinquiry.independent.gov.uk/ (accessed 30 October 2014).

[62] Mary O'Hara, 'We were slaves from a young age', *The Guardian*, 25 September 2013, p 40.

[63] Historical Institutional Abuse Inquiry, 'Terms of reference', available at: http://www.hiainquiry.org/index/acknowledgement_forum/terms-of-reference.htm (accessed 27 May 2014).

[64] Historical Institutional Abuse Inquiry, 'Statistics', available at: http://www.hiainquiry.org/index/statistics.htm (accessed 27 May 2014).

[65] Northern Ireland Historical Institutional Abuse Inquiry, 'General information and application form', available at: http://www.hiainquiry.org/index/documentation/hiai-general-information-leaflet-new.pdf (accessed 27 May 2014).

[66] Scottish Parliament, 'Petition 535', available at: http://archive.scottish.parliament.uk/business/petitions/docs/PE535.htm (accessed 27 May 2014).

[67] Survivor Scotland, 'A National Strategy for Survivors of Childhood Abuse', available at: http://www.survivorscotland.org.uk/ (accessed 27 May 2014).

[68] Tom Shaw, *Historic Abuse Systemic Review: Residential Schools and Children's Homes in Scotland 1950–1955*, Scottish Government, Edinburgh, 2007; see also Robin Sen, Andrew Kendrick, Ian Milligan and Moyra Hawthorn, 'Lessons learned? Abuse in residential child care in Scotland', *Child and Family Social Work*, vol 13, no 4, 2008, pp 411–22.

[69] SHRC, *A Human Rights Framework*, p 2; see also Zachari Duncalf, Moyra Hawthorn, Jennifer Davidson, Jim Goddard and Will McMahon, *Time for Justice: Historic Abuse of Children in Scotland*, Care Leavers' Association and the Scottish Institute for Residential Child Care, Manchester and Glasgow, 2009.

[70] Andrew Kendrick, Moyra Hawthorn, Samina Karim and Julie Shaw, 'Scotland: abuse in care and human rights', in Johanna Sköld and Shurlee Swain (eds), *Apologies and the Legacies of Abuse of Children in 'Care'*, Palgrave Macmillan, Basingstoke, 2015.

[71] Tom Shaw, *Time to be Heard: A Pilot Forum*, Scottish Government, Edinburgh, 2011, p 5.

[72] These concerns were raised in a petition titled 'Time for all to be heard' to the Scottish government by Chris Daly and Helen Holland in 2010; Scottish Parliament, 'Petition 1351', available at: http://www.scottish.parliament.uk/Petitions_Archive/PE1351.pdf (accessed 27 May 2014).

[73] See Angela Sdrinis, 'Scottish National Confidential Forum into abuse announced', available at: http://www.rct-law.com.au/sexual-abuse-update/scottish-national-confidential-forum-into-abuse-announced.html (accessed 27 May 2014).

[74] SHRC and Centre for Excellence for Looked After Children in Scotland, 'SHRC InterAction on historic abuse of children in care: action plan on justice

for victims of historical abuse of children in care', available at: http://www.shrcinteraction.org/Portals/23/Action-Plan-on-Historic-Abuse-of-Children-in-Care-Nov-2013.pdf (accessed 27 May 2014).

[75] Scottish Government, 'Education secretary statement on Historic Child Abuse Inquiry', available at: http://news.scotland.gov.uk/Speeches-Briefings/Education-Secretary-statement-on-Historic-Child-Abuse-Inquiry-194b.aspx (accessed 15 July 2015).

[76] Bronwyn Halfpenny, 'Child abuse inquiry – committee members' final report tabling speeches to the Parliament of Victoria', Family and Community Development Committee, 13 November 2013; a similar point is made in SCARC, *Forgotten Australians*, pp 14–16; see also Kathleen Daly, *Redressing Institutional Abuse of Children*, Palgrave Macmillan, Basingstoke, 2014, p 5. Indeed, Johanna Sköld, in reviewing similar inquiries in nine countries, makes the point that their 'reports are quite similar regardless of the geographical origins of the interviewees and the commissions'; Sköld, 'Historical abuse – a contemporary issue', p 7.

[77] RACP, *Report*, cited in O'Connor, 'Squaring the circle', p 189.

[78] RACP, *Report*, cited in O'Connor, 'Squaring the circle', p 189.

[79] Law Commission of Canada, *Restoring Dignity*, p 4.

[80] Office of the Minister for Children and Youth Affairs, *Report of the Commission to Inquire into Child Abuse, 2009: Implementation Plan*, Minister for Health and Children, Dublin, 2009, p 1.

[81] O'Connor, 'Squaring the circle', p 205.

[82] Law Commission of Canada, *Restoring Dignity*, p 51.

[83] Andrews, 'Foreword', p xi.

[84] Office of the Minister for Children and Youth Affairs, *Report of the Commission to Inquire into Child Abuse, 2009: Implementation Plan*, pp 22–9.

[85] Since the *Ryan Report*, two subsequent inquiries have investigated state involvement in the Magdalen Homes (or Magdalen Laundries as they are also known due to the nature of the work that women did there) and redress to the women affected. The findings of these reports are known as the McAleese (2012) and Quirke (2013) reports, respectively. While these institutions were not for adult care-leavers specifically, some young women who worked in the Magdalen Homes had also been in care. For further discussion of the Magdalen Homes, see Eoin O'Sullivan and Ian O'Donnell (eds), *Coercive Confinement in Ireland: Patients, Prisoners and Penitents*, Manchester University Press, Manchester, 2012; James Smith, *Ireland's Magdalen Laundries and the Nation's Architecture of Containment*, University of Notre Dame Press, Notre Dame, 2007.

[86] Australian Government, 'Australian government response to *Forgotten Australians: A Report on Australians who Experienced Institutional or Out-of-home Care as Children*', Commonwealth of Australia, Canberra, 2005, available at: http://www.aph.gov.au/Parliamentary_Business/Committees/Senate/Community_Affairs/Completed_inquiries/2004-07/inst_care/~/media/wopapub/senate/committee/clac_ctte/completed_inquiries/2004_07/inst_care/gov_response/gov_response_pdf.ashx (accessed 27 May 2014).

[87] Australian Government, 'Australian government response to *Forgotten Australians*', p 2.

[88] Australian Human Rights Commission, 'International review of Indigenous issues in 2000: Australia – 6. Indigenous children as victims of racism', available at: http://www.humanrights.gov.au/publications/international-review-Indigenous-issues-2000-australia-6-Indigenous-children-victims (accessed 27 May 2014). In relation to reparations, the Public Interest Advocacy Centre 'developed a proposal for a stolen generations reparations tribunal to provide full reparations for forcible removal of Indigenous children'; see Amanda Cornwall, *Restoring Identity: Final Report of the* Moving Forward *Consultation Project*, Public Interest Advocacy Centre, Sydney, 2009, p xi.

[89] Australian Human Rights Commission, 'International review of Indigenous issues in 2000'.

[90] United Nations Committee on the Elimination of Racial Discrimination, cited in Australian Human Rights Commission, 'International review of Indigenous issues in 2000'.

[91] Australian Human Rights Commission, 'International review of Indigenous issues in 2000'; see also Melissa Nobles, *The Politics of Official Apologies*, Cambridge University Press, New York, 2008, pp 93–9.

[92] Justice Peter McLennan, '2014 Families Australia oration', 31 March 2014, Melbourne, available at: http://www.childabuseroyalcommission.gov.au/media-centre/speeches/2014-families-australia-oration (accessed 27 May 2014).

Chapter Four

[1] Ray, interviewed by Suellen Murray, 15 March 2011, Melbourne.

[2] In this chapter, the focus is on state-offered apologies. Other apologies have been offered by the Church and other organisations that ran care institutions; for example, in Australia, see Care Leavers Australia Network, Senate Community Affairs References Committee, *Forgotten Australians: A Report on Australians who Experienced Institutional or Out-of-Home Care as Children*, Commonwealth of Australia, Canberra, 2004, pp 187–91; in New Zealand, see Catholic Church in Aotearoa New Zealand, 'Confronting abuse', available at: http://www.catholic.org.nz/nzcbc/dsp-default.cfm?loadref=32 (accessed 27 May

2014); in Canada, see CBC News, 'A history of residential schools in Canada', available at: http://www.cbc.ca/news/canada/a-history-of-residential-schools-in-canada-1.702280 (accessed 27 May 2014).

[3] Law Commission of Canada, *Restoring Dignity: Responding to Child Abuse in Canadian Institutions*, Minister of Public Works and Government Services, Ottawa, 2000, p 81.

[4] Law Commission of Canada, *Restoring Dignity*, p 81.

[5] Law Commission of Canada, *Restoring Dignity*, pp 80–1.

[6] Michael Murphy, 'Apology, recognition and reconciliation', *Human Rights Review*, no 12, 2011, pp 47–69, 53.

[7] Law Commission of Canada, *Restoring Dignity*, p 83.

[8] Alice MacLachlan, 'The state of "sorry": official apologies and their absence', *Journal of Human Rights*, no 9, 2010, pp 373–85, 376.

[9] Michael Cunningham, 'Saying sorry: the politics of apology', *Political Quarterly*, vol 70, no 3, 1999, pp 285–93, 289.

[10] Jan Löfström, 'Historical apologies as acts of symbolic inclusion – and exclusion? Reflections on institutional apologies as politics of cultural citizenship', *Citizenship Studies*, vol 15, no 1, 2011, pp 93–108, 94.

[11] Löfström, 'Historical apologies as acts of symbolic inclusion', p 96.

[12] MacLachlan, 'The state of "sorry"', p 374.

[13] Melissa Nobles, 'Reparation claims: politics by another name', *Political Power and Social Theory*, vol 18, 2007, pp 253–8, 254.

[14] Michael Cunningham, 'Apologies in Irish politics: a commentary and critique', *Contemporary British History*, vol 18, no 4, 2004, pp 80–92, 89; regarding 'transgenerational responsibility', see also Janna Thompson, *Taking Responsibility for the Past: Reparation and Historical Injustice*, Polity Press, Cambridge, 2002, cited in Cunningham, 'Apologies in Irish politics', p 89.

[15] Michael Murphy, 'Apology, recognition and reconciliation', pp 49–50.

[16] For objections to apologies, see Cunningham, 'Saying sorry'; see also Cunningham, 'Apologies in Irish politics'.

[17] Murphy, 'Apology, recognition and reconciliation', p 54.

[18] Dacia Viejo-Rose, 'Memorial functions: intent, impact and the right to remember', *Memory Studies*, no 4, 2011, pp 465–80, 469.

[19] Damien Short, 'When sorry isn't enough: official remembrance and reconciliation in Australia', *Memory Studies*, no 5, 2012, pp 293–304, 296.

[20] Emilie Pine, *The Politics of Irish Memory: Performing Remembrance in Contemporary Irish Culture*, Palgrave Macmillan, Basingstoke, 2011, p 3.

[21] Viejo-Rose, 'Memorial functions', p 469.

[22] Pine, *The Politics of Irish Memory*, p 4.

[23] Viejo-Rose, 'Memorial functions', p 466.

[24] Paul Ashton and Paula Hamilton, 'Memorials, public history and the state in Australia since 1960', *Public History Review*, vol 15, 2008, pp 1–29, 3.

[25] Joanne Laws, 'Memorial to the victims of abuse while in residential care', Publicart.ie, November 2013, available at: http://www.publicart.ie/main/ thinking/writing/writing/view//292a91ec0db768523e90722a44a43a95/? tx_pawritings_uid=3 (accessed 19 January 2014).

[26] Law Commission of Canada, *Restoring Dignity*, pp 95–6.

[27] Commission to Inquire into Child Abuse (CICA), *Commission to Inquire into Child Abuse Report*, vol 1 (Investigation Committee Report), Government of Ireland, Dublin, 2009, p 1.

[28] Office of the Minister for Children and Youth Affairs, *Report of the Commission to Inquire into Child Abuse, 2009: Implementation Plan*, Minister for Children and Health, Dublin, 2009, p xi.

[29] Jane Stewart, 'Notes for an address by the Honourable Jane Stewart, Minister of Indian Affairs and Northern Development, on the occasion of the unveiling of Gathering Strength – Canada's Aboriginal Action Plan', 7 January 1998, available at: http://sisis.nativeweb.org/clark/jan0798can.html (accessed 27 May 2014).

[30] Murphy, 'Apology, recognition and reconciliation', p 55.

[31] Neil Funk-Unrau, 'The Canadian apology to Indigenous Residential School survivors: a case study of renegotiation of social relations', in Mihaela Mihai and Mathais Thaler (eds), *On the Uses and Abuses of Apologies*, Palgrave Macmillan, Basingstoke, pp 141–2; MacLachlan, 'The state of "sorry"', p 379.

[32] Prime Minister of Canada, 'Prime Minister Harper offers full apology on behalf of Canadians for the Indian Residential Schools system', 11 June 2008, available at: http://www.pm.gc.ca/eng/news/2008/06/11/prime-minister-harper-offers-full-apology-behalf-canadians-indian-residential (accessed 27 May 2014).

[33] MacLachlan, 'The state of "sorry"', p 379 (emphasis in original).

[34] Aboriginal Affairs and Northern Development Canada, 'Settlement Agreement', available at: http://www.aadnc-aandc.gc.ca/ eng/1100100015638/1100100015639 (accessed 27 May 2014).

[35] For an evaluation of the effects of the Canadian apology, see Melissa Nobles, 'Revisiting the "Membership Theory of Apologies": apology politics in Australia and Canada', in Mihaela Mihai and Mathais Thaler (eds), *On the Uses and Abuses of Apologies*, Palgrave Macmillan, Basingstoke, 2014, pp 123–5.

[36] British Home Children in Canada, 'Apology petition to the House of Commons in Parliament assembled', available at: http://canadianbritishhomechildren.weebly.com/apology-petition.html (accessed 27 May 2014).

[37] 'Canadians not interested in "home children" apology: minister', *The Star*, 16 November 2009, available at: http://www.thestar.com/news/canada/2009/11/16/canadians_not_interested_in_home_children_apology_minister.html (accessed 27 May 2014).

[38] See, for example, Canadian Museum of Immigration at Pier 21, 'Online story collection: British home children', available at: http://www.pier21.ca/research/collections/online-story-collection/british-home-children (accessed 27 May 2014).

[39] BBC News, 'Gordon Brown apologises to child migrants sent abroad', available at: http://news.bbc.co.uk/2/hi/uk_news/8531664.stm (accessed 27 May 2014).

[40] BBC News, 'Gordon Brown apologises'.

[41] 'Kevin Rudd's national apology to Stolen Generations', *Australian*, 13 February 2008, available at: http://www.news.com.au/national/pm-moves-to-heal-the-nation/story-e6frfkw9-1111115539560 (accessed 27 May 2014).

[42] Denise Cuthbert and Marian Quartly, '"Forced adoption" in the Australian story of national regret and apology', *Australian Journal of Politics and History*, vol 58, no 1, 2012, pp 82–96, 86.

[43] Cuthbert and Quartly, '"Forced adoption"', p 86; see also, National Sorry Day Committee, 'History of Sorry Day', available at: http://www.nsdc.org.au/events-info/history-of-national-sorry-day (accessed 27 May 2014).

[44] Christine Fejo-King, 'The national apology to the Stolen Generations: the ripple effect', *Australian Social Work*, vol 64, no 1, 2011, pp 130–43.

[45] Australian Government, 'Apology to Australia's Indigenous people', 13 February 2008, available at: http://australia.gov.au/about-australia/our-country/our-people/apology-to-australias-Indigenous-peoples (accessed 27 May 2014).

[46] A. Dirk Moses, 'Official apologies, reconciliation and settler colonialism: Australian Indigenous alterity and political agency', *Citizenship Studies*, vol 15, no 2, pp 145–59, 152.

[47] Short, 'When sorry isn't enough', p 298.

[48] For a critique of the Northern Territory intervention, which arose out of an inquiry into child abuse, see Jon Altman and Melinda Hinckson (eds), *Coercive Reconciliation: Stabilise, Normalise, Exit Aboriginal Australia*, Arena Publications, Melbourne, 2007; Fejo-King, 'The national apology to the Stolen Generations'; for further critique, see Nobles, 'Revisiting the "Membership Theory of Apologies"', pp 128–33.

[49] Cuthbert and Quartly, '"Forced adoption"', p 83.

[50] Denise Cuthbert and Marian Quartly, 'Forced child removal and the politics of national apologies in Australia', *American Indian Quarterly*, vol 37, no 1/2, 2013, pp 178–202, 185.

[51] Cuthbert and Quartly, 'Forced child removal', p 190.

[52] For further discussion of the previously 'institutionalised' as 'innocent children', see also Melissa Nobles, *The Politics of Official Apologies*, Cambridge University Press, New York, 2008, cited in and quoted from Cuthbert and Quartly, '"Forced adoption"', p 95.

[53] Cuthbert and Quartly, 'Forced child removal', p 197.

[54] Cuthbert and Quartly, 'Forced child removal', p 198.

[55] Cuthbert and Quartly, 'Forced child removal', p 193; see also Nobles, *The Politics of Official Apologies*.

[56] Aboriginal Affairs and Northern Development, 'Fact sheet – Indian Residential Schools Settlement Agreement', available at: http://www.aadnc-aandc.gc.ca/eng/1332949137290/1332949312397 (accessed 27 May 2014).

[57] See, for example, Aboriginal Affairs and Northern Development, 'Commemoration 2012–2013 – project descriptions', available at: http://www.aadnc-aandc.gc.ca/eng/1370974253896/1370974471675 (accessed 27 May 2014).

[58] Government of Canada, 'Stained glass window in Parliament commemorating the legacy of the Indian Residential Schools', available at: http://www.aadnc-aandc.gc.ca/eng/1354805080035/1354805131174 (accessed 27 May 2014).

[59] Office of Public Works, 'Memorial to victims of abuse while in residential care: international competition', available at: http://www.education.ie/en/Learners/Information/Former-Residents-of-Industrial-Schools/Memorial-for-Survivors-of-Institutional-Abuse-Expressions-of-Interest.pdf (accessed 27 May 2014).

[60] 'Abuse memorial – a slap in the face for survivors', *Irish Examiner*, 28 November 2013, available at: http://www.irishexaminer.com/archives/2013/1128/opinion/abuse-memorial-a-slap-in-the-face-for-survivors-250938.html (accessed 27 May 2014); see also Paul Melia, 'Memorial to victims of abuse rejected on appeal', *Independent*, 28 November 2013, available at: http://www.independent.ie/irish-news/memorial-to-victims-of-abuse-rejected-on-appeal-29790979.html (accessed 27 May 2014).

[61] HREOC, *Bringing Them Home*, Recommendation 7a.

[62] National Capital Authority, 'Reconciliation Place', available at: http://www.nationalcapital.gov.au/index.php?Itemid=203 (accessed 27 May 2014).

[63] National Capital Authority, 'Artwork 3 – Separation', available at: http://www.nationalcapital.gov.au/index.php?Itemid=203 (accessed 27 May 2014). There was criticism of the memorials, see, for example, Debra Johnson and Michael Bradley, 'Stolen Generations fury at memorial "whitewash"', *Sydney Morning Herald*, 27 May 2002, available at: http://www.smh.com.au/articles/2002/05/26/1022243291792.html (accessed 27 May 2014).

[64] See, for example, Royal Botanic Gardens Sydney, 'Stolen Generations memorial', available at: www.rbgsyd.nsw.gov.au/__data/assets/pdf_file/0016/101464/Panel_36,_37.pdf (accessed 27 May 2014).

[65] Australian Government, 'Australian Government Responses to the Committee's Reports'; Coral Dow and Janet Phillips, *'Forgotten Australians' and 'Lost Innocents': Child Migrants and Children in Institutional Care in Australia*, Parliament of Australia, Canberra, 2009, available at: http://www.aph.gov.au/About_Parliament/Parliamentary_Departments/Parliamentary_Library/pubs/BN/0910/ChildMigrants?print=1 (accessed 27 May 2014).

[66] Government of Western Australia, 'Memorial for former child migrants', available at: http://www.mediastatements.wa.gov.au/pages/StatementDetails.aspx?listName=StatementsGallop&StatId=3966 (accessed 17 January 2014).

[67] Alliance for Forgotten Australians, 'Monuments', available at: http://www.forgottenaustralians.org.au/monuments.html (accessed 27 May 2014).

[68] Allan Laing, 'Survivors win memorial at last for forgotten orphans. Nuns agree to fund tribute to infants who died after year-long campaign', *Herald Scotland*, 23 April 2004, available at: http://www.heraldscotland.com/sport/spl/aberdeen/survivors-win-memorial-at-last-for-forgotten-orphans-nuns-agree-to-fund-tribute-to-infants-who-died-after-year-long-campaign-1.87468 (accessed 27 May 2014); see also Care Leavers' Association, 'Care leavers gather to commemorate children from the Smyllum orphanage', available at: http://www.careleavers.com/news/19-events/190-smyllum (accessed 27 May 2014).

[69] Laing, 'Survivors win memorial'.

[70] Other ways that time in care and its aftermath have been memorialised and remembered are through art, biographical works and plays; for a discussion of these in Ireland, see Pine, *The Politics of Memory*, ch 1.

[71] Alan S. Marcus, 'Representing the past and reflecting the present: museums, memorials, and the secondary history classroom', *Social Studies*, May/June 2007, pp 105–10, 105–6; MacLachlan, 'The state of "sorry"', p 374.

[72] National Museum of Australia, 'Inside: Life in Children's Homes and Institutions', available at: http://www.nma.gov.au/exhibitions/inside_life_in_childrens_homes_and_institutions/home (accessed 27 May 2014).

[73] Care Leavers Australia Network, 'CLAN National Orphanage Museum', available at: http://www.clan.org.au/reference/museum (accessed 14 October 2015).

74 National Library of Australia, 'Bringing Them Home oral history project', available at: http://pandora.nla.gov.au/pan/133365/20120410-1246/www.nla.gov.au/oh/bth/index.html (accessed 27 May 2014).

75 Doreen Mellor and Anna Haebich, *Many Voices: Reflections on Experiences of Indigenous Child Separation*, National Library of Australia, Canberra, 2002.

76 National Library of Australia, 'Forgotten Australians and former child migrants oral history project', available at: http://www.nla.gov.au/oral-history/forgotten-australians-and-former-child-migrants-oral-history-project (accessed 27 May 2014); National Library of Australia, *'You Can't Forget Things Like That'*, *Forgotten Australians and Former Child Migrants Oral History Project*, Australian Government, Canberra, 2012.

77 Commercially produced films, while not in the ambit of official acknowledgements, can also be very useful forms of acknowledgement and public education. For example, *Oranges and Sunshine* (2010) depicted the suffering of child migration, and its aftermath, and paid particular attention to the work of the Child Migrants Trust, initiated by Margaret Humphreys. In relation to Indigenous children, *Rabbit-Proof Fence* (2002) in Australia and *We Were Children* (2012) in Canada present powerful narratives about experiences of care.

78 Canada Post, 'Home children', available at: http://www.canadapost.ca/cpo/mc/personal/collecting/stamps/2010/2010_home_children.jsf (accessed 27 May 2014).

79 Canadian Centre for Home Children, 'January – Year of the Home Child', available at: http://www.canadianhomechildren.ca/index.php (accessed 27 May 2014) (capitalisation in original).

80 Government of Canada, 'News release – government of Canada designates 2010 as the Year of the British Home Child', available at: http://www.cic.gc.ca/ENGLISH/department/media/releases/2010/2010-01-26a.asp (accessed 14 January 2014). Canadian organisations ran events to celebrate the Year of the British Home Child with a similar focus, such as Edmonton Public Library, 'Year of the Home Child', available at: http://www.epl.ca/homechild (accessed 28 May 2014).

81 Service Ontario, 'British Home Child Act, 2011', available at: http://www.e-laws.gov.on.ca/html/statutes/english/elaws_statutes_11b14_e.htm (accessed 28 May 2014).

82 Jim Coyle, 'Story of home children part of our history', *Ontario Star*, 22 February 2010, available at: http://www.thestar.com/news/ontario/2010/02/22/coyle_story_of_home_children_part_of_our_history.html (accessed 28 May 2014).

[83] Ministry of Children and Youth Services, 'British Home Child Day – 28 September', available at: http://www.children.gov.on.ca/htdocs/English/britishhomechildday/index.aspx (accessed 28 May 2014).

[84] Personal correspondence, Communications and Marketing Branch, Ministry of Children and Youth Services, Ontario, 15 January 2014; St Lawrence Parks Commission, 'Upper Canada Village: British Home Child Day', available at: http://www.uppercanadavillage.com/index.cfm/en/activities/special-events/british-home-child-day/ (accessed 14 January 2014). Upper Canada Village is a recreation of an 1860s' English Canadian town and is a major tourist attraction and historical site.

[85] Law Commission of Canada, *Restoring Dignity*, p 75.

[86] Truth and Reconciliation Commission of Canada (TRCC), 'The Truth and Reconciliation Commission of Canada', available at: http://www.trc.ca/websites/trcinstitution/index.php?p=3 (accessed 28 May 2014).

[87] TRCC, 'Residential Schools', available at: http://www.trc.ca/websites/trcinstitution/index.php?p=4 (accessed 28 May 2014).

[88] TRCC, *Truth and Reconciliation Commission of Canada: Interim Report*, TRCC, Winnipeg, 2012, p 18; see also TRCC, *They Came for the Children: Canada, Aboriginal Peoples and Residential Schools*, TRCC, Winnipeg, 2012.

[89] Aboriginal Healing Foundation (AHF), 'Vision, mission, values', available at: http://www.ahf.ca/about-us/mission (accessed 28 May 2014).

[90] Another resource is AHF, *Speaking My Truth: Reflections on Reconciliation and Residential Schools*, AHF, Ottawa, 2012.

[91] Alliance for Forgotten Australians, 'Forgotten Australians: life stories', available at: http://www.forgottenaustralians.org.au/dvd.htm (accessed 28 May 2014).

Chapter Five

[1] Royal Commission into Institutional Responses to Child Sexual Abuse (RCIRCSA), 'Issues papers – next steps', released 6 December 2013, p 1, available at: www.childabuseroyalcommission.gov.au/.../Issues-Paper-Next-Steps.pdf (accessed 26 January 2014).

[2] Stephen Winter, *Transitional Justice in Established Democracies: A Political Theory*, Palgrave Macmillan, Basingstoke, 2014, p 7.

[3] RCIRCSA, 'Issues papers', p 1; see also Kathleen Daly, *Redressing Institutional Abuse of Children*, Palgrave Macmillan, Basingstoke, 2014, pp 115–16.

[4] 'Redress' and 'reparation' are used interchangeably. Here, I use the term more narrowly than, for example, the Law Commission of Canada or the Royal Commission into Institutional Responses to Child Sexual Abuse.

[5] Law Commission of Canada, *Restoring Dignity: Responding to Child Abuse in Canadian Institutions*, Minister of Public Works and Government Services, Ottawa, 2000, p 109.

[6] Reg Graycar and Jane Wangmann, 'Redress packages for institutional child abuse: exploring the Grandview Agreement as a case study in "alternative" dispute resolution', Sydney Law School Research Paper No 07/50, University of Sydney, Sydney, 2007, pp 1–53, 5.

[7] Graycar and Wangmann, 'Redress packages for institutional child abuse', p 4.

[8] Kathleen Daly suggests that negotiation was not a characteristic of the Australian redress schemes, but she notes that 'there is too little information to know what precisely happened in the early phases of redress scheme creation'; Daly, *Redressing Institutional Abuse of Children*, p 123.

[9] Graycar and Wangmann, 'Redress packages for institutional child abuse', pp 6–7.

[10] Graycar and Wangmann, 'Redress packages for institutional child abuse', p 15.

[11] Nathalie Des Rosiers, 'Moving forward with dignity: the report of the Law Commission of Canada and its aftermath', Australian Human Rights Commission, 'Moving forward – achieving reparations for the Stolen Generations' conference, August 2001, p 5, available at: http://www.humanrights.gov.au/moving-forward-dignity-report-law-commission-canada-and-its-aftermath (accessed 28 May 2014).

[12] Des Rosiers, 'Moving forward with dignity', p 4.

[13] Jennifer J. Llewellyn, 'Dealing with the legacy of native residential school abuse in Canada: litigation, ADR, and restorative justice', *University of Toronto Law Journal*, vol 52, no 3, 2002, pp 253–300, 253; see also Margaret Hall, 'Book review: Law Commission of Canada, *Restoring Dignity: Responding to Child Abuse in Canadian Institutions*', *International Journal of Children's Rights*, vol 10, no 3, 2002, pp 295–302, 295; Margaret Hall, 'The liability of public authorities for the abuse of children in institutional care: common law developments in Canada and the United Kingdom', *International Journal of Law, Policy and the Family*, no 14, 2000, pp 281–301.

[14] Simon Collins, 'Calls for abuse claims commission', *New Zealand Herald*, 21 April 2011, available at: http://www.nzherald.co.nz/nz/news/article.cfm?c_id=1&objectid=10720704 (accessed 28 May 2014). This also occurs elsewhere, see, for example, Llewellyn, 'Dealing with the legacy of native residential school abuse', pp 268–9.

[15] Collins, 'Calls for abuse claims commission'.

[16] Hall, 'Book review', p 298; see also Hall, 'The liability of public authorities for the abuse of children in institutional care'.

[17] Ben Matthews, 'Queensland government actions to compensate survivors of institutional abuse: a critical and comparative evaluation', *QUT Law and Justice Journal*, vol 4, no 1, 2004, pp 23–45, 28.

[18] Compensation Advisory Committee, *Towards Redress and Recovery: Report to the Minister for Education and Science*, Government of Ireland, Dublin, 2002, pp v–vi.

[19] Des Rosiers, 'Moving forward with dignity', pp 5–6.

[20] Law Commission of Canada, *Restoring Dignity*, p 391.

[21] Law Commission of Canada, *Restoring Dignity*, p 92.

[22] Des Rosiers, 'Moving forward with dignity', p 5.

[23] See, for example, Gail Green, Janice MacKenzie, Dion Leeuwenburg and Julie Watts, 'Reflections from the Redress WA experience in light of the Royal Commission into Institutional Responses to Child Sexual Abuse', *Australian Association of Social Workers, Western Australian Branch, e-News*, May 2014, p 7, available at: http://www.aasw.asn.au/document/item/5904 (accessed 22 June 2014); Martina O'Riordan and Ella Arensman, *Institutional Child Sexual Abuse and Suicidal Behaviour: Outcomes of a Literature Review, Consultation Meetings and a Qualitative Study*, National Suicide Research Foundation, Cork, 2007, p 25; RCIRCSA, *Consultation Paper*, p 159.

[24] Law Commission of Canada, *Restoring Dignity*, p 92.

[25] Graycar and Wangmann, 'Redress packages for institutional child abuse', pp 49–50.

[26] Compensation Advisory Committee, 'Towards redress and recovery', p vi, citing the Residential Institutions Redress Bill 2001; see also Residential Institutions Redress Board (RIRB), *A Guide to the Redress Scheme Under the Residential Institutions Redress Act, 2002 as Amended by the Commission to Inquire into Child Abuse (Amendment) Act, 2005* (3rd edn), RIRB, Dublin, 2005.

[27] Law Commission of Canada, *Restoring Dignity*, pp 392–3.

[28] Law Commission of Canada, *Restoring Dignity*, pp 391–2; see also Graycar and Wangmann, 'Redress packages for institutional child abuse', pp 40–5.

[29] For an alternative means of classifying redress schemes, see Daly, *Redressing Institutional Abuse of Children*, pp 25–51. Daly classifies according to whether: authorities failed to protect and care for children; wrongs were committed against certain groups of children; or these wrongs were embedded in discrimination against a minority group.

[30] See Joanna Penglase, *Orphans of the Living: Growing up in 'Care' in Twentieth-Century Australia*, Fremantle Arts Centre Press, Fremantle, 2005, pp 59–60, cited in Daly, *Redressing Institutional Abuse of Children*, p 3.

[31] See, for example, Amanda Cornwall, *Restoring Identity: Final Report of the Moving Forward Consultation Project*, Public Interest Advocacy Centre, Sydney, 2009; Lisa R. Jackson and Sally A. Fitzpatrick, 'Beyond *Sorry*: the first steps in laying claim to a future that embraces all Australians', *Medical Journal of Australia*, vol 188, no 10, 2008, pp 556–8; Richard Hil and Elizabeth Branigan (eds), *Surviving Care: Achieving Justice and Healing for the Forgotten Australians*, Bond University Press, Gold Coast, 2010.

[32] See RCIRCSA, *Consultation Paper: Redress and Civil Litigation*, RCIRCSA, Sydney, 2015.

[33] Coral Dow and Janet Phillips, *'Forgotten Australians' and 'Lost Innocents': Child Migrants and Children in Institutional Care in Australia*, Parliament of Australia, Canberra, 2009, available at: http://www.aph.gov.au/About_Parliament/Parliamentary_Departments/Parliamentary_Library/pubs/BN/0910/ChildMigrants?print=1 (accessed 27 May 2014).

[34] TVNZ, 'NZ govt statement regarding child migrants', One News, 16 November 2009, available at: http://tvnz.co.nz/national-news/nz-govt-statement-regarding-child-migrants-3148096 (accessed 27 May 2014).

[35] Graycar and Wangmann, 'Redress packages for institutional child abuse', p 2; see also Aboriginal Affairs and Northern Development Canada, 'Indian residential schools – key milestones', available at: http://www.aadnc-aandc.gc.ca/eng/1332939430258/1332939552554 (accessed 1 June 2014); Neil Funk-Unrau, 'The Canadian apology to Indigenous Residential School survivors: a case study of renegotiation of social relations', in Mihaela Mihai and Mathais Thaler (eds), *On the Uses and Abuses of Apologies*, Palgrave Macmillan, Basingstoke, pp 143–4; Llewellyn, 'Dealing with the legacy of native residential school abuse in Canada'.

[36] Goldie Shea, *Redress Programs Relating to Institutional Child Abuse in Canada*, Law Commission of Canada, Ottawa, 1999, pp 9–10.

[37] Dow and Phillips, *'Forgotten Australians' and 'Lost Innocents'*.

[38] Lotus Place, 'Lotus Place', available at: http://www.lotusplace.org.au (accessed 29 May 2014).

[39] Aboriginal Affairs and Northern Development Canada, 'Common Experience Payments', available at: https://www.aadnc-aandc.gc.ca/eng/1100100015594/1100100015595 (accessed 29 May 2014).

[40] Graycar and Wangmann, 'Redress packages for institutional child abuse', pp 10–11.

[41] Graycar and Wangmann, 'Redress packages for institutional child abuse', pp 13–15.

[42] Graycar and Wangmann, 'Redress packages for institutional child abuse', pp 16–19, 32.

[43] Child Migrants Trust, 'Family Restoration Fund', available at: http://www. childmigrantstrust.com/services/family-restoration-fund (accessed 29 May 2014).

[44] Compensation Advisory Committee, 'Towards redress and recovery', pp vii–viii.

[45] Caranua, 'Caranua: support for survivors of institutional abuse', available at: http://www.caranua.ie (accessed 29 May 2014).

[46] Green et al, 'Reflections from the Redress WA experience'.

[47] Ministry of Social Development, 'Historic claims', available at: http://www. msd.govt.nz/about-msd-and-our-work/contact-us/complaints/cyf-historic-claims.html (accessed 29 May 2014); Kerryn Pollock, 'Children's homes and fostering – experiences of institutional and foster care', Te Ara – the Encyclopedia of New Zealand, available at: http://www.teara.govt.nz/en/ childrens-homes-and-fostering/page-5 (accessed 29 May 2014).

[48] Indian Residential Schools Settlement Agreement, 'Guide to the Independent Assessment Process application'.

[49] Aboriginal Affairs and Northern Development Canada, 'Statistics on the implementation of the Indian Residential Schools Settlement Agreement'.

[50] BBC News, 'Irish redress scheme', available at: http://news.bbc.co.uk/2/hi/ programmes/law_in_action/8139216.stm (accessed 22 June 2014).

[51] Aboriginal Affairs and Northern Development Canada, 'Government of Canada Indian Residential Schools Settlement Agreement outreach and public education activities', available at: http://www.aadnc-aandc.gc.ca/ eng/1319729483116/1319729524914 (accessed 29 May 2014). Redress WA is an example of where it became evident that the dissemination processes were inadequate; see Green et al, 'Reflections from the Redress WA experience', p 2.

[52] Pauline Bagdonavicius, 'Looking back: looking forward – lessons learnt from Redress', paper presented at the 29th Australian and New Zealand Association of Psychiatry, Psychology and Law Congress, Fremantle, 27 November 2009.

[53] Bagdonavicius, 'Looking back: looking forward'.

[54] Law Commission of Canada, Restoring Dignity, p 110.

[55] Law Commission of Canada, Restoring Dignity, p 112.

[56] Matthew Colton, Maurice Vanstone and Christine Walby, 'Victimization, care and justice: reflections on the experiences of victims/survivors involved in large-scale historical investigations of child sexual abuse in residential institutions', British Journal of Social Work, vol 32, 2002, pp 541–51; Green et al, 'Reflections from the Redress WA experience'; O'Riordan and Arensman, Institutional Child Sexual Abuse and Suicidal Behaviour.

[57] Green et al, 'Reflections from the Redress WA experience', p 7.

[58] O'Riordan and Arensman, *Institutional Child Sexual Abuse and Suicidal Behaviour*, p 25.

[59] O'Riordan and Arensman, *Institutional Child Sexual Abuse and Suicidal Behaviour*, p 25.

[60] Green et al, 'Reflections from the Redress WA experience', pp 5–6.

[61] Green et al, 'Reflections from the Redress WA experience', p 2; see also RCIRCSA, *Consultation Paper*, p 135.

[62] Green et al, 'Reflections from the Redress WA experience', p 8; this was also noted in Ireland, see O'Riordan and Arensman, *Institutional Child Sexual Abuse and Suicidal Behaviour*, p 24.

[63] Green et al, 'Reflections from the Redress WA experience', pp 1–2.

[64] Green et al, 'Reflections from the Redress WA experience', p 2.

[65] Law Commission of Canada, *Restoring Dignity*, p 111; see also Andrew Kendrick and Moyra Hawthorn, 'Dilemmas of care: social work and historic abuse', in Johanna Sköld and Shurlee Swain (eds), *Apologies and the Legacies of Abuse of Children in 'Care'*, Palgrave Macmillan, Basingstoke, 2015.

[66] Green et al, 'Reflections from the Redress WA experience', p 7; see also Shurlee Swain, 'Transitional justice workers and vicarious trauma', in Johanna Sköld and Shurlee Swain (eds), *Apologies and the Legacies of Abuse of Children in 'Care'*, Palgrave Macmillan, Basingstoke, 2015.

Chapter Six

[1] Caroline Carroll, 'Unbearable cost', letters to the editor, *Sunday Age*, 27 July 2014, p 32.

[2] Martina O'Riordan and Ella Arensman, *Institutional Child Sexual Abuse and Suicidal Behaviour: Outcomes of a Literature Review, Consultation Meetings and a Qualitative Study*, National Suicide Research Foundation, Cork, 2007, p 25.

[3] Pamela O'Connor, 'Squaring the circle: how Canada is dealing with the legacy of its Indian Residential Schools experiment', *Australian Journal of Human Rights*, vol 6, no 1, 2000, pp 188–211, 195.

[4] Reg Graycar and Jane Wangmann, 'Redress packages for institutional abuse: exploring the Grandview Agreement as a case study in "alternative" dispute resolution', Sydney Law School, Legal Studies Research Paper No 07/50, University of Sydney Law School, Sydney, 2007, pp 1–53, 5.

[5] Thanos Karatzias, *In Care Survivors Service Scotland (ICSSS) Evaluation*, Napier University, Edinburgh, 2011, p 37.

[6] Roger Tucker, *Civil Liability for Sexual Assault in an Institutional Setting*, Canadian Institute Publications, Toronto, 1994, p 17, cited in Institute for

Human Resource Development, *Review of 'The Needs of Victims of Institutional Child Abuse'*, Law Commission of Canada, Ottawa, 1998, p 119. The importance of counselling and psychological care is also noted in RCIRCSA, *Consultation Paper*, ch 5.

[7] See, for example, the way in which the Irish Association for Counselling and Psychotherapy (IACP) distinguishes between the two: counselling is concerned 'more with immediate issues that may have arisen more recently'; psychotherapy, on the other hand, 'tends to deal with deeper, more long-term issues that may be rooted in the past'. See IACP, '"Talk to us": a guide to counselling and psychotherapy', IACP brochure, 2010.

[8] Health Canada, First Nations and Inuit Health, 'Indian Residential Schools Resolution Health Support Program', available at: http://www.hc-sc.gc.ca/fniah-spnia/services/indiresident/irs-pi-eng.php (accessed 29 May 2014).

[9] Historical Abuse Institutional Inquiry, 'Frequently asked questions', available at: http://www.hiainquiry.org/index/frequently-asked-questions.htm (accessed 30 May 2014).

[10] Historical Abuse Institutional Inquiry, 'Frequently asked questions'.

[11] RCIRCSA, 'Support services', available at: http://www.childabuseroyalcommission.gov.au/support/support-services/ (accessed 8 January 2014).

[12] Law Commission of Canada, *Restoring Dignity*, p 89.

[13] RCIRCSA, *Consultation Paper*, p 111.

[14] National Counselling Service, 'About our services', available at: http://www.hse-ncs.ie/en/ (accessed 29 May 2014).

[15] National Counselling Service, *Second Report*, Health Boards Executive, Dublin, 2004, p 6.

[16] Health Service Research Centre, *SENCS: Survivors' Experiences of the National Counselling Service*, Health Boards Executive, Dublin, 2003, p 3; see also National Counselling Service, *First Report*, Health Boards Executive, Dublin, 2002; National Counselling Service, *Second Report*. Even though this evaluation is a decade old, similar issues were reported in my meetings with advocates and service providers in Ireland in 2013. More recent data were not available.

[17] Connect, *Connect Service Report 2006–2010*, Connect, Dublin, 2011, p 4: see also Connect, *Connect: The National Adults Counselling Service – A Service Evaluation, Executive Summary*, Connect, Dublin, 2009.

[18] Connect, *Connect Service Report 2006–2010*, pp 9–10; Connect, *Connect: The National Adults Counselling Service*, pp v–vi.

[19] Connect, *Connect Service Report 2006–2010*, pp 6–7.

[20] See, for example, IACP's accreditation requirements: IACP, 'A guide to professional accreditation and membership', IACP brochure, 2010.

[21] Towards Healing, *Counselling and Support Services, Annual Report for 2012*, Towards Healing, Dublin, 2012.

[22] Towards Healing, *Counselling and Support Services, Annual Report for 2012*, p 5.

[23] Goldie Shea, *Redress Programs Relating to Institutional Child Abuse in Canada*, Law Commission of Canada, Ottawa, 1999, pp 9–10; Residential Historic Abuse Program, *Guidelines for Therapists*, Vancouver Coastal Health Authority, Vancouver, 2012; see also the Residential Historical Abuse Program brochure and application form, available at: http://vch.eduhealth.ca/%5CPDFs%5CCE/ CE.851.S49.pdf (accessed 30 May 2014).

[24] Deborah Leach and Associates, *Evaluation of the Grandview Agreement Process: Final Report*, 1997, p 42, cited in Graycar and Wangmann, 'Redress packages for institutional child abuse', p 23.

[25] Health Canada, 'Indian Residential Schools Resolution Health Support Program', available at: http://www.hc-sc.gc.ca/fniah-spnia/services/ indiresident/irs-pi-eng.php (accessed 30 May 2014). Examples of such work include: Indian Residential School Survivor Society, based in North Vancouver (see: http://irsss.ca/irsss/) and Anish Corporation, based in and around Winnipeg (see: http://anishcorp.ca/).

[26] See Department of Health and Aging (DoHA), *Social and Emotional Wellbeing Program – Handbook for Counsellors*, Commonwealth of Australia, Canberra, 2012; DoHA, *Social and Emotional Wellbeing Program – Handbook for Link Up Service Providers*, Commonwealth of Australia, Canberra, 2012.

[27] DoHA, *Social and Emotional Wellbeing Program – Handbook for Counsellors*, p 7.

[28] In Care Survivors Service Scotland, 'Aim of the National Strategy', background paper provided by ICSSS, September 2013.

[29] ICSSS, 'Service outcomes', background paper provided by ICSSS, September 2013.

[30] ICSSS, 'February to April 2011 – In Care Survivors Service Scotland – focus groups', evaluation report provided by ICSSS, p 2.

[31] ICSSS, 'February to April 2011 – In Care Survivors Service Scotland – focus groups', p 8.

[32] Aislinn Education and Support Centre, 'Aislinn Education Centre Dublin', available at: http://www.aislinneducation.com/ (accessed 14 October 2015).

[33] Right of Place, available at: http://www.rightofplace.com (accessed 30 May 2014).

[34] Irish Survivors Advice and Support Service, brochure.

35 Examples of these services include Wattle Place in Sydney, Open Place in Melbourne and Lotus Place in Brisbane.

36 Forde Foundation, 'Personal development grant: guidelines', available at: http://fordefoundation.org.au/u/lib/cms/guidelines-personal-development-grant-v53.pdf (accessed 30 May 2014); see also Forde Foundation, available at: http://fordefoundation.org.au/

37 See Caranua, available at: http://www.caranua.ie/ (accessed 30 May 2014).

38 Healing Foundation, 'Healing programs', available at: http://healingfoundation.org.au/healing-programs/ (accessed 30 May 2014).

39 Lorraine Peeters, 'The Marumali program: an Aboriginal model of healing', in Nola Purdie, Pat Dudgeon and Roz Walker (eds), *Working Together: Aboriginal and Torres Strait Islander Mental Health and Wellbeing Principles and Practice*, Department of Health Aging (DoHA), Canberra, 2010, pp 285–92, 286.

40 Peeters, 'The Marumali program', p 286.

41 Institute for Human Resource Development, *Review of 'The Needs of Victims of Institutional Child Abuse'*, Law Commission of Canada, Ottawa, 1998, p 54.

42 Institute for Human Resource Development, *Review*, p 54.

43 Law Commission of Canada, *Restoring Dignity*, p 72.

44 Anish Corporation, 'Vision, mission statement and core values and principles'.

45 Open Place, 'Our principles', available at: http://www.openplace.org.au/AboutUs (accessed 26 June 2014). Open Place also has a code of conduct for adult care-leavers who use their service; see Open Place, 'Our code of conduct', available at: http://www.openplace.org.au/OurCodeofConduct (accessed 26 June 2014).

46 For a description of the work of CLAS, see Catherine Masters, 'Treated worse than animals', *Listener*, 25 May 2013, pp 16–21.

47 Alliance for Forgotten Australians (AFA), *Forgotten Australians: Supporting Survivors of Childhood Institutional Care in Australia*, AFA, Canberra, 2008, p 13.

48 Health Service Research Centre, *SENCS*, p iv.

49 Alan Carr, Barbara Dooley, Mark Fitzpatrick, Edel Flanagan, Roisin Flanagan-Howard, Kevin Tierney, Megan White, Margaret Daly and Jonathan Egan, 'Adult adjustment of survivors of institutional abuse in Ireland', *Child Abuse and Neglect*, vol 34, 2010, pp 477–89, 488.

50 RCIRCSA, *Consultation Paper*, pp114–15.

51 RCIRCSA, *Consultation Paper*, p 114; see also Andrew Kendrick and Moyra Hawthorn, 'Dilemmas of care: social work and historic abuse', in Johanna Sköld and Shurlee Swain (eds), *Apologies and the Legacies of Abuse of Children in 'Care'*, Palgrave Macmillan, Basingstoke, 2015.

[52] St Stephens Green Trust, Survivors of Abuse Grant Scheme, 'Summary of projects grantaided – Jan 2012', available at: http://www.ssgt.ie/files/survivor_grant_scheme_2012_projects_summary.pdf (accessed 30 May 2014).

[53] Jeff Moore, Christine Thornton, Mary Hughes and Eugene Waters, *Open Hearts and Open Minds: A Toolkit of Sensitive Practice for Professionals Working with Survivors of Institutional Child Abuse*, London Irish Centre and Immigrant Counselling and Psychotherapy, London, 2014, available at: http://www.icap.org.uk/wp-content/uploads/2014/10/Appendix-3-Open-Hearts-and-Open-Minds.pdf (accessed 7 December 2014).

[54] Winangali-Marumali, 'Marumali program for Aboriginal and Torres Strait Islander service providers (5 days)', available at: http://www.marumali.com.au/workshop-formats (accessed 22 June 2014).

[55] Winangali-Marumali, 'People: Lorraine Peeters, Winangali-Marumali managing director and facilitator', available at: http://marumali.com.au/people (accessed 22 June 2014).

[56] A. Wilczynski, K. Reed-Gilbert, K. Milward, B. Tayler, J. Fear and J. Schartzkoff, *Evaluation of Bringing Them Home and Indigenous Mental Health Programs*, Office for Aboriginal and Torres Strait Islander Health, Department of Health and Aging, Canberra, cited in Peeters, 'The Marumali program', p 287.

[57] AFA, 'Forgotten Australians', available at: http://www.forgottenaustralians.org.au/PDF/MiniAfaBooklet.pdf (accessed 30 May 2014); AFA, 'Forgotten Australians: life stories', available at: http://www.forgottenaustralians.org.au/dvd.htm (accessed 1 June 2014).

[58] Alliance for Forgotten Australians, 'Welcome to the Alliance for Forgotten Australians', available at: http://www.forgottenaustralians.org.au/index.html (accessed 30 May 2014).

[59] AFA, *Forgotten Australians*, frontispiece.

[60] AFA, *Forgotten Australians*, p 4.

Chapter Seven

[1] Roseanne, interviewed by Suellen Murray, 28 March 2011, Ballarat.

[2] Roy Parker, *Uprooted: The Shipment of Poor Children to Canada, 1867–1917*, The Policy Press, Bristol, 2010, p xii.

[3] Parker, *Uprooted*, p 212.

[4] Julia Feast, *Access to Information for Post-care Adults: A Guide for Social Workers and Access to Records Officers (AROs)*, British Association for Adoption and Fostering, London, 2009, p 3.

[5] Suellen Murray, Jenny Malone and Jenny Glare, 'Building a life story: providing records and support to former residents of children's homes', *Australian Social Work*, vol 61, no 3, 2008, pp 239–55, 243.

[6] Murray, Malone and Glare, 'Building a life story'; see also Gill Pugh, *Unlocking the Past: The Impact of Access to Barnardo's Childcare Records*, Ashgate, Aldershot, 1999.

[7] Murray, Malone and Glare, 'Building a life story'; Christine Horrocks and Jim Goddard, 'Adults who grew up in care: constructing the self and accessing care files', *Child and Family Social Work*, vol 11, no 2, 2006, pp 264–72.

[8] Frank Golding, *An Orphan's Escape: Memories of a Lost Childhood*, Lothian, Melbourne, 2005.

[9] While I made it clear in my request for information to record-holders that I was interested in the processes of release, not the records themselves, it was commonly assumed that I wanted to see records. Hence, my experience is probably not that different to an adult care-leaver who was actually trying to find out how to access their records.

[10] Correspondence between anonymous Archive and Suellen Murray, 30 October 2013 (emphasis added).

[11] Tom Shaw, *Historic Abuse Systemic Review: Residential Schools and Children's Homes in Scotland 1950–1995*, Scottish Government, Edinburgh, 2007, p 117. Other inquiries, including the three in Australia, reported similar difficulties.

[12] Correspondence between anonymous Archive and Suellen Murray, 30 October 2013.

[13] See Cathy Humphreys, Gavan McCarthy, Melissa Dowling, Margaret Kertesz and Rachel Tropea, 'Improving the archiving of records in the out-of-home care sector', *Australian Social Work*, vol 67, no 4, 2014, pp 509–24.

[14.] Victorian Auditor-General, *Freedom of Information*, Victorian Government Printer, Melbourne, 2012, p xi, see also pp 33–42; Victorian Ombudsman, *Investigation into the Storage and Management of Ward Records by the Department of Human Services*, Victorian Government Printer, Melbourne, 2012, which expressed similar concerns.

[15] The legislative context regarding records is complex and varies from jurisdiction to jurisdiction. The scope of this book does not allow for a detailed discussion of all relevant laws. (On this, see, eg, in Scotland, Shaw, *Historic Abuse Systemic Review*, pp 123–6.) My main focus is on privacy legislation, both for the benefit it provides and its impact on the information given to adult care-leavers.

[16] Jim Goddard, Suellen Murray and Zachari Duncalf, 'Access to child-care records: a comparative analysis of UK and Australian policy and practice', *British Journal of Social Work*, vol 43, no 4, 2013, pp 759–74.

[17] Jenny Glare, 'Making links with the past: the challenge for a present day child welfare service with a history dating back to the 1850s to provide a background information service to former clients', paper presented at Australian Association of Social Workers conference, 9 November 1998, Melbourne, pp 4–5.

[18] Murray, Malone and Glare, 'Building a life story', pp 242–3.

[19] Suellen Murray and Cathy Humphreys, '"My life's been a total disaster but I feel privileged": care-leavers' access to personal records and their implications for social work practice', *Child and Family Social Work*, vol 19, no 2, 2014, pp 215–24, 221.

[20] Murray and Humphreys, '"My life's been a total disaster"', p 219.

[21] Murray and Humphreys, '"My life's been a total disaster"', p 216.

[22] Derek Kirton, Julia Feast and Jim Goddard, 'The use of discretion in a "Cinderella" service: data protection and access to child-care files for post-care adults', *British Journal of Social Work*, vol 41, no 5, 2011, pp 912–30, 920. For further discussion, see Shurlee Swain and Nell Musgrove, 'We are the stories we tell ourselves: child welfare records and the construction of identity among Australians who, as children, experienced out-of-home "care"', *Archives and Manuscripts*, vol 40, no 1, 2012, pp 4–14, 8–9.

[23] Suellen Murray, 'Compassion and compliance: releasing records to care-leavers under privacy and freedom of information legislation', *Social Policy and Society*, vol 13, no 4, 2014, pp 493–503.

[24] Murray and Humphreys, '"My life's been a total disaster"', p 220.

[25] Algoma University, 'The Shingwauk Project', available at: http://archives.algomau.ca/main/shingwauk_project (accessed 30 May 2014). See also Residential School Research, Archive and Visitors Centre and the Shingwauk Project, 'The Spanish Indian Residential Schools, Spanish, Ontario, photo album 7, student and staff', 2006, available at: http://www.nrsss.ca/Resource_Centre/SpanishIRS/SpanishIRS_STAFF_Dec2007_wm.pdf (accessed 30 May 2014).

[26] Australian Institute of Aboriginal and Torres Strait Islander Studies, 'Collections', available at: http://www.aiatsis.gov.au/collections (accessed 14 October 2015).

[27] AITSIS, 'Search the collection', available at: http://aiatsis.gov.au/collections/using-collection/search-collection (accessed 13 October 2015).

[28] MacKillop Family Services' Heritage and Information Service, discussed later, for example, drew on the family searching and reunion work done with adults who had been adopted as children from St Joseph's Foundling Home, one of the founding agencies of this organisation; see Glare, 'Making links with the past'; see also Liz Trinder, Julia Feast and David Howe, *The Adoption Reunion Handbook*, John Wiley, Chichester, 2004.

29 For further detail on undertaking family reunions, or 'tracing and intermediary services', see Feast, *Access to Information for Post-care Adults*, pp 35–8.

30 Ellen Boucher, *Empire's Children: Child Emigration, Welfare and the Decline of the British World, 1869–1967*, Cambridge University Press, New York, 2014, p 247.

31 DoHA, *Social and Emotional Wellbeing Program: Handbook for Link Up Service Providers*, Commonwealth of Australia, Canberra, 2012, p 1.

32 DoHA, *Social and Emotional Wellbeing Program*, p 20.

33 Peter Read, *A Rape of the Soul so Profound: The Return of the Stolen Generations*, Allen & Unwin, Sydney, 1999, p 72, cited in Keith Windschuttle, 'The impact of Peter Read's pamphlet', available at: http://www.stolengenerations.info/index.php?option=com_content&view=article&id=64&Itemid=19#_ftnref1 (accessed 25 June 2014).

34 The government funding programme now uses the name Link Up; I have retained the original hyphenation.

35 Australian Institute for Aboriginal and Torres Strait Islander Studies, 'Link-Up services', available at: http://aiatsis.gov.au/research/finding-your-family/link-services (accessed 14 October 2015).

36 Office of Aboriginal and Torres Strait Islander Health (OATSIH), *Evaluation of the Bringing Them Home and Indigenous Mental Health Programs: Final Report*, Commonwealth of Australia, Canberra, 2007.

37 DoHA, *Social and Emotional Wellbeing Program – Handbook for Link Up Service Providers*.

38 DOHA, *Social and Emotional Wellbeing Program – Handbook for Link Up Service Providers*, p 3.

39 DoHA, *Social and Emotional Wellbeing Program – Handbook for Link Up Service Providers*, p 3.

40 OATSIH, *Evaluation*, pp 32–3.

41 DoHA, *Social and Emotional Wellbeing Program – Handbook for Link Up Service Providers*, p 25.

42 For a history of MacKillop Family Services and its founding agencies, see Jill Barnard and Karen Twigg, *Holding onto Hope: A History of the Founding Agencies of MacKillop Family Services, 1854–1997*, Australian Scholarly Publishing, Melbourne, 2004.

43 MacKillop Family Services, 'Heritage display', available at: http://www.mackillop.org.au/heritagedisplay (accessed 30 May 2014).

44 MacKillop Family Services, 'Heritage display'.

[45] MacKillop Family Services, 'A message from our founding congregations', available at: https://www.mackillop.org.au/apology-to-former-residents (accessed 14 October 2015).

[46] Child Migrants Trust, 'UK apology to former child migrants, 3rd anniversary', 24 February 2013, available at: http://www.childmigrantstrust.com/news/uk-apology-to-former-child-migrants--3rd-anniversary--24022013 (accessed 30 May 2014).

[47] The account of her experiences is told in her book, Margaret Humphreys, *Empty Cradles*, Doubleday, London, 1994, and the film *Oranges and Sunshine*, directed by Jim Loach.

[48] Child Migrants Trust, 'What we do', available at: http://www.childmigrantstrust.com/our-work/what-we-do (accessed 30 May 2014).

[49] For further discussion on the Child Migrants Trust's funding difficulties, see Senate Community Affairs References Committee, *Lost Innocents: Righting the Record, Inquiry into Child Migration*, Commonwealth of Australia, Canberra, 2001, pp 129–32.

[50] Child Migrant Trust, 'Family Restoration Fund', available at: http://www.childmigrantstrust.com/services/family-restoration-fund (accessed 30 May 2014).

[51] Child Migrants Trust, 'Services', available at: http://www.childmigrantstrust.com/services (accessed 30 May 2014).

[52] AIATSIS, 'Mura® FAQ', available at: http://www.aiatsis.gov.au/collections/faq.html (accessed 30 May 2014).

[53] Find and Connect, 'A resource for Forgotten Australians, former child migrants and anyone interested in the history of child welfare in Australia', available at: http://www.findandconnect.gov.au/ (accessed 30 May 2014). As part of a wider Find and Connect programme, the Australian government has also funded a network of services, some of which were already established, to assist adult care-leavers to access their records. While the intention had also been to provide support to reunite families, the funding available does not allow for this in most instances. For background to the development of Find and Connect, see Michael Jones and Cate O'Neill, 'Identity, records and archival evidence: exploring the needs of Forgotten Australians and former child migrants', *Archives and Records*, vol 35, no 2, 2014, pp 110–25.

[54] See, for example, Library and Archives Canada, 'Conducting research on residential schools: a guide to the records of the Indian and Inuit Affairs Program and related resources at Library and Archives Canada', available at: http://www.collectionscanada.gc.ca/obj/020008/f2/020008-2000-e.pdf (accessed 30 May 2014); Library and Archives Canada, 'Researching your Aboriginal ancestry at Library and Archives Canada', available at: http://www.collectionscanada.gc.ca/obj/022/f2/022-607.002-e.pdf (accessed 30 May 2014).

[55] National Archives of Australia, 'Bringing Them Home name index – fact sheet 175', available at: http://www.naa.gov.au/collection/fact-sheets/fs175.aspx (accessed 30 May 2014).

[56] AIATSIS, 'Fact sheet 8: ABI – Aboriginal and Torres Strait Islander Biographical Index', available at: http://www.aiatsis.gov.au/sites/default/files/docs/family_history/fact_sheet_8_atsi_bio_index.pdf (accessed 14 October 2015).

[57] AIATSIS, 'Family history kit', available at: http://www.aiatsis.gov.au/research/finding-your-family/family-history-kit (accessed 14 October 2015).

[58] Public Records Office Victoria, *Finding Your Story: A Resource Manual to the Records of the Stolen Generations in Victoria*, State of Victoria, Melbourne, 2005.

[59] Lori Oschefski, 'Researching your home child – the basics', available at: http://canadianbritishhomechildren.weebly.com/researching-your-home-child---the-basics.html (accessed 30 May 2014).

[60] Care Leavers' Association (CLA), *It's Your Information! How to View Your Childhood Records: A Guide for Care Leavers*, CLA, Manchester, 2009.

[61] CLA, *CLEARmark Access to Records Quality Mark: A Framework for Improved Services for Care Leavers*, CLA, Manchester, c 2009.

[62] Feast, *Access to Information for Post-care Adults*.

Chapter Eight

[1] Care Leavers Australia Network, 'Why do we protest?', brochure, available at: http://www.clan.org.au/perch/resources/why-do-we-protest-brochure.pdf (accessed 14 October 2015).

[2] Susan Arai, Peggy Hutchinson, Alison Pedlar, John Lord and Val Shepard, 'Shared values, networks and trust among Canadian consumer driven disability organizations', *Disability Studies Quarterly*, vol 28, no 1, 2008, no page.

[3] Angela Guy, 'Case advocacy and active citizenship', *British Columbia Association of Social Workers Newsletter*, Summer 2004, p 1.

[4] Guy, 'Case advocacy and active citizenship', p 1.

[5] Andrew Hewett and John Wiseman, 'Memory, reflection, imagination and action: advocacy and social action in a globalising world', *Just Policy*, September 2000, pp 154–62, 155.

[6] Neil Bateman, *Advocacy Skills for Health and Social Care Professionals*, Jessica Kingsley Publishing, London, 2000, p 18.

[7] Nancy Tomes, 'The patient as a policy factor: a historical case study of the consumer/survivor movement in mental health', *Health Affairs*, vol 25, no 3, 2006, pp 720–9.

[8] Bateman, *Advocacy Skills for Health and Social Care Professionals*, p 19.

[9] Bateman, *Advocacy Skills for Health and Social Care Professionals*, p 20; Suellen Murray and Jim Goddard, 'Life after growing up in care: informing policy and practice through research', *Australian Social Work*, vol 67, no 1, 2014, pp 102–17.

[10] Arai et al, 'Shared values, networks and trust among Canadian consumer driven disability organisations', no page.

[11] Judith Allsop, Kathryn Jones and Rob Baggott, 'Health consumer groups in the UK: a new social movement?', *Sociology of Health and Illness*, vol 26, no 6, 2004, pp 737–56, 743; see also Tomes, 'The patient as a policy factor'.

[12] Allsop et al, 'Health consumer groups in the UK'.

[13] Law Commission of Canada, *Restoring Dignity*, pp 4–5.

[14] Allsop et al, 'Health consumer groups in the UK', p 738.

[15] Allsop et al, 'Health consumer groups in the UK', pp 738–9.

[16] Allsop et al, 'Health consumer groups in the UK', pp 752–3.

[17] Michael DeGagné, 'Implementing reparations: international perspectives', paper presented at 'Moving Forward: Achieving Reparations for the Stolen Generations', 15 August 2011, Australian Human Rights Commission, Sydney, available at: http://www.humanrights.gov.au/implementing-reparations-international-perspectives (accessed 30 May 2014).

[18] Allsop et al, 'Health consumer groups in the UK', p 740; Geoffrey Nelson, Rich Janzen, John Trainor and Joanna Ochocka, 'Putting values into practice: public policy and the future of mental health consumer-run organizations', *American Journal of Community Psychology*, no 42, 2008, pp 192–201, 193.

[19] Nelson et al, 'Putting values into practice', p 193.

[20] Institute for Human Resource Development, *Review of 'The Needs of Victims of Institutional Abuse'*, Law Commission of Canada, Ottawa, 1998, p 42.

[21] Nelson et al, 'Putting values into practice', p 197.

[22] See, for example, Aidan Ricketts, *The Activists' Handbook: A Step by Step Guide to Participatory Democracy*, Zen Books, London, 2012, ch 9.

[23] Hewett and Wiseman, 'Memory, reflection, imagination and action', p 156.

[24] Hewett and Wiseman, 'Memory, reflection, imagination and action', p 156.

[25] Ricketts, *The Activists' Handbook*, p 129.

[26] Verity Burgmann, *Power, Profit and Protest: Australian Social Movements and Globalisation*, Allen & Unwin, Sydney, 2003, p 8.

[27] Burgmann, *Power, Profit and Protest*, pp 8–9.

[28] Allsop et al, 'Health consumer groups in the UK', pp 741–2.

[29] CBC Digital Archives, 'Phil Fontaine opens up about abuse', available at: http://www.cbc.ca/archives/categories/politics/parties-leaders/phil-fontaine-native-diplomat-and-dealmaker/abused-to-abuser.html (accessed 30 May 2014); see also Canadian Encyclopedia, 'Phil Fontaine', available at: http://www.thecanadianencyclopedia.ca/en/article/phil-fontaine/ (accessed 30 May 2014); Theodore Fontaine, *Broken Circle: The Dark Legacy of Indian Residential Schools, A Memoir*, Heritage House, Victoria, 2010.

[30] RTÉ, 'Tributes following campaigner Christine Buckley's death', 11 March 2014, available at: http://www.rte.ie/news/2014/0311/601465-christine-buckley/ (accessed 30 May 2014); see also Connall Ó Fátharta, 'Warrior, survivor, advocate, charmer – Christine Buckley was a hero among heroes', *Irish Examiner*, 12 March 2014, available at: http://www.irishexaminer.com/ireland/warrior-survivor-advocate-charmer-christine-buckley-was-a-hero-among-heroes-261631.html (accessed 30 May 2014).

[31] Simon Collins, 'Calls for abuse claims commission', *New Zealand Herald*, 21 April 2011, available at: http://www.nzherald.co.nz/nz/news/article.cfm?c_id=1&objectid=10720704 (accessed 30 May 2014); see also Netta England, *Stolen Lives: A New Zealand Foster Child's Story from the '40s and '50s*, Netta Christian, Hamilton, 2014.

[32] For further information about his parliamentary career, see Parliament of Australia, 'Senator Andrew Murray', available at: http://www.aph.gov.au/Senators_and_Members/Parliamentarian?MPID=3M6 (accessed 30 .May 2014).

[33] Jim Coyle, 'Story of home children part of our history', *The Star*, 22 February 2010, available at: http://www.thestar.com/news/ontario/2010/02/22/coyle_story_of_home_children_part_of_our_history.html (accessed 30 May 2014).

[34] Bateman, *Advocacy Skills for Health and Social Care Professionals*, p 23.

[35] Care Leavers' Association, 'Vision and mission', available at: http://www.careleavers.com/ourmission (accessed 30 May 2014).

[36] Care Leavers' Association, 'Vision and mission'.

[37] Care Leavers' Association, 'Vision and mission'.

[38] Care Leavers' Association, 'Careleavers Reunited', available at: http://www.careleavers.com/clreunited (accessed 30 May 2014).

[39] Mary Raftery and Eoin O'Sullivan, *Suffer the Little Children: The Inside Story of Ireland's Industrial Schools*, New Island, Dublin, 1999, p 305.

[40] Care Leavers' Association, 'Which one grew up in care? They all did!', available at: http://www.careleavers.com/component/content/article/77 (accessed 30 May 2014).

[41] Care Leavers' Association, 'It's our history, it's our right', available at: http://www.careleavers.com/accesstorecords/its-our-history-its-our-right (accessed 30 May 2014).

[42] Care Leavers' Association, *It's Your Information! How to View Your Childhood Records: A Guide for Care Leavers*, Manchester, CLA, 2009.

[43] Care Leavers' Association, *CLEARmark Access to Records Quality Mark: A Framework for Improved Services for Care Leavers*, Manchester, CLA, c 2009.

[44] Rachel Williams, 'Care leavers to get access to their records', *Guardian*, 19 March 2014, available at: http://www.theguardian.com/society/2014/mar/18/care-leavers-access-records-new-rules (accessed 30 May 2014); see also UK Parliament, 'Baroness Young of Hornsey', available at: http://www.parliament.uk/biographies/lords/baroness-young-of-hornsey/3696 (accessed 30 May 2014).

[45] Baroness Young of Hornsey, House of Lords, 14 October 2013, *Hansard*, Columns GC154–5, available at: http://www.publications.parliament.uk/pa/ld201314/ldhansrd/text/131014-gc0001.htm (accessed 30 May 2014).

[46] Williams, 'Care leavers to get access to their records'.

[47] Joanna Penglase, *Orphans of the Living: Growing up in 'Care' in Twentieth-Century Australia*, Fremantle Arts Centre Press, Fremantle, 2005, frontispiece.

[48] CLAN, 'About CLAN: our history and objectives', available at: http://www.clan.org.au/page.php?pageID=1 (accessed 30 May 2014).

[49] CLAN, 'About CLAN'.

[50] CLAN, 'Our name: Care Leavers Australia Network', available at: http://www.clan.org.au/page.php?pageID=16 (accessed 9 May 2014).

[51] CLAN, 'About CLAN'; CLAN, 'CLAN annual report, 2012–2013', available at: http://www.clan.org.au/images/2012-13%20CLAN%20Annual%20Report%20V5%2012-11-13.pdf (accessed 30 May 2014).

[52] Nick Galvin, 'TV previews', *Sydney Morning Herald*, 16 November 2010, p 8, available at: http://www.clan.org.au/images/Media_Monitor_Report_15_11_10.pdf (accessed 30 May 2014).

[53] CLAN, 'CLAN annual report, 2012–2013'.

[54] CLAN, 'Politician birthday campaign', available at: http://www.clan.org.au/page.php?pageID=240 (accessed 30 May 2014).

[55] CLAN, 'CLAN protest history', available at: http://www.clan.org.au/protests.php?pageID=117 (accessed 30 May 2014).

[56] See the report of the Victorian Inquiry: Family and Community Development Committee, *Betrayal of Trust*, Parliament of Victoria, Melbourne, 2013.

[57] CLAN, 'Why do we protest?', brochure, available at: http://www.clan.org.au/images/New%20Protest%20Flyer%20march%20update.pdf (accessed 30 May 2014) (capitals in original).

[58] Suzy Braye, 'Participation and involvement in social care: an overview', in Hazel Kemshall and Rosemary Littlechild (eds), *User Involvement and Participation in Social Care: Research Informing Practice*, Jessica Kingsley Publishers, London, 2000, p 9.

[59] Braye, 'Participation and involvement in social care', p 9.

[60] See, for example, the chapters in Hazel Kemshall and Rosemary Littlechild (eds), *User Involvement and Participation in Social Care: Research Informing Practice*, Jessica Kingsley Publishers, London, 2000.

[61] Law Commission of Canada, *Restoring Dignity*, p 71.

[62] Donna McIntosh, 'The difference between case and cause advocacy is u (you)', *New Social Worker*, available at: http://www.socialworker.com/feature-articles/practice/The_Difference_Between_Case_and_Cause_Advocacy_is_U_(You)/ (accessed 30 May 2014).

[63] Law Commission of Canada, *Restoring Dignity*, pp 71–2.

[64] See, for example, Youth in Care Canada, 'Youth in Care Canada', available at: http://www.youthincare.ca/ (accessed 4 November 2014); The Who Cares? Trust, 'The Who Cares? Trust', available at: http://www.thewhocarestrust.org.uk/ (accessed 4 November 2014).

[65] Suellen Murray and Jim Goddard, 'Life after growing up in care: informing policy and practice through research', *Australian Social Work*, vol 67, no 1, 2014, pp 102–17.

[66] Centre for Excellence in Child and Family Welfare, 'Who Am I?', available at: http://www.cfecfw.asn.au/know/research/sector-research-partnership/partnership-projects/out-home-care/who-am-i (accessed 30 May 2014); see also Michael Jones and Cate O'Neill, 'Identity, records and archival evidence: exploring the needs of Forgotten Australians and former child migrants', *Archives and Records*, vol 35, no 2, 2014, pp 110–25.

[67] See Melissa Downing, Lynda Campbell and Margaret Kertesz, *Self Assessment Tool for Archives Report*, Who Am I? Project – Archives Strand, University of Melbourne, Melbourne, 2012.

[68] This is research I conducted; see Suellen Murray, 'Compassion and compliance: releasing records to care-leavers under privacy and freedom of information legislation', *Social Policy and Society*, vol 13, no 4, 2014, pp 493–503; Suellen Murray and Cathy Humphreys, '"My life's been a disaster but I feel privileged": care-leavers access to personal records and their implications for social work practice', *Child and Family Social Work*, vol 19, no 2, 2014, pp 215–24.

[69] See, for example, Cathy Humphreys and Margaret Kertesz, '"Putting the heart back into the record": personal records to support young people in care', *Adoption and Fostering*, vol 36, no 1, pp 27–39.

[70] Lesley Laing, Cathy Humphreys and Kate Cavanagh, *Social Work and Domestic Violence: Developing Critical and Reflective Practice*, Sage, London, 2013, p 9; see also Humphreys and Kertesz, '"Putting the heart back into the record"', p 31.

[71] Cate O'Neill, Vlad Selakovic and Rachel Tropea, 'Access to records for people who were in out-of-home care: moving beyond "third dimension" archival practice', *Archives and Manuscripts*, vol 40, no 1, 2012, pp 29–41.

[72] Vlad Selakovic, presentation at workshop 'Archiving: moving forward as a community', Victorian Archives Centre, 15 April 2010, cited in O'Neill, Selakovic and Tropea, 'Access to records for people who were in out-of-home care', p 30.

[73] O'Neill, Selakovic and Tropea, 'Access to records for people who were in out-of-home care', p 31.

[74] O'Neill, Selakovic and Tropea, 'Access to records for people who were in out-of-home care', p 31.

[75] Frank Golding, 'Telling stories: accessing personal records', in Richard Hil and Elizabeth Branigan (eds), *Surviving Care: Achieving Justice and Healing for the Forgotten Australians*, Bond University Press, Gold Coast, 2010, pp 79–99, 89, cited in O'Neill, Selakovic and Tropea, 'Access to records for people who were in out-of-home care', p 31.

Chapter Nine

[1] Law Commission of Canada, *Restoring Dignity: Responding to Child Abuse in Canadian Institutions*, Minister of Public Works and Government Services, Ottawa, 2000, p 2.

[2] Law Commission of Canada, *Restoring Dignity*, p 72.

[3] Assembly of First Nations, *Breaking the Silence: An Interpretive Study of Residential School Impact and Healing as Illustrated by the Stories of First Nations Individuals*, Assembly of First Nations, Ottawa, 1994, p 189, cited in Rhonda Claes and Deborah Clifton, *Needs and Expectations for Redress of Victims of Abuse*, Law Commission of Canada, Ottawa, 1998, p 2.

Select bibliography

Aboriginal Healing Foundation (2012) *Speaking My Truth: Reflections on Reconciliation and Residential School*, Aboriginal Healing Foundation, Ottawa.

Aboriginal Legal Service of Western Australia (1995) *Telling Our Story: A Report by the Aboriginal Legal Service of Western Australia (Inc) on the Removal of Aboriginal Children from their Families in Western Australia*, Aboriginal Legal Service of Western Australia, Perth.

Alliance for Forgotten Australians (2008) *Forgotten Australians: Supporting Survivors of Childhood Institutional Care in Australia*, Alliance for Forgotten Australians, Canberra.

Allsop, J., Jones, K. and Baggott, R. (2004) 'Health consumer groups in the UK: a new social movement?', *Sociology of Health and Illness*, vol 26, no 6, pp 737–56.

Altman, J. and Hinckson, M. (eds) (2007) *Coercive Reconciliation: Stabilise, Normalise, Exit Aboriginal Australia*, Arena Publications, Melbourne.

Arai, S., Hutchinson, P., Pedlar, A., Lord, J. and Shepard, V. (2008) 'Shared values, networks and trust among Canadian consumer driven disability organizations', *Disability Studies Quarterly*, vol 28, no 1.

Ashton, P. and Hamilton, P. (2008) 'Memorials, public history and the state in Australia since 1960', *Public History Review*, vol 15, pp 1–29.

Australian Government (2005) *Australian Government Response to Forgotten Australians: A Report on Australians who Experienced Institutional or Out-of-Home Care as Children*, Commonwealth of Australia, Canberra.

Bagnell, K. (2001) *The Little Immigrants: The Orphans Who Came to Canada*, Dundurn Press, Toronto.

Barnard, J. and Twigg, K. (2004) *Holding onto Hope: A History of the Founding Agencies of MacKillop Family Services, 1854–1997*, Australian Scholarly Publishing, Melbourne.

Bateman, N. (2000) *Advocacy Skills for Health and Social Care Professionals*, Jessica Kingsley Publishing, London.

Biehal, N. (2014) 'A sense of belonging: meanings of family and home in the long-term foster care', *British Journal of Social Work*, vol 44, pp 955–71.

Boucher, E. (2014) *Empire's Children: Child Emigration, Welfare and the Decline of the British World, 1869–1967*, Cambridge University Press, New York.

Brennan, C. (2007) 'Facing what cannot be changed: the Irish experience of confronting institutional child abuse', *Journal of Social Welfare and Family Law*, vol 29, nos 3/4, pp 245–63.

Brennan, C. (2015) 'Trials and contestations: Ireland's Ryan Commission', in J. Sköld and S. Swain (eds), *Apologies and the Legacies of Abuse of Children in 'Care'*, Palgrave Macmillan, Basingstoke.

Buchanan, A. (1999) 'Are leavers significantly dissatisfied and depressed in later life?', *Adoption and Fostering*, vol 23, no 4, pp 35–40.

Budiselik, W., Crawford, F. and Chung, D. (2014) 'The Australian Royal Commission into Institutional Responses to Child Sexual Abuse: dreaming of child safe organisations?', *Social Science*, vol 3, no 3, pp 565–83.

Buehler, C., Orme, J.G., Post, J. and Patterson, D.A. (2000) 'The long-term correlates of family foster care', *Children and Youth Services Review*, vol 22, no 8, pp 595–625.

Burgmann, V. (2003) *Power, Profit and Protest: Australian Social Movements and Globalisation*, Allen & Unwin, Sydney.

Buti, A. (2002) 'The removal of Aboriginal children: Canada and Australia compared', *University of Western Sydney Law Review*, no 6, pp 25–37.

Buti, A. (2003) 'Bridge over troubled Australian waters: reparations for Aboriginal child removals and British child migrants', *E Law Murdoch University Electronic Journal of Law*, vol 10, no 4, pp 5–20.

Care Leavers Australia Network (2008) *A Terrible Way to Grow Up: The Experience of Institutional Care and its Outcomes for Care Leavers in Australia*, Care Leavers Australia Network, Sydney.

Carr, A., Dooley, B., Fitzpatrick, M., Flanagan, E., Flanagan-Howard, R., Tierney, K., White, M., Daly, M. and Egan, J. (2010) 'Adult adjustment of survivors of institutional abuse in Ireland', *Child Abuse and Neglect*, vol 34, no 7, pp 477–89.

Cashmore, J. and Paxman, M. (1996) *Longitudinal Study of Wards Leaving Care*, New South Wales Department of Community Services, Sydney.

Cassidy, J. (2006) 'The best interests of the child? The Stolen Generations in Canada and Australia', *Griffith Law Review*, vol 15, no 1, pp 111–52.

Children's Commissioner for Wales (2015) *Learning the Lessons: Operation Pallial*, Children's Commissioner for Wales, Swansea.

Claes, R. and Clifton, D. (1998) *Needs and Expectations for Redress of Victims of Abuse at Residential Schools*, Law Commission of Canada, Ottawa.

Coldrey, B. (1999) *Good British Stock: Child and Youth Migration to Australia*, National Archives of Australia, Canberra.

Colton, M., Vanstone, M. and Walby, C. (2002) 'Victimization, care and justice: reflections on the experiences of victims/ survivors involved in large-scale historical investigations of child sexual abuse in residential institutions', *British Journal of Social Work*, vol 32, no 5, pp 541–51.

Commission to Inquire into Child Abuse (2009) *Commission to Inquire into Child Abuse Report*, Government of Ireland, Dublin.

Compensation Advisory Committee (2002) *Towards Redress and Recovery: Report to the Minister for Education and Science*, Government of Ireland, Dublin.

Corby, B., Doig, A. and Roberts, V. (2001) *Public Inquiries into Residential Abuse of Children*, Jessica Kingsley Publishers, London.

Cornwall, A. (2009) *Restoring Identity: Final Report of the Moving Forward Consultation Project*, Public Interest Advocacy Centre, Sydney.

Cregan, K. and Cuthbert, D. (2014) *Global Childhoods: Issues and Debates*, Sage, London.

Cunningham, M. (1999) 'Saying sorry: the politics of apology', *Political Quarterly*, vol 70, no 3, pp 285–93.

Cunningham, M. (2004) 'Apologies in Irish politics: a commentary and critique', *Contemporary British History*, vol 18, no 4, pp 80–92.

Cuthbert, D. and Quartly, M. (2012) '"Forced adoption" in the Australian story of national regret and apology', *Australian Journal of Politics and History*, vol 58, no 1, pp 82–96.

Cuthbert, D. and Quartly, M. (2013) 'Forced child removal and the politics of national apologies in Australia', *American Indian Quarterly*, vol 37, nos 1/2, pp 178–202.

Dalley, B. (1998) *Family Matters: Child Welfare in Twentieth Century New Zealand*, Auckland University Press, Auckland.

Daly, K. (2014) *Redressing Institutional Abuse of Children*, Palgrave Macmillan, Basingstoke.

Del Valle, J.F., Bravo, A., Alvarez, E. and Fernanz, A. (2008) 'Adult self-sufficiency and social adjustment in care leavers from children's homes: a long-term assessment', *Child and Family Social Work*, vol 13, no 1, pp 12–22.

Department of Health and Aging (2012) *Social and Emotional Wellbeing Program – Handbook for Counsellors*, Commonwealth of Australia, Canberra.

Department of Health and Aging (2012) *Social and Emotional Wellbeing Program – Handbook for Link Up Service Providers*, Commonwealth of Australia, Canberra.

Dixon, J. (2008) 'Young people leaving care: health, well-being and outcomes', *Child and Family Social Work*, vol 13, no 2, pp 207–17.

Doyle, P. (1989) *The God Squad: The Bestselling Story of One Child's Triumph Over Adversity*, Corgi, London.

Draper, B., Pfaff, J., Pirkis, J., Snowdon, J., Lautenschlager, N., Wilson, I. and Almeida, O. (2008) 'Long-term effects of childhood abuse on the quality of life and health of older people: results from the depression and early prevention of suicide in general practice project', *Journal of the American Geriatrics Society*, vol 56, no 2, pp 262–71.

Duncalf, Z. (2010) *Listen Up! Adult Care Leavers Speak Out. Research Gathered from 310 Care Leavers aged 17–78*, Care Leavers' Association, Manchester.

Duncalf, Z., Hawthorn, M., Davidson, J., Goddard, J. and McMahon, W. (2009) *Time for Justice: Historic Abuse of Children in Scotland*, Care Leavers' Association and the Scottish Institute for Residential Child Care, Manchester and Glasgow.

Durie, M. (2011) 'Indigenizing mental health services: New Zealand experience', *Transcultural Psychiatry*, vol 48, nos 1/2, pp 24–36.

Durie, M., Milroy, H. and Hunter, E. (2009) 'Mental health and the Indigenous peoples of Australia and New Zealand', in L.J. Kirmayer and G.G. Valakakis (eds), *Healing Traditions: The Mental Health of Aboriginal Peoples in Canada*, UBC Press, Vancouver, pp 36–55.

Edwards, D. (2012) 'The girls of Nazareth House, 1940–1960: (auto)biographical understandings of care experiences and identities', PhD thesis, School of Sociology, Social Policy and Social Work, Queen's University, Belfast.

England, N. (2014) *Stolen Lives: A New Zealand Foster Child's Story from the '40s and '50s*, Netta Christian, Hamilton.

Family and Community Development Committee (2013) *Betrayal of Trust: Inquiry into the Handling of Child Abuse by Religious and Other Non-Government Organisations*, Parliament of Victoria, Melbourne.

Feast, J. (2009) *Access to Information for Post-Care Adults: A Guide to Access to Records Officers*, British Association for Adoption and Fostering, London.

Feast, J. (2010) 'Access to information: progress and perils', *Adoption and Fostering*, vol 34, no 3, pp 74–9.

Fejo-King, C. (2011) 'The national apology to the Stolen Generations: the ripple effect', *Australian Social Work*, vol 64, no 1, pp 130–43.

Fontaine, F. (2010) *Broken Circle: The Dark Legacy of Indian Residential Schools*, Heritage House, Victoria.

Forde, L. (1999) *Report of the Commission of Inquiry into Abuse of Children in Queensland Institutions*, Queensland Government, Brisbane.

Funk-Unrau, N. (2014) 'The Canadian apology to Indigenous residential school survivors: a case study of renegotiation of social relations', in Mihaela Mihai and Mathais Thaler (eds), *On the Uses and Abuses of Apologies*, Palgrave Macmillan, Basingstoke, pp 138–53.

Gilligan, R. (2014) 'The "public child" and the reluctant state?', in Maria Luddy and James M. Smith (eds), *Children, Childhood and Irish Society*, Four Courts Press, Dublin, pp 145–63.

Goddard, J., Feast, J. and Kirton, D. (2005) 'A childhood on paper: accessing care records under the Data Protection Act 1998', *Adoption and Fostering*, vol 29, no 3, pp 82–4.

Goddard, J., Murray, S. and Duncalf, Z. (2013) 'Access to child-care records: a comparative analysis of UK and Australian policy and practice', *British Journal of Social Work*, vol 43, no 4, pp 759–74.

Golding, F. (2005) *An Orphan's Escape: Memories of a Lost Childhood*, Lothian Books, Melbourne.

Gone, J.P. (2013) 'A community-based treatment for Native American historical trauma: prospects for evidence-based practice', *Spirituality in Clinical Practice*, vol 1(S), pp 78–94.

Graycar, R. and Wangmann, J. (2007) 'Redress packages for institutional child abuse: exploring the Grandview Agreement as a case study in "alternative" dispute resolution', Sydney Law School Research Paper No 07/50, University of Sydney, Sydney.

Green, G., MacKenzie, J., Leeuwenburg, D. and Watts, J. (2014) 'Reflections from the Redress WA experience in light of the Royal Commission into Institutional Responses to Child Sexual Abuse', *Australian Association of Social Workers, Western Australian Branch, e-News*, May 2014, available at: http://www.aasw.asn.au/document/item/5904 (accessed 22 June 2014).

Haebich, A. (2000) *Broken Circles: Fragmenting Indigenous Families, 1800–2000*, Fremantle Arts Centre Press, Fremantle.

Hall, M. (2000) 'The liability of public authorities for the abuse of children in institutional care: common law developments in Canada and the United Kingdom', *International Journal of Law, Policy and the Family*, no 14, pp 281–301.

Hall, M. (2002) 'Book review: Law Commission of Canada, *Restoring Dignity: Responding to Child Abuse in Canadian Institutions*', *International Journal of Children's Rights*, vol 10, no 3, pp 295–302.

Harrison, P. (ed) (2003 [1979]) *The Home Children: Their Personal Stories*, J. Gordon Shillingford Publishing, Winnipeg.

Hawthorn, M. (2006) 'Historic abuse in residential care: sharing good practice', *In Residence*, no 4.

Hearn, J., Pösö, T., Smith, C., White, S. and Korpinen, J. (2004) 'What is child protection? Historical and methodological issues in comparative research on *lastensuojelu*/child protection', *International Journal of Social Welfare*, vol 13, pp 28–41.

Hewett, A. and Wiseman, J. (2000) 'Memory, reflection, imagination and action: advocacy and social action in a globalising world', *Just Policy*, September, pp 154–62.

Hewitt, P. (2002) *The Looked After Kid*, Mainstream Publishing, Edinburgh.

Hil, R. and Branigan, E. (eds) (2010) *Surviving Care: Achieving Justice and Healing for the Forgotten Australians*, Bond University Press, Gold Coast.

Hill, D. (2007) *The Forgotten Children: Fairbridge Farm School and its Betrayal of British Child Migrants to Australia*, Random House, Sydney.

Hocking, D. (2014) 'The social and emotional well-being of Aboriginal Australians and the collaborative consumer narrative', in N. Procter, T. Froggatt, D. McGarry, H.P. Hamer and R.L Wilson (eds), *Mental Health: A Person-Centred Approach*, Cambridge University Press, Melbourne, pp 52–71.

Hood, M. (2014) 'Feminism and the Royal Commission into Institutional Responses to Child Sexual Abuse', *AASW National Bulletin*, Spring, p 29.

Horrocks, C. and Goddard, J. (2006) 'Adults who grew up in care: constructing the self and accessing care files', *Child and Family Social Work*, vol 11, no 2, pp 264–72.

Human Rights and Equal Opportunity Commission (1997) *Bringing Them Home: The Report of the National Inquiry into the Separation of Aboriginal and Torres Strait Islander Children from their Families*, Commonwealth of Australia, Sydney.

Humphreys, C. and Kertesz, M. (2012) '"Putting the heart back into the record": personal records to support young people in care', *Adoption and Fostering*, vol 36, no 1, pp 27–39.

Humphreys, C., McCarthy, G., Dowling, M., Kertesz, M. and Tropea, R. (2014) 'Improving the archiving of records in the out-of-home care sector', *Australian Social Work*, vol 67, no 4, pp 509–24.

Humphreys, M. (1994) *Empty Cradles*, Doubleday, London.

Inquiry on Child Abuse and Neglect in Institutions and Foster Homes (2009) *Abuse and Neglect in Institutions and Foster Homes During the Twentieth Century*, Swedish Government, Stockholm.

Institute for Human Resource Development (1998) *Review of 'The Needs of Victims of Institutional Abuse'*, Law Commission of Canada, Ottawa.

Jackson, L.R. and Fitzpatrick, S.A. (2008) 'Beyond *Sorry*: the first steps in laying claim to a future that embraces all Australians', *Medical Journal of Australia*, vol 188, no 10, pp 556–8.

Jacobs, M.D. (2014) *A Generation Removed: The Fostering and Adoption of Indigenous Children in the Postwar World*, University of Nebraska Press, Lincoln.

Jones, M. and O'Neill, C. (2014) 'Identity, records and archival evidence: exploring the needs of Forgotten Australians and former child migrants', *Archives and Records*, vol 35, no 2, pp 110–25.

Kendrick, A. and Hawthorn, M. (2015) 'Dilemmas of care: social work and historic abuse', in J. Sköld and S. Swain (eds), *Apologies and the Legacies of Abuse of Children in 'Care'*, Palgrave Macmillan, Basingstoke.

Kendrick, A., Hawthorn, M., Karim, S. and Shaw, J. (2015) 'Scotland: abuse in care and human rights', in J. Sköld and S. Swain (eds), *Apologies and the Legacies of Abuse of Children in 'Care'*, Palgrave Macmillan, Basingstoke.

Kidd, J., Butler, K. and Harris, R. (2014) 'Māori mental health', in N. Procter, T. Froggatt, D. McGarry, H.P. Hamer and R.L. Wilson (eds), *Mental Health: A Person-Centred Approach*, Cambridge University Press, Melbourne, pp 72–91.

Kirmayer, L.J. (2012) 'Cultural competence and evidence-based practice in mental health: epistemic communities and the politics of pluralism', *Social Science and Medicine*, vol 75, pp 249–56.

Kirmayer, L.J. and Valakakis, G.G. (eds) (2009) *Healing Traditions: The Mental Health of Aboriginal Peoples in Canada*, UBC Press, Vancouver.

Kirmayer, L.J., Simpson, C. and Cargo, M. (2003) 'Healing traditions: culture, community and mental health promotion with Canadian Aboriginal people', *Australasian Psychiatry*, vol 11(S), pp 15–23.

Kirmayer, L.J., Tait, C.L. and Simpson, C. (2009) 'The mental health of Aboriginal peoples in Canada: transformations of identity and community', in L.J. Kirmayer and G.G. Valakakis (eds), *Healing Traditions: The Mental Health of Aboriginal Peoples in Canada*, UBC Press, Vancouver, pp 3–35.

Kirton, D., Peltier, E. and Webb, E. (2001) 'After all these years: accessing care records', *Adoption and Fostering*, vol 25, no 4, pp 39–49.

Kirton, D., Feast, J. and Goddard, J. (2011) 'The use of discretion in a "Cinderella" service: data protection and access to child-care files for post-care adults', *British Journal of Social Work*, vol 41, no 5, pp 912–30.

Laing, L., Humphreys, C. and Cavanagh, K. (2013) *Social Work and Domestic Violence: Developing Critical and Reflective Practice*, Sage, London.

Law Commission of Canada (2000) *Restoring Dignity: Responding to Child Abuse in Canadian Institutions*, Minister of Public Works and Government Services, Ottawa.

Llewellyn, J.L. (2002) 'Dealing with the legacy of native residential school abuse in Canada: litigation, ADR, and restorative justice', *University of Toronto Law Journal*, vol 52, no 3, pp 253–300.

Löfström, J. (2011) 'Historical apologies as acts of symbolic inclusion – and exclusion? Reflections on institutional apologies as politics of cultural citizenship', *Citizenship Studies*, vol 15, no 1, pp 93–108.

Luddy, M. (2014) 'The early years of the NSPCC in Ireland', in Maria Luddy and James M. Smith (eds), *Children, Childhood and Irish Society*, Four Courts Press, Dublin, pp 100–20.

Luddy, M. and Smith, J.M. (2014) 'Introduction', in Maria Luddy and James M. Smith (eds), *Children, Childhood and Irish Society*, Four Courts Press, Dublin, pp 15–28.

Maclachlan, A. (2010) 'The state of "sorry": official apologies and their absence', *Journal of Human Rights*, no 9, pp 373–85.

MacVeigh, J. (1982) *Gaskin*, Jonathan Cape, London.

Marcus, A.S. (2007) 'Representing the past and reflecting the present: museums, memorials, and the secondary history classroom', *Social Studies*, May/June, pp 105–10.

Mathews, B. (2004) 'Queensland government actions to compensate survivors of institutional abuse: a critical and comparative evaluation', *QUT Law and Justice Journal*, vol 4, no 1, pp 23–45.

McCall, J. (1999) 'Research on the psychological effects of orphanage care: a critical review', in R. McKenzie (ed), *Rethinking Orphanages for the 21st Century*, Sage, London, pp 127–50.

McCormick, R. (2009) 'Aboriginal approaches to counselling', in L.J. Kirmayer and G.G. Valakakis (eds), *Healing Traditions: The Mental Health of Aboriginal Peoples in Canada*, UBC Press, Vancouver, pp 337–54.

McCullagh, J. (2002) *A Legacy of Caring: A History of the Children's Aid Society of Toronto*, Dundurn, Toronto.

McDonald, T.P., Allen, R.I., Westerfelt, A. and Piliavin, I. (1996) *Assessing the Long-Term Effects of Foster Care: A Research Synthesis*, CWLA Press, Washington.

McKenzie, R. (1999) 'Orphanage alumni: how they have done and how they evaluate their experience', in R. McKenzie (ed), *Rethinking Orphanages for the 21st century*, Sage, London, pp 103–26.

McKenzie, R. (2003) 'The impact of orphanages on the alumni's lives and assessments of their childhoods', *Children and Youth Services Review*, vol 25, no 9, pp 703–53.

Mellor, D. and Haebich, A. (2002) *Many Voices: Reflections on Experiences of Indigenous Child Separation*, National Library of Australia, Canberra.

Middleton, W., Stavropolous, P., Dorahy, M.J., Krüger, C., Lewis-Fernández, R., Martínez-Taboas, A., Sar, V. and Brand, B. (2014) 'The Australian Royal Commission into Institutional Responses to Child Sexual Abuse', *Australian and New Zealand Journal of Psychiatry*, vol 48, no 1, pp 17–21.

Moore, J., Thornton, C., Hughes, M. and Waters, E. (2014) *Open Hearts and Open Minds: A Toolkit of Sensitive Practice for Professionals Working with Survivors of Institutional Child Abuse*, London Irish Centre and Immigrant Counselling and Psychotherapy, London.

Moses, A.D. (2011) 'Official apologies, reconciliation and settler colonialism: Australian Indigenous alterity and political agency', *Citizenship Studies*, vol 15, no 2, pp 145–59.

Mullighan, T. (2008) *The Report of the Commission of Inquiry (Children in State Care)*, Government of South Australia, Adelaide.

Murphy, M. (2011) 'Apology, recognition and reconciliation', *Human Rights Review*, no 12, pp 47–69,

Murray, K. and Hill, M. (1991) 'The recent history of Scottish child welfare', *Children and Society*, vol 5, no 3, pp 266–81.

Murray, S. (2014) 'Compassion and compliance: releasing records to care-leavers under privacy and freedom of information legislation', *Social Policy and Society*, vol 13, no 4, pp 493–503.

Murray, S. and Goddard, J. (2014) 'Life after growing up in care: informing policy and practice through research', *Australian Social Work*, vol 67, no 1, pp 102–17.

Murray, S. and Humphreys, C. (2014) '"My life's been a disaster but I feel privileged": care-leavers access to personal records and their implications for social work practice', *Child and Family Social Work*, vol 19, no 2, pp 215–24.

Murray, S., Malone, J. and Glare, J. (2008) 'Building a life story: providing records and support to former residents of children's homes', *Australian Social Work*, vol 61, no 3, pp 239–55.

Murray, S., Murphy, J., Branigan, E. and Malone, J. (2009) *After the Orphanage: Life Beyond the Children's Home*, UNSW Press, Sydney.

Musgrove, N. (2013) *The Scars Remain: A Long History of Forgotten Australians and Children's Institutions*, Australian Scholarly Publishing, Melbourne.

Nelson, G., Janzen, R., Trainor, J. and Ochocka, J. (2008) 'Putting values into practice: public policy and the future of mental health consumer-run organizations', *American Journal of Community Psychology*, no 42, pp 192–201.

Niezen, R. (2013) *Truth and Indignation: Canada's Truth and Reconciliation Commission on Indian Residential Schools*, University of Toronto Press, Toronto.

Nobles, M. (2007) 'Reparation claims: politics by another name', *Political Power and Social Theory*, vol 18, pp 253–8.

Nobles, M. (2008) *The Politics of Official Apologies*, Cambridge University Press, New York.

Nobles, M. (2014) 'Revisiting the "Membership Theory of Apologies": apology politics in Australia and Canada', in Mihaela Mihai and Mathais Thaler (eds), *On the Uses and Abuses of Apologies*, Palgrave Macmillan, Basingstoke, pp 119–37.

O'Connor, P. (2000) 'Squaring the circle: how Canada is dealing with the legacy of its Indian residential schools experiment', *Australian Journal of Human Rights*, vol 6, no 1, pp 1–25.

Office of Aboriginal and Torres Strait Islander Health (2009) *Evaluation of the Bringing Them Home and Indigenous Mental Health Programs: Final Report*, Commonwealth of Australia, Canberra.

Office of the Minister for Children and Youth Affairs (2009) *Report of the Commission to Inquire into Child Abuse, 2009: Implementation Plan*, Government of Ireland, Dublin.

Oldfield, B. (2004) *Rootless*, Hutchinson, London.

O'Neill, C., Selakovic, V. and Tropea, R. (2012) 'Access to records for people who were in out-of-home care: moving beyond "third dimension" archival practice', *Archives and Manuscripts*, vol 40, no 1, pp 29–41.

O'Riordan, M. and Arensman, E. (2007) *Institutional Child Sexual Abuse and Suicidal Behaviour: Outcomes of a Literature Review, Consultation Meetings and a Qualitative Study*, National Suicide Research Foundation, Cork.

O'Sullivan, E. (2009) *Residential Child Welfare in Ireland, 1965–2008: An Outline of Policy, Legislation and Practice*, Commission to Inquire into Child Abuse, Dublin.

O'Sullivan, E. (2014) 'Residential child welfare in Ireland: from Kennedy to the task force', in Maria Luddy and James M. Smith (eds), *Children, Childhood and Irish Society*, Four Courts Press, Dublin, pp 121–44.

O'Sullivan, E. and O'Donnell, I. (2012) 'Explaining coercive confinement: why was the past such a different place?', in E. O'Sullivan and I. O'Donnell (eds), *Patients, Prisoners and Penitents: Coercive Confinement in Ireland*, Manchester University Press, Manchester.

Parker, R. (2010) *Uprooted: The Shipment of Poor Children to Canada, 1867–1917*, The Policy Press, Bristol.

Pecora, P.J., Williams, J., Kessler, R.C., Hiripi, E., O'Brien, K., Emerson, J., Herrick, M.A. and Torres, D. (2006) 'Assessing the educational achievements of adults who were formerly placed in family foster care', *Child and Family Social Work*, vol 11, pp 220–31.

Pecora, P.J., Kessler, R.C., Williams, J., Downs, A.C., English, D.J., White, J. and O'Brien, K. (2010) *What Works in Foster Care? Key Components of Success from the Northwest Foster Care Alumni Study*, Oxford University Press, Oxford.

Peeters, L. (2010) 'The Marumali program: an Aboriginal model of healing', in N. Purdie, P. Dudgeon and R. Walker (eds), *Working Together: Aboriginal and Torres Strait Islander Mental Health and Wellbeing Principles and Practice*, Department of Health and Ageing, Canberra, pp 285–92.

Penglase, J. (2005) *Orphans of the Living: Growing up in 'Care' in Twentieth-Century Australia*, Fremantle Arts Centre Press, Fremantle.

Perry, J.C., Sigal, J.J., Boucher, S., Pare, N., Ouimet, M., Normand, J. and Henry, M. (2005) 'Personal strengths and traumatic experiences among institutionalised children given up at birth (Les enfants de Duplessis – Duplessis' children), II: adaptation in late adulthood', *Journal of Nervous and Mental Disorders*, vol 193, no 12, pp 783–9.

Perry, J.C., Sigal, J.J., Boucher, S., Pare, N. and Ouimet, M. (2005) 'Personal strengths and traumatic experiences among institutionalised children given up at birth (Les enfants de Duplessis – Duplessis' children), I: early experiences', *Journal of Nervous and Mental Disorders*, vol 193, no 12, pp 777–82.

Perry, J.C., Sigal, J.J., Boucher, S. and Paré, N. (2006) 'Seven institutionalized children and their adaptation in late adulthood; the Children of Duplessis (Les Enfants de Duplessis)', *Psychiatry*, vol 69, no 4, pp 283–301.

Pilkington, D. (1996) *Follow the Rabbit-Proof Fence*, University of Queensland Press, Brisbane.

Pine, E. (2011) *The Politics of Memory: Performing Remembrance in Contemporary Irish Culture*, Palgrave Macmillan, Basingstoke.

Powell, F. and Scanlon, M. (2015) *Dark Secrets of Childhood: Media Power, Child Abuse and Public Scandals*, The Policy Press, Bristol.

Powell, F., Geoghegan, M., Scanlon, M. and Swirak, K. (2012) 'The Irish charity myth, child abuse and human rights: contextualising the Ryan Report into care institutions', *British Journal of Social Work*, vol 43, no 1, pp 7–23.

Pugh, G. (1999) *Unlocking the Past: The Impact of Access to Barnardo's Childcare Records*, Ashgate, Aldershot.

Purdie, N., Dudgeon, P. and Walker, R. (eds) (2010) *Working Together: Aboriginal and Torres Strait Islander Mental Health and Wellbeing Principles and Practice*, Department of Health and Ageing, Canberra.

Quinton, D. (1987) 'The consequences of care: adult outcomes from institutional rearing', *Maladjustment and Therapeutic Education*, vol 5, no 2, pp 18–28.

Quinton, D. and Rutter, M. (1984) 'Parents with children in care – I. Current circumstances and parenting', *Journal of Child Psychology and Psychiatry*, vol 25, no 2, pp 211–29.

Raftery, M. and O'Sullivan, E. (1999) *Suffer the Little Children: The Inside Story of Ireland's Industrial Schools*, New Island, Dublin.

Raman, S. and Forbes, C. (2008) *It's Not Too Late to Care: Report on the Research into Life Outcomes for People Brought Up in Institutional Care in Victoria*, Centre for Excellence in Child and Family Welfare, Melbourne.

Regan, P. (2010) *Unsettling the Settler Within: Indian Residential Schools, Truth Telling and Reconciliation in Canada*, UBC Press, Vancouver.

Ricketts, A. (2012) *The Activists' Handbook: A Step by Step Guide to Participatory Democracy*, Zen Books, London.

Royal Commission into Institutional Responses to Child Sexual Abuse (2015) *Consultation Paper: Redress and Civil Litigation*, Royal Commission into Institutional Responses to Child Sexual Abuse, Sydney.

Royal Commission on Aboriginal Peoples (1996) *Report of the Royal Commission on Aboriginal Peoples*, Indian and Northern Affairs Canada, Ottawa.

Saied-Tessier, A. (2014) *Estimating the Costs of Child Sexual Abuse in the UK*, National Society for the Prevention of Cruelty to Children, London.

Scottish Human Right Commission (2010) *A Human Rights Framework for the Design and Implementation of the Proposed 'Acknowledgement and Accountability Forum' and other Remedies for Historic Child Abuse in Scotland*, Scottish Human Rights Commission, Edinburgh.

Sen, R., Kendrick, A., Milligan, I. and Hawthorn, M. (2008) 'Lessons learned? Abuse in residential child care in Scotland', *Child and Family Social Work*, vol 13, no 4, pp 411–22.

Senate Community Affairs References Committee (2001) *Lost Innocents: Righting the Record, Report on Child Migration*, Commonwealth of Australia, Canberra.

Senate Community Affairs References Committee (2004) *Forgotten Australians: A Report on Australians Who Experienced Institutional or Out-of-Home Care as Children*, Commonwealth of Australia, Canberra.

Senate Community Affairs References Committee (2009) Lost Innocents and Forgotten Australians *Revisited: Report on the Progress with the Implementation of the Recommendations of the* Lost Innocents and Forgotten Australians *Reports*, Commonwealth of Australia, Canberra.

Shaw, T. (2007) *Historical Abuse Systemic Review: Residential Schools and Children's Homes in Scotland 1950–1995*, Scottish Government, Edinburgh.

Shaw, T. (2011) *Time to be Heard: A Pilot Forum*, Scottish Government, Edinburgh.

Shea, G. (1999) *Redress Programs Relating to Institutional Child Abuse in Canada*, Law Commission of Canada, Ottawa.

Short, D. (2012) 'When sorry isn't enough: official remembrance and reconciliation in Australia', *Memory Studies*, no 5, pp 293–304.

Sinclair, R. (2007) 'Identity lost and found: lessons from the sixties scoop', *First Peoples Child and Family Review*, vol 3, no 1, pp 65–82.

Sinha, V. and Kozlowski, A. (2013) 'The structure of Aboriginal child welfare in Canada', *International Indigenous Policy Journal*, vol 4, no 2, pp 1–21.

Sköld, J. (2013) 'Historical abuse – a contemporary issue: compiling inquiries into abuse and neglect of children in out-of-home care worldwide', *Journal of Scandinavian Studies in Criminology and Crime Prevention*, vol 14, sup 1, pp 5–23.

Sköld, J., Foberg, E. and Hedström, J. (2012) 'Conflicting or complementing narratives? Interviewees' stories compared to their documentary records in the Swedish Commission to Inquire into Child Abuse and Neglect in Institutions and Foster Homes', *Archives and Manuscripts*, vol 40, no 1, pp 15–28.

Smith, D., Varcoe, C. and Edwards, N. (2005) 'Turning around the intergenerational impact of residential schools on Aboriginal people: implications for health policy and practice', *Canadian Journal of Nursing Research*, vol 37, no 4, pp 38–60.

Smith, J.M. (2007) *Ireland's Magdalen Laundries and the Nation's Architecture of Containment*, University of Notre Dame Press, Notre Dame.

Smith, M. (2010) 'Victim narratives of historical abuse in residential care: do we really know what we think we know?', *Qualitative Social Work*, vol 9, no 3, pp 303–20.

Spear, W.K. (2014) *Full Circle: The Aboriginal Healing Foundation and the Unfinished Work of Hope, Healing and Reconciliation*, Aboriginal Healing Foundation, Ottawa.

Spila, B., Makara, M., Kozak, G. and Urbanska, A. (2008) 'Abuse in childhood and mental disorder in adult life', *Child Abuse Review*, vol 17, no 2, pp 133–8.

Stanley, N., Manthorpe, J. and Penhale, B. (1999) *Institutional Abuse: Perspectives Across the Life Course*, Routledge, London.

Stein, M. (2012) *Young People Leaving Care: Supporting Pathways to Adulthood*, Jessica Kingsley Publishing, London.

Stein, M. and Munro, E. (eds) (2008) *Young People's Transitions from Care to Adulthood: International Research and Practice*, Jessica Kingsley Publishing, London.

Stout, R. and Peters, S. (2011) *Intergenerational Effects on Professional Women Whose Mothers Are Residential School Survivors*, Prairie Women's Health Centre of Excellence, Winnipeg.

Swain, S. (1998) 'The state and the child', *Australian Journal of Legal History*, vol 4, pp 57–77.

Swain, S. (2014) *History of Australian Inquiries Reviewing Institutions Providing Care for Children*, Australian Catholic University, Melbourne.

Swain, S. (2014) *History of Child Protection Legislation*, Australian Catholic University, Melbourne.

Swain, S. (2015) 'Transitional justice workers and vicarious trauma', in J. Sköld and S. Swain (eds), *Apologies and the Legacies of Abuse of Children in 'Care'*, Palgrave Macmillan, Basingstoke.

Swain, S. and Howe, R. (1995) *Single Mothers and their Children: Disposal, Punishment and Survival in Australia*, Cambridge University Press, Melbourne.

Swain, S. and Musgrove, N. (2012) 'We are the stories we tell ourselves: child welfare records and the construction of identity among Australians who, as children, experienced out-of-home "care"', *Archives and Manuscripts*, vol 40, no 1, pp 4–14.

Swain, S., Sheedy, L. and O'Neill, C. (2012) 'Responding to "Forgotten Australians": historians and the legacy of out-of-home "care"', *Journal of Australian Studies*, vol 36, no 1, pp 17–28.

Szablicki, R. (2010) *Orphanage Boy: Through the Eyes of Innocence*, New Holland Publishers, Sydney.

Tasmanian Ombudsman (2006) *Review of Claims of Abuse from Adults in State Care as Children: Final Report*, Tasmania Ombudsman, Hobart.

Tomes, N. (2006) 'The patient as a policy factor: a historical case study of the consumer/survivor movement in mental health', *Health Affairs*, vol 25, no 3, pp 720–9.

Tomison, A.M. (2001) 'A history of child protection: back to the future?', *Family Matters*, no 60, pp 46–57.

Trinder, L., Feast, J. and Howe, D. (2004) *The Adoption Handbook*, John Wiley and Sons, Chichester.

Truth and Reconciliation Commission of Canada (2012) *They Came for the Children: Canada, Aboriginal Peoples and Residential Schools*, Truth and Reconciliation Commission of Canada, Winnipeg.

Truth and Reconciliation Commission of Canada (2015) *Honouring the Truth: Reconciling for the Future. Summary of the Final Report of the Truth and Reconciliation Commission of Canada*, Truth and Reconciliation Commission of Canada, Winnipeg.

Victorian Auditor-General (2012) *Freedom of Information*, Victorian Government Printer, Melbourne.

Victorian Koorie Records Taskforce (2012) *Final Report*, Department for Victorian Communities, Melbourne.

Victorian Ombudsman (2012) *Investigation into the Storage and Management of Ward Records by the Department of Human Services*, Victorian Government Printer, Melbourne.

Viejo-Rose, D. (2011) 'Memorial functions: intent, impact and the right to remember', *Memory Studies*, no 4, pp 465–80.

Viner, R.M. and Taylor, B. (2005) 'Adult health and social outcomes of children who have been in public care: population-based study', *Pediatrics*, vol 115, no 4, pp 894–9.

Wade, J., Biehal, N., Farrelly, N. and Sinclair, I. (2011) *Caring for Abused and Neglected Children: Making the Right Decisions for Reunification or Long-term Care*, Jessica Kingsley Publishers, London.

Winter, K. and Cohen, O. (2005) 'Identity issues for looked after children with no knowledge of their origins', *Adoption and Fostering*, vol 29, no 2, pp 44–52.

Winter, S. (2009) 'Australia's *ex gratia* redress', *Australian Indigenous Law Review*, vol 13, no 1, pp 49–61.

Winter, S. (2014) *Transitional Justice in Established Democracies: A Political Theory*, Palgrave Macmillan, Basingstoke.

Wolfe, D.A., Francis, K.J. and Straatman, A. (2006) 'Child abuse in religiously affiliated institutions: long-term impact on men's mental health', *Child Abuse and Neglect*, vol 30, pp 205–12.

Index

NOTE: page numbers in *italic type* refer to tables, page numbers followed by 'n' refer to a note and its number.

see also Australian Senate
Community Affairs References
Committee; Human Rights and
Equal Opportunity Commission;
Royal Commission into
Institutional Responses to Child
Sexual Abuse
Canadian *43*, 48–51
see also Law Commission of
Canada; Royal Commission on
Aboriginal Peoples
care-leavers' voice and
participation in 36, 39, 47–8, 52,
56, 57, 188
and international policy variations
187–8
Irish *45*, 51–3
see also Commission to Inquire
into Child Abuse
key findings and outcomes 58–63,
71–2
lobbying for 37, 46–7, 55, 165–6,
176–7
New Zealand perspective on *43*,
53–5
purpose and nature of 38–40
as source of knowledge 29–30, 37
support for participants 31, 116
UK *44*, 55–8

Q

Quarriers (Scotland) 141
Quartly, Marian 76

R

RCAP *see* Royal Commission on
Aboriginal Peoples
RCIRCSA *see* Royal Commission
into Institutional Responses to
Child Sexual Abuse
Read, Peter 149–50
records
advocacy campaigns relating to
172–4
and adoptees 34, 136, 139
difficulties of accessing 137–8,
181
and family reunification 34, 103,
134–5, 147–9, 191
finding aids and guides 155–8
importance of 133–5, 136–40

incomplete and fragmented
143–4
key elements of access to *159*
legislation relating to 139–40,
143–4, 146, 157, 173
motivations for accessing 135–6
ownership of 144
photographs 145–7, 156
storage and management of
137–8, 139, 146, 180, 181–2
supported release of 4–5, 34,
140–5, 149–55, 191
'Who Am I?' research project
179–82
redaction 143–4, 146
redress 189
apologies as form of 67
compensation payments *see*
financial compensation
development of programmes
89–91
elements of 88–9, *110*
implementation of 106–9
models of 95–7
international comparisons 53–5,
97–105
role of advocacy groups 177–8
support during process 107–9,
122
use of term 87–8
Redress WA 105, 107, 108–9
relationships, impact of care on
33–5
religious organisations
care provided by 16, 19, 22
support provided by 118–19
remembrance initiatives 69, 80–3
see also memorials
reparation 189
see also apologies; financial
compensation; memorials;
redress; support for adult care-
leavers
reparation politics 68
research
consumer participation in 179–82
need for 195
residential care *see* foster care;
institutional care
Residential Historic Abuse Program
(RHAP) (Canada) 119